ONE NIGHT AT THE PALACE

A Referee's Story

Alan Wilkie with George Miller
WITH A FOREWORD BY MARTIN TYLER

The Parrs Wood Press
Manchester

First Published 2002

THE PARRS WOOD PRESS
St Wilfrid's Enterprise Centre
Royce Road, Manchester, M15 5BJ
www.parrswoodpress.com

ISBN: 1 903158 35 4

This book was produced by The Parrs Wood Press
and Printed in Great Britain by:

Fretwell Print & Design
Healey Works
Goulbourne Street
Keighley
West Yorkshire

"What makes a sane and rational person subject himself to such humiliation? Why on earth does anyone want to become a football referee?"

Roy Hattersley

This book is dedicated to my wife Margaret, sons Ben and Carl, my mother Violet and to my late father, Tom, who was always so proud of my achievements in football.

My appreciation goes to all those club and league secretaries who gave me the opportunity to be involved in the game I love. Also to my refereeing colleagues who provided me with moral support when I needed it.

I owe a huge debt of gratitude to George Miller, whose persistence and determination made this book happen, and to his family who had to suffer my presence on so many occasions. Thanks also to Peter and Frank for their contributions.

Finally, special thanks to my publisher, Andy Searle of the Parrs Wood Press, for having faith and for providing expert guidance in production of the finished article.

CONTENTS

FOREWORD by Martin Tyler vii
1. THE BEGINNING 1
2. THE INITIATION 3
3. A DIFFERENT LEAGUE 27
4. HOME AND AWAY 39
5. A PREMIER APPOINTMENT 56
6. INCE RETURNS 64
7. 'GO ON, TISS, SHOOT!' 78
8. CANTONA SEES RED 91
9. 'THERE'S A BULLET WAITING...' 98
10. VINNIE'S PLEA 119
11. BEARDSLEY IN THE BOOK 135
12. BETRAYAL 153
13. THE JOY AND THE PAIN 170
14 THE END OF THE ROAD 196
15. EPILOGUE 205

vi

FOREWORD

by Martin Tyler

I WAS IN MY CAR driving home from Chelsea's match with Nottingham Forest that January evening in 1995. You tend to remember exactly where you were when you heard about Alan Wilkie sending off Eric Cantona at Selhurst park and the Manchester United star then taking violent exception to a remark from a hostile fan.

You now have the chance to read Alan's story of that night, a tale I have been fortunate enough to hear as our paths crossed many times on the highways and by-ways of the Premiership. It is by no means the only yarn told by a witty raconteur with a nice line in self-deprecation.

Above all Alan Wilkie was a top-class referee and it is to the credit of the Football Association that he is still involved in a full-time capacity, including the role of match observer.

Football commentators and referees have a lot in common. We are asked to judge quickly, accurately and fairly incidents that happen at high speed. On television we have the replays to call on of course, unlike the men with the whistle. However, it is my experience that though slow-motion works in matters of fact such as was the ball over the line, it is not a perfect guide in matters of interpretation. You basically have to call it as you see it. Alan Wilkie was very good at that.

This foreword also gives me the chance to publicly express my gratitude to Alan and his colleagues for the help and clarification given by referees to commentators, often in pressurised situations.

One game sticks in the memory, an FA Cup tie that was scheduled for Sky Sports on a particularly foggy day at Bradford City. Alan not only kept we broadcasters regularly updated as to his plans while the weather improved and worsened but he had the courage of his convictions to get the game played.

In wishing Alan every success with this venture, I hope it also encourages some of the younger readers to go into refereeing. It is a simple but often overlooked truth that the game cannot continue to prosper without its officials. Nowadays the best can earn a very good living from their skills. Alan Wilkie was certainly one of the very best.

1

THE BEGINNING

'KEEPER'S BALL'. The unmistakable voice of Bob Flynn boomed out loud and clear across the penalty area. Knowing this man's reputation for steamrollering anyone who got in his way, and sometimes forgetting to collect the ball in the process, I immediately retreated to the goal line to cover any sort of mishap. Sure enough, under considerable pressure, Bob didn't make the catch. The ball rolled loose towards the line with two incoming forwards closing in at what seemed to be a hundred miles per hour.

We were 3-2 up with two minutes to go. This was not the time to be thinking of shirking any challenges and, to the gratitude of my team mates, I managed to get there in time to save the day. Unfortunately there was no way to halt the charge of the opposition and the impact was only a matter of time. The next thing I knew I was in a crumpled heap. I was initially surprised at the lack of any real pain but it soon dawned on me that this was due to the fact that my lower right leg and foot were in fact totally numb. With the ball still in play I tried to get to my feet but within a matter of seconds I was dragging myself over the touchline so that I didn't interfere with play.

As the whistle went for the end of the proceedings I found myself surrounded by my colleagues, not so much concerned about the state of my health, but more interested in bestowing hero status on me for saving the match. Not one to turn down such rare adulation I tried to put any thoughts of serious injury out of my mind. In the clubhouse, over a pint or two, and revelling in the re-enactment of the great escape, I wallowed in the glory of my deeds. Regardless of the standard of football, the pride and the passion are just the same - the only thing missing at the lower level is the roar of the crowd, a sound I was to get very accustomed to over the coming years.

It wasn't until I was visiting friends with my wife, later that evening, that the pain started to come through and I eventually had to make my excuses and leave early. The next day I realised that this was a hospital job and proceeded to Newcastle General Hospital. I spent the Sunday morning enduring the indignity suffered by many minor sportsmen in being advised that 'self-inflicted injuries' are at the back of the queue and that I might as well settle down for a long wait. Three hours later I emerged on crutches with my leg in plaster from toe to knee, a situation in which I remained for the next four months.

Returning to work on light duties after six months sick leave, the surgeon's words were ringing in my ears. 'I can do an operation to re-attach the tendons but there would be a chance you would end up with a permanent limp.' Not getting immediate treatment after the game, followed by driving home with two broken bones in my foot, had apparently caused serious damage to the muscle tissues. I declined the operation in the hope that after a while I might be able to run properly again. I couldn't avoid the feeling, though, that here I was at the age of 25 and my football career, such as it was, was on the scrap-heap.

As every amateur footballer knows, Saturday afternoon is a miserable time when you're not able to join the action. In passing conversation one day with a local referee, Elliott Blackburn, he suggested that I would fail miserably if I was to take a referees' course. Never one to turn down a challenge, not to mention the prospect of a free pint from Elliott if I passed the exam, I allowed myself to be persuaded. And so it was that under Elliott's expert guidance I qualified in June 1977 as a class 3 referee and the Durham Football Association let me loose on an unsuspecting world.

2

THE INITIATION

I SPENT THE NEXT SEASON (1977/78) torn between refereeing and running my local side. However, one day as I surveyed the pile of sweaty, muddy strips lying in a heap on the dressing room floor, with the tension high thanks to another unexpected defeat of my team, the decision was made. The referee bug had bitten and I wanted to be out there amongst the action. If I couldn't play I could still get on the pitch and make a contribution, even if it was in a rather different way. Little was I to know that this decision would propel me into the public spotlight and see me travelling the country and also in Europe on match day assignments. The flak I had received as a local team manager was to pale into insignificance compared with what was to come!

Like every new referee I felt mightily important with the never ending phone calls asking me to help out, although there were times when I did wonder if I had made the right decision. The early days consisted of such delights as getting changed in a cupboard behind the stage in a Working Men's club and refereeing on pitches where a car would need to be in first gear to get up the hill. There were also character-building tests such as being harangued in a snowstorm, by a team losing 5-0, into abandoning the game. My deliberations, in this case, were helped by the knowledge that my personal safety would not be a good insurance risk if I was to concur.

A particularly soul-searching point came when I refereed at Philadelphia, a suburb of Sunderland. I sent off a home-team player for violent conduct, thus making myself less than popular. Although the atmosphere was threatening I managed to avoid any serious recriminations about my decision. Or so I thought. After the game I got changed leisurely whilst going over in my mind the events of the previous ninety minutes. When I came to leave the Portakabin changing accommodation I found that everyone had gone and they had locked me in. I spent the next hour wondering if I was going to have to spend the night there before I finally attracted someone's attention and the caretaker was called to let me out. Whether it was an intentional act or pure accident I'll never be sure but I've got a pretty good idea.

I must have been doing quite well, though, as I was invited to participate in cup finals by all four of the leagues I was involved with. This was not as referee but as linesman, or referee's assistant as they are horribly known these days. This was a different kettle of fish. I had never even refereed in a game with linesmen involved. Running the line is a different experience altogether and carries different hazards to those of refereeing.

As a referee you bear the brunt of the crowd's displeasure but at least you are in the middle of the pitch and free to move around. As a linesman you are much more of a captive audience and can be the subject of the crowd's entertainment, particularly on a Sunday morning when they are warming up for a lunchtime session at the club. Running up and down the touchline could, on occasion, be the equivalent of the 100 metres hurdles, jumping over the sudden outstretched foot of a spectator. If you went flying you knew it was going to be the subject of great mirth in the next few hours as the story spread from the bar to the concert room. I like to consider this sort of experience as part of my refereeing apprenticeship; it certainly got me used to being close to hostile crowds!

One game in particular sticks in my mind. This was the final of the Stanley Aged Miner's Cup where I encountered for the first time the luxury of an enclosed pitch with a barrier around the touchline and even a running track around the perimeter. The only down side was the need to run the gauntlet of the partisan fans between the changing room and the pitch. This was intimidating to say the least, hearing at close quarters the muttered suggestions of what might happen to me if their team didn't win.

In my second season, having been promoted to class 2 referee, I had the distinction of being asked to referee the Washington Aged Miners' Cup final. This was a game usually reserved for class 1 referees and this selection gave me a lot of confidence as people had obviously recognised that I was capable of handling such locally prestigious games.

The next season saw me progress to class 1 referee status and this put me in the frame for a possible move up to a higher class of football. I had set my sights on becoming a referee in the old Northern League, which was populated by players moving down from professional status or those on the way up to greater things. Included in the latter category were people like Chris Waddle, who would turn out for Tow Law when he wasn't working overtime in the local sausage factory.

It was first necessary, however, to serve my time as a linesman and I had a great disappointment in this respect when I missed out in the 1980/81 season owing to an oversight on my part. This resulted in my application being received by the league secretary one day late. In a state of panic I had driven to the secretary's house and handed in my letter the day after the deadline. The response I received was one that lives on in my mind as if it was just yesterday. 'Aas sorry, bonny lad, you're too late - what makes yer think the league wants people like yersell who cannot get the correspondence right, try again next year!'

Try again I did and I was successfully appointed to the dizzy heights of the Northern League as a linesman for the 1981/82 season. My first appointment turned out to be a Wednesday evening game between Bishop Auckland and Horden Colliery Welfare. The referee picked me up in his car, in accordance with league rules to keep costs down, and I was almost overawed as we took the pitch under floodlights and a half decent crowd. To everyone in the North East, Bishop Auckland is synonomous with great deeds of the past, having an incredible eighteen FA Amateur Cup victories to their credit, including three consecutive years in the 1950s. The game went well and there were many other similar matches over the coming months.

I discovered that apart from the actual involvement in the games I was beginning to enjoy the 'apres-match', chatting to players and spectators in the bar afterwards. It was fascinating for me to mix with players who had stories to tell about life in the big time when they had been professionals with League clubs. Some of these players were by necessity what I would call 'pretty hard' but they were all genuine and very affable off the pitch.

One thing led to another and in 1982 I was invited to be a Northern League referee for the forthcoming 1982/83 season. I began to realise that after only four years refereeing I was only one step away from involvement in the Football League itself. My first priority though was survival in the Northern League where the standard of football was generally acknowledged to be as high as the old Fourth Division, a fact borne out by results in the FA Cup against League opposition.

ONE NIGHT AT THE PALACE

My first match in charge was Ashington v Ferryhill, a game that went pretty much according to plan. The following Tuesday, however, I was to get a taste of the pressures to come. I was appointed to take the Blyth Spartans home game against Ferryhill. Now this was a test, Blyth were just about the most famous non-league club in the country and had recently reached the fifth round of the FA Cup, beating respected League opposition on the way. Their heroics had ended in a narrow defeat by Wrexham in a replay at St James Park in front of 30,000 spectators.

As it happened, I gave a penalty against Blyth after just ten minutes. Amid the mayhem even the Ferryhill captain said to me 'Are you sure, ref, nobody gives an away penalty up here!' I found myself surrounded by Blyth players and eventually decided I had to brandish my first yellow card. When I asked the player his name he turned to his team mates and declared: 'He doesn't even know who I am, help him out lads.' This was Tommy Dixon, a stalwart of the cup run, captain of the side and a formidable character. In the end Blyth won the match 2-1 but they still gave me a frosty reception in the clubhouse afterwards.

After this encounter I was sent to Blyth another five times that season and it was only later that I found out why. After the Ferryhill match Blyth had apparently given me one mark out of ten and had declared to the League that they didn't want to see me up there again. In his inimitable fashion the League administrator, Gordon Nicholson, had decided to show them who was in charge. It wasn't exactly a sheltered life up there.

Having survived that first tempestuous Northern League season, I had decided to put everything I could into refereeing and, if it was at all possible, to reach the Football League in some capacity or other. I concentrated on dealing with all correspondence promptly, keeping fit (the foot was not causing me problems apart from on the odd cold day), making sure of a smart appearance at all matches and treating everyone with respect whether it was officials, players or spectators. I also made sure that I watched as much football on television as I could, only now I was watching the ref rather than the match itself.

I consolidated my position in the Northern League in 1983/84, even, I believe, winning over Blyth, a conclusion I came to due to my games up there turning out to be more evenly distributed. I also developed a growing reputation through controlling games which involved other well known teams such as Spennymoor, Whitby, Bishop Auckland, North Shields and Whitley Bay, all teams of great stature in those days.

I was looking forward to the following season when an unexpected letter arrived in the post inviting me to a fitness test with a view to becoming a Football League linesman. Although I had refereed 650 games in my six seasons so far, I was still taken by surprise and I felt elated and terrified at the same time. I attended the fitness test at Durham and was surprised to find I was in the company of many well known people, including George Courtney and Peter Willis, both of whom I had seen refereeing on Match Of The Day. The thing I remember most about the test was that I was 'busting a gut' but the advice from the seasoned campaigners, such as the burly Peter Willis, was: 'Just do what is necessary and save your energy for when the season starts.' I won't repeat what Peter said when I lapped him for the second time and suggested he should put a move on!

When I got the news that I had passed the test and had qualified I was incredibly happy, not just for myself but also for my family, particularly my father, and also my brother Tom who had accompanied me to many matches, helping out as linesman when necessary. I was delighted that I would be able to repay his support by taking him on trips to Football League grounds where he could actually have a seat and watch the game in relative comfort.

I was just about to set off on a holiday to set me up for the start of the season when a letter arrived from the Association of Football League Referees and Linesmen inviting me to attend the annual conference to become a member. So off I went to the National Exhibition Centre at Birmingham where the feeling of achieving something really hit home when all the newly-appointed officials were asked to stand whilst they received applause from their established colleagues.

There I was, in the company of people I had admired from a distance, not just referees but a sprinkling of managers, players and members of the press. Little was I to know that one day I would become President of this organisation.

The 1984/85 pre-season period took on a different perspective for me. Instead of letting people come to me, I was ringing all over the place asking if I could referee or run the line as I was so desperate to try to be match sharp for when my fixture list came in. I had been advised that on the first day of the season I would be going to York to run the line against Walsall and I was looking forward to it with a mixture of excitement and trepidation. The big day was to be Saturday 28 August 1984 and it couldn't come soon enough.

When the day came I set off in my blue, four-door Vauxhall Chevette which, complete with its black vinyl roof, was my pride and joy. I had our Tom sitting alongside me and we spent the next hour talking excitedly about what was to come that afternoon. Tom seemed to be almost as thrilled as myself. After a while we decided to pull into a lay-by to have our packed lunch, consisting of cheese and chutney sandwiches and a flask of tea. I had no idea that at this level of competition refreshments would be supplied at the ground; this was to be a different world altogether.

On arrival at Bootham Crescent I felt very awkward, just like a schoolboy attending school for the first time. Like a school kid I was resplendent in my new uniform, in this case a blazer, with Football League badge sewn on, flannels and crisp white shirt. As we drew into the car park my sense of importance was given a boost when I saw a car parking space marked out for linesmen. This was a complete surprise and was something I was certainly not used to. What a huge improvement on parking in a muddy field, trying to avoid getting your car stuck, or in a dubious neighbourhood where you worried throughout the match whether your car would be standing on bricks when you got back to it. Luxury indeed.

The club secretary Tom Hughes, all six foot four inches of him, came out to meet me. Tom was a real gentleman and did his best to put me at ease. As I was the first of the officials to arrive, Tom took me to the lounge to await my colleagues. The referee was to be David Scott from Burnley whom I had not met previously. This was my first experience of working with a real League referee and when David arrived it surprised me that he was so quiet, polite and unassuming. I think I had the impression that most referees would be more outgoing and boisterous. Where would I fit in on this scale, I wondered.

At 1.30 p.m. we went out to have a look at the pitch with the other linesman, Ken Lupton. Looking at the terraces and stands I got an even greater feeling of excitement which I found difficult to contain. I asked David at 1.45 if it was OK if I went to get changed and to mentally prepare for the game. He said this was all right and off I went on my own to get myself ready. This was a habit I was to indulge in for the rest of my career.

THE INITIATION

Regardless of what the other officials were doing I would always be in the changing room from 1.45. On this occasion I lost count of the number of times I trotted off to the Gents; it's funny how nerves and anticipation can affect you!

David came in at 2 p.m. to hold what would these days no doubt be called a team briefing. This is where the referee lays down specific instructions to the linesmen telling them how he intends to operate, what his style is, what sort of signals he wants, and all sorts of other detail. I think this particular meeting took twice as long as usual because of all my questions. I was really keen and wanted to know the back end of everything. He never said anything but I can imagine David thought I was a real pain and would have been glad to get out on the pitch for a bit of relief.

The managers of both teams came in at 2.15 to present their team-sheets, a procedure I had not witnessed before. This was quite daunting and brought home to me the fact that I was now operating in a professional and highly organised environment. Gone were the days of 'Can I tell you who the sub is later, ref, we're not sure who's going to get here first.'

All of the match preliminaries were fascinating but they only served to get me more hyped up and I was desperate for the clock to tick on and get us to kick-off time. Eventually 2.55 arrived and we went out onto the pitch, just the three of us, to a mixed reception. The older generation of supporter can generally muster polite applause, whilst the younger generation wouldn't want to damage their credibility by any such behaviour. Being an optimist I liked to think this was an age thing and that when they got older these same individuals would perhaps learn to appreciate the officials.

Your first game is one that you will never forget and I had to give full marks to David Scott for his superb handling of the game, particularly as he had a babbling, excited and jumpy character masquerading as a linesman. The crowd of four thousand was huge by my standards and this added to the excitement, to the point where I was sure I could hear the blood coursing through my veins. David had advised me not to be too anxious in waving my first ever League flag and I managed to contain my enthusiasm until ten minutes into the game. At this point a Walsall attacker moved into an offside position and I could feel myself willing his colleague to pass the ball to him. My telepathic powers brought immediate success and, whilst everything seemed as if it was happening in slow motion, I could feel my arm reaching for the sky. As the whistle sounded, the Hallelujah Chorus resounded through my head. It was only an offside decision but I felt like doing a lap of honour. The remainder of the game passed without any major incidents. I had not been involved in any contentious decisions and the game had gone really well. The result was one goal each but that was totally incidental to me; I had achieved my dream of officiating in the Football League and felt I was on my way.

As Tom and I drove back up the A19 I was so elated I could hardly speak. When we were almost home we stopped at a pub in Chester-le-Street where, over a pint of beer, the enormity of it all suddenly sank in. I apparently repeated the same questions again and again, trying to establish whether I had let anyone down. A couple of drinks helped calm me down and I then returned home to my wife Margaret and two sons, Ben and Carl, who were waiting anxiously to see how I had fared.

The next day I raided the local newsagent's for a selection of Sunday papers to see if I had been mentioned. Not a word. I am not sure whether I was pleased or not. On the one hand I wanted to see my contribution mentioned, on the other hand no mention presumably meant no controversy, which in turn meant no mistakes (of any significance anyway). Tom Hughes was later good enough to send me the local newspaper report and, again, there was no mention of any of the officials. I had decided this was good news and should be the way all referees and linesmen like it.

After about ten days the formal League report came in and I was pleased, not to mention relieved, to learn that I had been deemed to have had a satisfactory game by the match assessor. Having had reasonable feedback on my first performance I was anxious to get involved again. Unfortunately I had to wait a month before my next fixture. In the meantime I filled in with games in the lower leagues where I would continue to operate for quite some time.

The extra experience and confidence gained from my League debut rubbed off onto my Northern League performances and by now I was apparently being recognised as a 'canny referee'. I couldn't ask for more. I was also enjoying the fact that I was suddenly surrounded by a sort of aura when I turned up at local venues. It seemed as if by my appearance the match assumed a new dimension. I think this was fun for the players involved and I certainly didn't mind the extra respect that seemed to come with it.

I had been appointed to twelve games in the Football League and they all passed fairly uneventfully. The most unusual event in these games occurred during only my second game, a match between Doncaster and Bolton, where the referee, Tony Ward, decided to lie down in the centre circle. I was bemused by this figure lying on his back and blowing his whistle in the process. Unfortunately for Tony he had jarred his back, partly owing to the hard ground conditions. Most referees would have been embarrassed by this but not Tony, who you could say was laid-back in more ways than one.

A feeling of panic set in as I thought about the possible implications if he was unable to continue. In those days there was no such thing as a reserve referee or fourth official. The practice was for the senior linesman, in this case a chap called Peter Holland, to take over. The junior linesman would then take over the role of the senior and this included the responsibility for dealing with control of the dugouts, something that filled me with dread at this early stage of my League career.

A recruit would then be sought from the crowd to take over on the line. Preferably this person would be a qualified referee of some sort but this could not always be assured. It now seems unthinkable that an unqualified person could be asked to take part as an official but it really did happen in those days, even at the highest level. This resulted in some interesting situations, not least of which saw Jimmy Hill running the line in a Football League fixture. At least Jimmy was a qualified referee, or so he says.

The trainer came on and the crowd entertained themselves while Tony underwent an on-pitch massage. He seemed to thoroughly enjoy this and to my relief he somehow managed to get up and carried on for the rest of the match. Only Tony could have nonchalantly brushed himself down and carried on as if nothing had happened. I didn't know at the time that I would one day suffer the indignity of lying on my back in front of thousands of people, many more thousands as it happened.

I was lucky enough to meet one of the all-time heroes of English soccer when I ran the line at the Hartlepool v Southend game in October 1984. The late, great, Bobby Moore, who was manager of Southend at the time, brought in his team sheet to be greeted by 'Is tha' all reet lad' from the inimitable John Key, a referee from Rotherham. John was a real joker and when Bobby walked in he was amused (I think that was the expression) to be confronted by John wearing a pair of spectacles purchased from the local joke shop. This was the type with long eyeballs on springs hanging down from the frames. Bobby's immediate reaction was something like, 'Oh, I see the proper ref hasn't turned up then.' He must have thought, '******* Hell, I've come a long way down the ladder since '66!'

Later that month, at the Carlisle v Notts County game, I found the officials' dressing room door locked. After trying the handle I heard a voice say, 'Come back in ten minutes.' This I did, only to spot a young lady leaving the dressing room with a beaming referee. I take it she had been treated to a pre-match team talk and perhaps a rub down.

At Oakwell, when Barnsley were entertaining Manchester City, the referee, ten minutes before the kick-off, passed me and the other linesman a flask and said, 'Take a little sip of this, lads, it will clear your passages.' Next thing I knew I was choking on neat whisky. I have to say, though, that the referee had a splendid game and I think we all enjoyed our pre-match warm-up.

In January 1985 I had the 'privilege' of an evening game at Hartlepool in the Freight-Rover Cup. The pitch was frozen but the referee had advised the home team that if they rolled the pitch and flattened the ridges and troughs they could play. They were really keen to do this as the game had already been postponed five times because of the weather. It had reached the point where the game was to be decided by the toss of a coin if it didn't go ahead on this occasion. A steam-roller was somehow found from somewhere and the pitch was flattened enough to become playable. However the temperature that night dropped to -11C, which was not so brilliant as the only official kit I possessed at that stage was a short-sleeved shirt!

Whilst all this was going on I was giving my all in twenty-eight Northern League games. I was really enjoying these games as my new-found status and confidence added an extra dimension to my performance. I was a busy man but that's the way I like it.

One of the most tragic events ever to happen at an English football ground happened shortly before the end of the season. The Bradford City fire, which resulted in the loss of 56 lives, took place on Saturday 11 May 1985. Ironically this happened on a day meant for celebration as the club had just won the Third Division Championship and were presented with the trophy before the match.

As it happened, I had been linesman at Bradford shortly before the fire and my father had been in the crowd watching me. It brought home just how the unthinkable can happen and how much in life is down to luck. All of football was shocked by this event and it must have been horrific for everyone who was present, including the officials, who I know were badly affected.

It is pleasing to see that the club has recovered, as far as it is possible to recover from such an event, but it goes without saying that the tragedy will live on forever in the memories of the people of Bradford and everyone associated with the club. One positive thing coming out of the tragedy is that it prompted a full enquiry and legislation was subsequently introduced to protect the safety of people at other grounds where a similar tragedy might have been possible.

This tragic season had now come to an end and it was rounded off for me with the Durham FA Challenge Cup Final between Spennymoor United and Bishop Auckland. It was unfortunate for me that this was the first season where the person appointed to this fixture was not automatically invited to interview with a view to becoming a Football League referee. This policy had been replaced by the 'Panel' system and I believe this change cost me three years of refereeing at the highest level.

I had done all I could to enhance my prospects and I was now anxious to find out if I was to be retained on the League list of linesmen for the forthcoming 1985/86 season. The notification of the movement in status, either up or down, after the season ends is very rapid so when the letters arrive it is a scary experience opening them.

When you've put so much into something the bad news can be devastating but on the other hand the relief is immense if the news is good. On this particular occasion I can only describe the feeling as one of euphoria when I read that I had not only been retained but also promoted again, this time to the list of 'Panel' referees! This involved working in the GM Vauxhall Conference, the Central League and the Football Combination. To cut a long story short, independent scrutiny in every game could lead to becoming a referee on the Football League. The Stairway to Heaven, or the Pathway to Hell, whichever way you prefer to look at it.

ONE NIGHT AT THE PALACE

When the season started I was inundated with appointments from all directions. I was a Football League linesman and a referee in the GM Conference, Central League, Northern League, Gateshead and District Sunday League and the Durham County FA competition. It was with a certain amount of sadness that I had to abandon the Sunday League as I had many friends in the local Gateshead football scene. They seemed to understand though and many of them have supported me and followed my fortunes since then.

During this season I was to complete 117 appointments covering 25,000 miles backwards and forwards to football matches. It was a wonderful experience but one which required a great deal of patience from my family. The fixtures were heavily biased towards the Panel games and my first such was at Sunderland against Burnley at Roker Park. Being a born and bred Newcastle United fan it was a strange experience to visit the 'Mackems' at their stronghold. However, I have to say they were as genuinely pleasant as anyone could wish for and all went very well.

The highlight of the season was being appointed as referee at St James' Park for a reserve match between Newcastle United and Manchester United. It was a wonderfully emotional feeling to walk out onto the hallowed St James' pitch. In those days the old main stand was a wooden affair with a big dome-like structure housing the press box. The floodlights consisted of four huge towers which were located at each corner of the ground. The lighting had a weird effect; everything but the pitch seemed to be blanked out. All I could see was a lush green surface and, outside of that, total blackness. This was really eerie as there was a crowd of 4,000 and I couldn't see one of them. Still, it meant that I didn't get easily distracted.

Following this wonderful experience I went to the other extreme with a nightmare match at Barrow against Northwich Victoria in the Conference. The Barrow supporters have a well earned reputation for hating all things other than Barrow but have a particular propensity for disliking referees. I was therefore not surprised when they screamed at me for the full 90 minutes and appeared as if they wanted to lynch me when they lost 2-1. I was only too pleased to get out of this hell-hole and couldn't get on to the A69 quick enough.

As usual, after the game I discussed with my colleagues whether the baying crowds did in fact have a point. The answer I got was not to worry, I was excellent and the crowd were just fanatical misfits. I was brought back to earth a few days later when I got my assessment from the official observer, tearing my performance to bits. I was so angry that I only just stopped myself ripping it up and had to put it on one side to read again later.

At this point I learned two lessons: firstly, do not ask your colleagues after a game how you performed (bearing in mind that they know you are responsible for marking them) and secondly, always be honest with yourself when the assessment is not what you want to read. I therefore owe a debt to a man called Jerry Jones, the assessor that evening, for his honest criticism and advice. I decided that in future all such advice would be taken as objective and constructive.

My most vivid recollection of the season was fighting my way through snow storms across the North Yorkshire moors with Russell Tiffin and Eric Pickersgill for a mid-week evening game between Scarborough and Frickley Athletic, two local rivals. After much consultation with the ground staff, team officials and the police it was finally decided to play the match after the Scarborough Chairman walked in and said, 'Tha's no way you can call it off, I've just paid for two hundred fresh pies!'

And so the decision was made. The scene at kick-off put even the most colourful rainbow to shame. A white pitch, lines marked out of purple dye, Scarborough in red shirts and socks with white shorts and the goalkeeper in yellow. Frickley in green, the goalkeeper in blue. Then there were the officials in black and, finally, an orange ball! Anyway, the game went well, the spectators had their pies and the result of a 2-2 draw seemed to keep everybody happy.

We were advised by the police not to try to get home owing to the continuing snow but with us all being at work the next day we had little choice. When we got back to Durham, where Eric's car was parked at his workplace, all that could be seen through the blizzard was a line of snow-covered pyramids. Eric hadn't a clue which was his vehicle among all the cars belonging to the nightshift workers. Russell and I left him to it and drove away in stitches. It was 2 a.m. and it was good to finish a gruelling night with a laugh, even if it was at Eric's expense!

I finally got home at 3 a.m, and went to work as usual at 8 a.m. I hadn't got any sleep in between times due to the adrenalin still pumping around my body. Either I can put on a good act of being fairly coherent whilst half asleep or my colleagues and bosses at British Telecom were very understanding. Perhaps a bit of both.

Towards the end of 1985 I received my first ever FA Cup appointment. This was to run the line at my 'old stamping ground' of York City where it had all started for me just fifteen months earlier. City were playing non-league Morecambe, a tricky hurdle to overcome. It is always a difficult situation for a league club when they are paired with non-league sides. It is a no win situation as their supporters expect a comfortable victory and even if the League side win, if it is not convincing they can take a lot of criticism. Sure enough Morecambe performed heroics on the day and fought out a creditable 0-0 draw to take City for a day out at the seaside. It was nice to see that on this occasion, rather than harangue their own team for a poor display, the City fans instead applauded Morecambe for their gritty play.

I visited Bradford again in March 1986, almost a year after the fire disaster. The game should have been held at the Bradford Rugby League ground, Odsal Stadium, as the Valley Parade ground was still closed. However, the game had to be diverted to Huddersfield Town's ground as at the previous home game against Leeds United the away fans had senselessly set fire to a chip van and rolled it down an embankment. This was particularly obscene in view of what had happened a year earlier. As a result Bradford were forced to hold their home games at Huddersfield and Elland Road.

It had been a busy and interesting season for me and as it ended I reviewed my progress. I was aware that 1986/87 would be my chance to really make it as a referee if only I could get the breaks.

When the season came round I found there were problems because of my geographical location. Because of the financial restrictions now applying to most of the leagues I was to get only two Conference games and nine Central League games. Fortunately, the Football League had a bigger budget than most for expenses and they gave me fifteen appointments. For Football League linesmen the operational area extended from Newcastle in the north to Barnsley in the south and from Huddersfield in the west to Hull in the east.

Most of the League games passed without much to report, a statistic, I suppose, which could indicate success from a refereeing point of view. One game which did have major significance was that between Middlesbrough and Bury at Ayresome Park. Boro had been on the verge of extinction, with the liquidator having given a stay of execution. The embargo on home games, owing to the freezing of assets, had just been lifted and this was to be the first game of Middlesbrough FC (1986) Ltd.

When I arrived at Ayresome I couldn't use the official car park as it was chained up and I ended up parking in a nearby school car park. Outside the ground, huge queues were forming as there were only two turnstiles open. This prompted the police to order a delay in the kick-off as there was the possibility of problems outside the ground if the majority were still waiting to get in when the game started. The modest crowd of 8,000 that afternoon witnessed the resurgence of the club and although they only drew on the day they never looked back after being rescued financially by ICI, who at that time were a major employer on Teesside.

It was during this season that I came across two referees who for reasons best known to themselves actually gave their pre-match instructions in the nude! I still haven't fathomed out why but they were both in the habit of stripping off and parading around the changing room in all their glory. One of these individuals also had a thing about the personal appearance of all his officials before they took the field. I was present on one occasion when he produced a clothes brush and proceeded to brush the shoulders of one of the linesmen. I decided I wasn't having any of this so I looked at the ref and said, 'Come near me with that thing and I'll stick it up your ****.' I'm pleased to say he didn't take me up on the offer..

A memorable event in the Central League that year was when I came across a young lad called Gascoigne in the Newcastle v Forest reserve game. He had the audacity to say to me, whilst he was defending a corner, 'Watch me ref, watch what happens next.' The ball duly arrived and Gazza gained possession in his own six yard area. He proceeded to advance up the pitch at speed, beating anyone who dared to challenge him. Unfortunately he didn't score but he did graze the crossbar. He turned around with a smile on his face and an impish wink, effectively saying, 'Not bad eh?' Concealing my admiration for a piece of sheer brilliance I nonchalantly said, 'You missed.' '**** off' came the response through his broad grin.

Another interesting Central League game featured Sunderland and Manchester City where the Roker crowd were giving some stick to one of their not so favourite players, Terry Curran. At 2-2 the crowd were jeering Curran and, as he made his way up the field to be substituted, I spotted him making a two fingered salute to the crowd with both hands. I decided to take the unusual step of sending off someone who was in the process of being substituted. As he was running down the tunnel I ran after him waving the red card. Before I could reach him he had been arrested and taken to the police station where he spent the rest of the evening.

Curran appealed against the dismissal, his defence being that he was indicating the score to the crowd! He was actually found not guilty because of a lack of preparation on my behalf, the crux of his defence revolving around the position of the officials and what they could and could not have seen. To be fair to Terry he took me and my fellow officials into the bar after the hearing, bought us a drink and admitted how lucky he was. He added that he had parted company with his friends in Sunderland and was on his way to America to try his luck.

At the end of the season I reflected on the fifteen League games I had been involved in and felt that I had acquitted myself very well. This was confirmed when I received a telephone call from the national assessment co-ordinator advising that my rapid improvement had catapulted me into a position where I would be considered for interview to become a Football League referee.

I therefore looked forward to the summer break, full of optimism and hope for the coming season.

As the new season approached I was waiting with anticipation, hoping against hope for the call to interview. My hopes were dashed when I found out that a chap called Joe Timmins, a Scottish League referee who had moved south of the border with his work as a banker, had been 'fast-tracked' ahead of me - the bastard!

The 1987/88 season was, however, to be my most enjoyable yet. I had decided to put the disappointment behind me and I adopted a positive attitude in an effort to achieve my eventual target. This season I would carry out 17 Football League games as linesman and 14 panel games as referee and, to my amazement, I would in September 1987 be appointed to run the line in a UEFA cup match.

The first three games of the season didn't fire the imagination very much when I was sent on safari to Hartlepool, Darlington and

Middlesbrough. In August I had a pleasant diversion when I received an appointment to referee the GM Conference Shield, the non-league equivalent of the Charity Shield. The game was between Scarborough, the current Conference champions, who had just been promoted to Football League Division Four, and the 1987 FA Trophy winners Kidderminster Harriers. This provided a wonderful opportunity to shine in front of the Conference and Football League hierarchy. I was very fortunate that everything went perfectly; I had a good game and, from comments received, it seemed I had done myself no harm at all.

In early September I received a phone call from a chap called Reg Payne in the FA Referees Department. 'I have a UEFA Cup appointment if you would like it,' said the voice at the other end of the phone. I had never met Reg before although I had heard his voice on one occasion. I was therefore frantically trying to assess whether this was a wind-up, to the point where he said, 'Are you still there?' Awakening from my stupor I managed to say, 'Yes, yes, I would be delighted to accept,' and yes I knew it would mean three days off work, travelling abroad, might need a vaccination, might need a visa. 'Whoa, one step at a time. You're off to Dundee,' he said, 'details will be in the post, cheerio.'

When the letter arrived it contained the information: 'Alan Wilkie, linesman no. 2, Chester-le-Street, County Durham. Drive to Manchester, fly to Edinburgh, meet Dundee liaison officer.' 'Hang on,' I thought, 'Manchester airport is 160 miles away from where I live and Dundee is only 180 miles away, seems like rather a strange arrangement.' I decided to ring Reg Payne and outline my thoughts. I was put in my place in no uncertain terms - 'We decide how and when and at what cost our people travel; if you don't want to go ring me tomorrow.' With that he put the phone down.

I was horrified, what had I done? Was my first plum appointment in jeopardy? I never slept a wink all night. However, when the mail arrived the next day there was a letter from the FA explaining that owing to geographical considerations, and ever mindful awareness of costs, would I be prepared to drive to Dundee, arriving on Tuesday at 3 p.m., signed Reg Payne! Relief, joy, and satisfaction were all experienced in equal measure. At the same time I was more than a little angry. Not to worry, Dundee here I come.

When I eventually got to Dundee, I negotiated my way to Broughty Ferry and checked in at the hotel where I and the other officials were staying. In the evening we were taken out by the Dundee United representative and found ourselves guests of honour at the opening of the brand new Stakis hotel on the waterfront. We were dined like royalty and this was a very nice introduction to the 'European' way of life. The next day we were whisked off to Perth to tour a glass making factory and a distillery before retiring to the hotel at 3 p.m. for a pre-match nap. I was getting to like this European match hospitality.

The game was uneventful, dour even, and we three officials were booed more than the opposing team because we were English! I saw Willie McFaul, the Newcastle manager, in the Directors' Lounge after the game and, being rather naive in these matters, I asked him what he was doing there. 'Looking at a player,' he said. 'Which one?' I asked. 'Can't say,' replied Willie, 'because the price will go up.' It turned out to be, in fact, Michael O'Neill, an eighteen year old who was playing in the match for the visitors, Coleraine. The Irish side managed a 1-1 draw on the night although they lost on aggregate. Michael must have made an impression as he did eventually end up at Newcastle where he never quite fulfilled his considerable potential, although he was very popular with the fans.

Following the game I was luxuriating in one of the three individual baths in the referee's changing room, with a glass of whisky in my hand; this was after all Scotland. I was telling myself this is as good as it gets when suddenly in walked the Dundee chairman and presented each of us with a gift consisting of a Timex wrist watch, Timex being one of the major employers in the city at the time. I was completely taken aback by this as I was new to the European circuit and had no idea of the level of hospitality involved. A relaxing evening in an Italian restaurant completed a perfect day. The following morning it was back to the real world and I drove home, dropping off John Gow, the match observer from Wales, at Edinburgh airport on the way.

Back in England, League games as a linesman were progressing well and I was learning all the time. I was also at this time continuing to referee in the Northern League as well as the Panel games. Whilst these games were very nice I was craving greater challenges. My chance came when the Football League made efforts to combat the lack of flexibility that the regionalisation policy was causing. The only trouble was that they tried to solve the issue in the most penny-pinching way.

THE INITIATION

They came up with a system whereby a linesman could actually cross the Pennines and spread his wings, so to speak, to the north-east or north-west as appropriate. However, we would have to travel by rail, standard class, on the day of the game. The thinking behind this was that a cheap day return would be more economical than paying a mileage rate for use of a car!

My appointed trip was to Liverpool for Everton v Derby on 12 December and I enthusiastically agreed to co-operate with the experiment. I got up early on the Saturday morning and caught the 7.15 a.m. train from Durham. This was the Trans-Pennine to Liverpool, a train apparently stopping at every station in the universe. I arrived at Liverpool at mid-day, stiff and weary. I was supposed to get the bus to Goodison Park which, looking back, seems a bit of an archaic arrangement. Getting on public transport on Merseyside just before the match, dressed in a Football League blazer, didn't seem such a wonderful idea. I decided to take the prudent course which was to fund a cab from my own pocket.

The match itself was brilliant and I was enthralled to participate in the running of the game in front of 40,000 fans. Derby had a good side, with Mark Wright being the captain at the time. Everton had the likes of Neville Southall, Dave Watson, Kevin Ratcliffe and Graeme Sharpe. The game lived up to expectations and was an exciting and entertaining 2 - 2 draw. Then the down side, the 6 p.m. train from Liverpool Lime Street back to Durham, just in time to catch Match Of The Day at 11 p.m. A pretty tiring affair, all told.

I fed my report into the League and suggested that such travelling arrangements weren't conducive to effective performance at this level. Apparently I was not alone in this belief and some people were circumventing the arrangements and using their own transport, at a financial loss, in order to make the travelling civilised and to provide the facility to take guests. The experiment was therefore consigned to the League dustbin of bright ideas.

One of the most exciting games I have been involved in was on Boxing Day 1987 when I refereed Lincoln, who had just been relegated from the old Division Four, against Kidderminster who were one of the most disciplined footballing sides I had ever come across. Lincoln were lying third in the Conference and Kidderminster were top. Lincoln, however, were starting to hit form in a big way so I was really up for this match. The game was magnificent, provided nine goals (there could have been many more) and a Conference record crowd of 6,500. Lincoln ran out winners by 6-3 and went on to become worthy champions, breaking their own Conference attendance record at every subsequent home game to the end of the season.

This was great stuff; the only down side was that I realised I was becoming obsessive about my markings and this was beginning to eat into my enjoyment. The Lincoln game, however, along with the earlier Vauxhall Champion Shield, were to prove decisive. I apparently received a mark of nine out of ten for both games. This, allied to other respectable performances, would later see me called to an interview for a position as a referee in the Football League.

As this was my fourth season as linesman I was becoming reasonably senior to the other linesmen and with that came the extra responsibility of controlling the personnel on the benches. I was appointed to an FA Cup fourth round replay at Middlesbrough against Everton in February 1988, my most senior match so far. This would be a mid-week match under floodlights, a large crowd guaranteed and a game vitally important to both teams.

The adrenaline began to flow as I approached the packed streets surrounding Ayresome Park. This time the car park was open and the turnstiles fully manned. The referee specifically asked us to be aware of the importance of the game when dealing with irate players or staff. His anticipation was spot on. As we had expected, the game was tight, even and hard-fought. After about 75 minutes the referee played an advantage following a dubious tackle on Peter Reid by a Middlesbrough player.

The Everton bench were livid and rose as one to complain. I played it softly, remembering my instructions, but also I think because I agreed with them that it was a free kick and probably a yellow card. However, my senior colleague, the referee, saw it differently and it was my job to accept this and restore order. I thought I had done this when Terry Darracott jumped up and screamed, 'If you saw it why didn't you put your ******* flag up?' I responded that the offence was on the other half of the pitch and not within my jurisdiction. His response was to become even more irate and he repeatedly screamed, 'Get your ******* flag up.' At that point that's exactly what I did. The referee came over and, after I described what had happened, dismissed Terry for abusive language to a linesman. Barry Davies, who was commentating for the BBC, was heard to say 'He must have said something pretty hurtful as Mr Wilkie appears to be extremely upset.' I didn't realise it showed! The game eventually went to extra time and then to a second replay which Everton won after winning the toss to see who should play at home.

I felt the season was going pretty well and that I was becoming more assured. Then a letter arrived from the Football League inviting me to the centenary celebrations taking place at Wembley on a forthcoming Saturday and Sunday in April. At first I thought it was an invitation to watch. It was only when my wife read the letter that she pointed out it was actually an invitation to be a linesman. Me, Alan Wilkie, a linesman at Wembley! I must apologise to all of my friends, or even vague acquaintances, who were unfortunate enough to come across me in the next forty-eight hours. I was so excited that I had to go rushing around telling everyone.

I was very conscious that the Northern League still had to be satisfied with my performances and I couldn't afford to relax at this lower end of the scale. If I failed there, everything else would topple. I was delighted with what appeared to be continuing improvement with my performances and was thrilled when I received the Silver Whistle award which goes to the highest marked referee in the League, recognition indeed from the people who matter.

In early April, as I was looking forward to the Wembley adventure, another letter arrived with a Lytham St Annes postmark. As I had already received my forthcoming fixtures, I was intrigued as to what this might be. Could it be what I had been waiting for all this time? When I opened the letter the first thing I saw was the signature of Graham Kelly, then secretary of the Football League. The excitement mounted as I began to read the text of the letter and I saw that it was indeed an invitation to Football Association Headquarters at Lancaster Gate in London to be interviewed for inclusion on the Football League referees' list for the season 1988/89. What a year this was turning out to be.

The interviews were to be held on the Wednesday following the centenary celebrations at Wembley. I therefore thought that I could perhaps use the time at Wembley to impress and possibly get some information as to what to expect.

ONE NIGHT AT THE PALACE

The Wembley event, properly titled 'The Mercantile Credit Football League Centenary Festival', took place on the weekend of 16-17 April 1988. It was quite unique and consisted of a knock-out competition with games between specially invited teams from all Football League Divisions. The criteria for qualification was based on the number of league points accumulated in the fifteen games between the beginning of November and the end of February. A strange formula but scientifically researched, I am sure.

The complement was made up of eight First Division teams, four teams from Division Two and two each from the Third and Fourth Divisions. Day one would see eight teams knocked out and going home, while the second day would consist of quarter-finals, semis, and final. The games were 20 minutes each way and provided a few shocks. It was convenient that Liverpool, who were knocked out by Newcastle on day one, went home on the Saturday as this allowed Fourth Division Tranmere to take over their hotel beds after their surprise victory over First Division Wimbledon.

There was also a Ladies international between England and Ireland on the Sunday morning, which would be refereed by Jack Taylor, the 1974 World Cup Final referee. I managed to coerce the Football League into letting me work with Jack on the Ladies International and I ended up running the line. I learnt many things from Jack but the one thing that sticks in my mind is his advice to 'be sure of yourself and then calmly set about your business.'

Wembley was a great experience even though the crowds ranged from only 10,000 to about 35,000. On the Saturday I was involved with the Wimbledon v Tranmere and Luton v Manchester United games. On the Sunday I was involved in a quarter-final and semi-final after which I was handed a medal and told I was free to go. I was somewhat deflated that after this wonderful Wembley experience I was denied the opportunity of climbing the famous steps for presentation of my medal.

I drove back to the North East with Jack's words ringing in my ears, 'Be sure of yourself and do the business.' Repeating these words mantra fashion I tried to brainwash myself into a calm and assured frame of mind for the interview at Lancaster Gate in the coming week.

Bearing in mind the old adage, 'failure to prepare is to prepare for failure,' I approached various people in the business world to get advice on interviewing techniques. I then travelled to London by train on the Tuesday, staying overnight in a hotel prior to the interview to ensure I wouldn't be rushed on the day. I was as ready as I could be.

There were four people present at the interview: David Dein (Arsenal), Ron Noades (Crystal Palace), Ken Ridden (FA) and John Goggins (Football League). The interview lasted just eight minutes and I didn't quite know what to make of it. It seemed that the introductions took longer than the questions. I had heard that if you're in and out quickly then that means that they want you but you can never be sure.

I was advised that they would let me know in seven days but I couldn't pluck up the courage to ask whether that would be on the seventh day or within seven days, like tomorrow for instance. 'Be patient,' I told myself, 'I've waited a long time for this.' My mind then meandered to the fact that twelve people had been invited for interview and I knew that only eight were required. Knowing the two other candidates from the North East, Alan Dawson and Ian Cruickshank, self-doubt began to creep into my mind because I knew how good they were.

When the letter arrived, after six days, I wasn't sure whether to open it myself or to get someone else to do it. In the end I plucked up the courage and, as I unfolded the piece of paper, words jumped out at me like 'pleased', 'referees list', 'fitness test', 'happy to'. Piecing these together the message was that I had been successful and was to be promoted to the League list for 1988/89 subject to passing a fitness test.

It had taken a football accident and six months of abortive treatment to push me towards becoming a referee. It had taken disenchantment with running a minor league soccer team to encourage me to concentrate on being the man in the middle. But here I was; in under ten years, this daft but dedicated Geordie from Denton Burn, Newcastle, had somehow managed to comply with the laws of the game in a manner which players and officials were happy to accept. I had achieved the ultimate in becoming one of only 92 referees to make the league list out of 30,000 referees in the country.

I still had one fixture left as linesman and I had to get my feet back on the ground for this. It was a Fourth Division game between Carlisle United and Swansea City. This was the last game of the season and for Swansea it had been an exceptional year with them having just achieved promotion to the Third Division.

ONE NIGHT AT THE PALACE

I was trying hard to concentrate on my task but as the minutes ticked away I could sense myself having to hold back a smile as my career as a linesman drew to a close and the thoughts of refereeing in the next campaign loomed large in front of me. As Carlisle mounted an attack late in the game, the Swansea bench, led by their manager Terry Yorath, remonstrated with me for not raising my flag at what they thought should have been an offside decision. In closing, Yorath shouted forcibly, and in obvious ignorance of my impending promotion, 'You've got no future in this game, you'll never make a referee!'

3

A DIFFERENT LEAGUE

I HAD A wonderful summer and ensured that I kept up my level of fitness so that the annual fitness test would be a formality, which it proved to be. As the new season approached I reflected on how everything seemed so unreal. Here I was on the verge of refereeing in the Football League and I hadn't quite taken it all in. My life seemed to have taken off at an alarming pace. Days merged into one another with all the demands upon my time. Apart from preparation for the season, I was in great demand by various organisations, particularly local Referees' Societies, who wanted me to come and talk to them. I rarely turned them down as it was quite something for them to get a colleague appointed to the League and I had found the Societies to be very supportive in my early days.

In mid-July I received the fixture list for the coming August and September; hopefully this would indicate my first fixtures as a League referee. I opened the letter with anticipation, hoping against hope to be in action on the first day. I studied the Division Four fixtures and to my horror saw that my name was not included. I had to scour the list further before I came across, scheduled for later in the month, my name against Scarborough v Rochdale. Idly browsing through the list for other items of interest involving people I knew, something started flashing in neon lights in the Division Three list. To my amazement I saw that I was nominated for the Division Three match Mansfield Town v Northampton Town on the first day of the season. I was, for some reason, the only one of the new starters to be given a Division Three game as their first fixture. This gave me a tremendous boost as well as coming as a welcome surprise.

Once the euphoria had settled, the concerns set in. Where is Mansfield? I hadn't a clue. How far is it? Do I stay overnight? What is expected of me? This is when I turned to local colleagues and newly appointed referees for eagerly accepted advice and support. I then mapped out my pre-season training and by the time the Mansfield game arrived I was in pretty good shape. On Friday 26 August 1988 I packed the car with my kit bag and set off to Mansfield some 150 miles away. I was travelling alone now as my brother Tom had changed his job and was no longer free on a Saturday. I arrived at 9 p.m., strangely calm and relaxed; even more so after having a couple of beers as a night-cap.

I surprised myself in the morning by being able to eat breakfast. I had expected that the nerves would dissipate my appetite. I watched the clock, willing it to speed round to 12 noon, and when it eventually did so I paid the bill and left to find the ground. I was the first one there and my first impressions were how big it was from the outside. Having never been there before this was all exciting and new. The beauty of a 'first day' fixture is that the ground, pitch and everything attached to the game is as good as it will ever be. After the opening day it will deteriorate relentlessly but on the opening day it might as well be Wembley. That's the feeling I got at Mansfield and was the same emotion I would experience at the beginning of every subsequent season.

My two colleagues that first day were Alf Hackett and Paul Rejer, experienced men who much to my relief assisted me greatly throughout the day. I had hoped to keep the fact that it was my first match fairly low profile. However, the first thing the Secretary said when he came in with the expenses book was, 'Good luck lad, I know it's your first game.' A few minutes later the security man came in for a briefing and passed on the same comments. Eventually it was time for the exchange of team sheets. When both teams' managers and captains walked in I could feel them looking me up and down. I therefore decided to grab the bull by the horns and before anyone could speak I said in a loud and, I think, assertive tone, 'Good afternoon gentlemen, these are my colleagues for today. I'm extremely pleased to be starting my career at Mansfield and I know I can rely on every assistance from you all. I'll ring the bell at 2.55 and I wish you luck, thank you.' When they left Alf turned to me and said, 'Bloody hell, I would think they know who's boss now lad.'

I went out on to the pitch to do some warming up, something that was very unusual in those days. One man in the crowd, obviously confused at this stranger on the pitch, shouted, 'Whats tha' name lad, when did we sign thee?' The look on his face was a picture when I told him I was the referee. 'Well, bugger me,' was his response. I returned to the dressing room and the enormity of the occasion and the expectation began to settle on my shoulders. 'Will my experience in the Conference and Central League be enough?' I thought. I then told myself they wouldn't have selected me if they didn't have faith in my ability, so trust their judgement.

No turning back now, it's 2.55 p.m., time to press the bell. In those days the teams didn't walk out together. This was the day of the home team being cheered onto the pitch and the opposition, and most likely the officials, being jeered on their emergence from the tunnel. I seem to recall my reception was one of polite applause, something for which I am forever grateful to the people of Mansfield.

The march onto the pitch was magnificent; my chest felt tight and my heart was pumping. My legs were like lead but when I arrived at the centre spot this all seemed to disappear. I checked the nets, went back to the middle, met the two captains, who still seemed to be trying to work out what to make of the new boy, and began the ritual of tossing the coin.

'This is it,' I thought, 'this is what I have worked so hard for, so just enjoy it.' With that thought and Jack Taylor's words coming back into my mind I gave a signal to the linesmen to start their watches and then I blew the whistle. We were off.

The first thing that struck me was the noticeable difference in pace, compared to what I was used to, and the movement off the ball by players. I could see them trying to comply with the respective managers' well thought out game plans. This was fascinating and to my surprise I found I was able to recognise what was going on in terms of the tactics whilst still controlling the game. The pitch was splendid, running was easy but it was very hot. At half-time I arranged for some water to be placed at the touchline for the players to take a drink during stoppages and play. This turned out to be a smart move and was very well received by the players and managers. The first half went well apart from having to speak to a couple of players for poor challenges. It was quite an open game but I knew the crunch would come when either side scored. After about 55 minutes the inevitable happened and Northampton scored. Sure enough the pace increased once more and I could feel the temperature rising..

A lesson I learned early in my refereeing career was that when the going gets tough there will be personal contests developing all over the field.

These will often develop into feuds and then flare-ups are inevitable. I became aware that Billy Gilbert, the little midfield general at Northampton, was in the ascendancy. I noticed that every ball from defence was coming through him and he was doing all the prompting for the Northampton attacks. His opponent, Kevin Kent of Mansfield, a tall athletic competitor, was now being over-run and whereas his previous challenges had resulted in winning the ball he was now struggling.

It wasn't long before Kevin flattened Billy without ceremony. As I had been aware of the developing situation I was well prepared for it and I vaulted over the moaning Gilbert to administer a caution to Kent. However, my concentration was so intense I was in a world of my own. The next thing I knew I felt a tap on the shoulder and when I turned round I was confronted by a Northampton player who politely asked, 'Excuse me ref, but do you think Billy could have the trainer on?' What an embarrassment, I had been so busy taking disciplinary action and was so pleased with myself for having anticipated the situation that I had completely forgotten about the poor victim lying on the ground.

Looking at the positive side, it was a good learning point and I vowed never to make the same mistake again. I am pleased to say that the expected reprisals over Kent's rough tackle did not materialise. Eventually Mansfield equalised and the game was over, finishing in a 1-1 draw. A number of players took the time to congratulate me on my performance, which was pleasing.

The officials of both clubs made favourable comments to me for which I was grateful but, on later reflection, I kept coming back to the fact that they always added at the end '...for your first game!' The final comment for me was from Alf Hackett, who said, 'You've set yourself a very high standard, I hope you're able to maintain it, because if you can the sky's the limit, good luck.' I dwelt on these words all the way home: was he just being nice or was there substance in this experienced linesman's opinion? Time would tell.

I arrived home and talked incessantly about the game and probably did so throughout the night. Apart from my personal pride about what I had achieved I was also feeling what all referees feel; that we really care about the effect we have on a game and recognise that the game is for the players and spectators. It is up to the referee to create the right atmosphere, direction and discipline of the match to ensure that everyone enjoys it. I hoped that I had achieved these standards in my first match.

On Thursday the assessment arrived. I had been observed by one of the top assessors in the country, Reg Leafe, who actually refereed in the 1950 World Cup Finals in Brazil. His report was very favourable indeed with the only criticism being, as expected, about the treatment of the injury to Billy Gilbert. And so the book closed on the first of what would be 456 top-flight games.

The next fixture was coming up fast and that was to be another visit to Scarborough. My familiarity with the very nice Scarborough club lessened the tension somewhat but I did have a perceived problem in that my senior linesman was Ian Cruickshank, who was one of the unsuccessful applicants at my interview session at Lancaster Gate. I knew Ian through the Northern League but not really very well at that time. I have to say, however, that his attitude couldn't have been better and we had a wonderful game, a lovely sunny day, with six goals to keep the crowd entertained.

Games followed thick and fast over the following weeks. These included Burnley v Colchester, Rotherham v Exeter and Blackpool v Sheffield United. These all passed without particular incident and I seemed to be getting reasonable reports from the assessors. Then came Bury v Southend, a mid-week fixture under floodlights. I arrived at Gigg Lane full of anticipation and feeling pretty good with myself so far.

This was the day I met Wilf McGuiness, who was formerly manager of Manchester United. A more amusing and genuine man I have yet to meet. Wilf had no hair left owing to the strain of his time in charge at Old Trafford. When I asked him if he missed it he said, 'Not really, it's only been three years, four months, nineteen days and ten hours since I got the bullet.'

The game had no history and no expectancy of any trouble. Bury scored first and then I awarded Southend a penalty for a foul on Danny O'Shea by Paul Rogers. The usual complaints took place but to my mind it was a certain penalty and the players eventually backed off.

Southend equalised from the spot and I was on red alert, knowing that things were rather heated. O'Shea and Rogers seemed to be getting engaged in animated conversation so I decided to keep an eye on them. The ball was cleared upfield for a Bury attack when, to everyone's surprise, I blew the whistle. A sixth sense had made me stay with the Bury defence and this enabled me to witness O'Shea elbow Rogers in the face, breaking his nose in the process. Before anyone could react I had shown the red card and O'Shea to his credit turned and ran off without question.

The problem was that none of his colleagues had seen what had happened and they all surrounded me, questioning my actions. I blew the whistle loudly and attracted the captain and told him what had happened. His response was, 'You'd better be right or there will be trouble.' As the teams lined up for the second half the Southend captain came over and shook my hand. 'You were totally correct,' he said, 'You'll have no problem from my team this half.' It's nice to know that this responsible and sporting attitude can prevail in a really competitive situation.

During the second half I awarded a penalty to Bury and they went ahead, eventually winning the game. There was no dissent at all and I have to say this was thanks to Danny O'Shea for being honest and telling the truth about the elbow incidence.

After the game I decided to go into the Bury supporters' club bar, a practice which I don't think was very usual among referees! When I walked in it was like the parting of the Red Sea and everything descended into a hushed silence.

There was a big screen in the corner and a re-run of the game was being played. As I went to buy a drink, a man at the bar asked why I had sent the Southend player off. I turned to the screen, recognised the passage of play, and said, 'In about two or three minutes you'll find out.' At this he shouted to one and all, 'It's coming, it's coming.' I had just ordered a pint of bitter when there was a large cheer as everyone watched the sending-off incident. I turned to pay the barman and the man who had asked the question said, 'I'll pay for that, that was a brilliant spot.' I spent the next half hour chatting, had another drink paid for, and then I bid my unexpected friends farewell and set off to Blackpool where I was spending the weekend with my family. It rained and rained, as it always does in Blackpool. We were soaked to the skin but who cared, it was an excellent trip.

Although I was heavily engrossed in the domestic scene I was delighted to be offered another European appointment, this time a European Cup game between Porto and PSV Eindhoven. Rather more exotic than Dundee and certainly an exciting prospect.

A DIFFERENT LEAGUE

The format of these European trips is that they last for three days and the visiting officials are really well looked after. None of this getting your own taxi or public transport business. The flights were all Business Class or better, so a Bucks Fizz with lunch on the way out to Porto was very welcome. My colleagues for this trip were George Courtney, who would be referee, and Brian Hill, who would be senior linesman. We were met at the airport by an ex-FIFA referee, Julio Guemerez, who would be our guide for the next three days. We booked into the Hotel Atlantico and went into the centre of Porto for a meal and a drink in two different establishments, both owned by the club. If our hosts had got their way there would have been other 'hospitality' on the menu but we graciously declined. On the morning of the game I attended the safety briefing followed by lunch and a short trip around the sights and then it was time for the usual short nap before the match.

I expected this to be a fairly low-key game with next to no crowd as Porto were 5-0 down from the first leg. We took to the pitch and I was stunned when I discovered there were 100,000 people in the stadium. They were screaming for their team and for the blood of everyone else around. What an atmosphere.

The Eindhoven team looked in control throughout and I think they did the sensible thing in allowing Porto to score after 44 minutes and again after 88 minutes. This sent the crowd home with a moral victory and everyone was happy.

A feature of the European games, which I had discovered at the Dundee match, is the presentation of gifts to the officials after the game. Obviously this is a pretty delicate area. It turns out that the more prestigious the game, the more expensive the gift and there is a serious and definite protocol in place. I have to say that there seems to be a great deal of respect for English officials abroad, which makes a nice change from the attitude back home. With this thought I headed off to the airport for the flight back to Teesside.

My next game was Wigan v Bristol City. The memorable thing about this was that when I arrived at the ground I was surprised to find the goalposts were the wrong shape. I hadn't appreciated that in Wigan anyone asking for directions to Wigan's ground automatically ends up at the rugby stadium! The rugby staff were highly amused but very helpful. Apparently I wasn't the first to make this mistake.

ONE NIGHT AT THE PALACE

When I eventually arrived at Springfield Park, the correct venue, I observed that the set-up was very good and the commercial side seemed particularly buoyant. At the team sheet exchange the Wigan captain, Dave Hamilton, said to me, 'Great, another Geordie, at least we'll be able to talk to each other out there.' I'm afraid we didn't get much chance as I sent him off after six minutes. The Bristol captain, Steve Galliers, had slid along the ground to kick the ball out for a throw-in and the Wigan captain had stamped on Galliers' chest with both feet. I was no more than five yards away and sent him off immediately. City won 1-0 and there were no complaints from the players about my decisions. To my surprise, when leaving the field I was confronted by Joe Jordan, the Bristol manager, who said, 'Pity, the sending off spoilt the game.' I replied that I had no choice and he said, 'Yes, but it spoilt the game.' I will never understand managers' logic.

December's fixtures arrived and I saw that I had a game scheduled for New Year's Eve at Chesterfield, against Fulham. I made enquiries with the League to see if I had a match on 2 January and I was told, 'Yes you're at Nottingham Forest.' Forest were playing Everton in the old First Division. This was tremendous news and would be my first game as referee in the top division. As both games were in the same area I decided to take the family with me for New Year. We decided to stay at Wakefield, not renowned as the most exciting of places, but to us it was excellent. This was an exciting time and things were going really well.

The Chesterfield game on the Saturday got a bit out of hand when they quickly went into a three goal lead. Fulham pulled a goal back but soon went 4-1 down. At this point, spurred on by their captain Jeff Eckhardt, they became over-physical and for the first time in my refereeing career I had to caution six players in a match. I returned to the dressing room mentally drained, wondering what I could have done differently in order to avoid cautioning so many people.

Margaret and I had a splendid New Year's Eve, wining and dining in the Swallow Hotel in Wakefield while the boys created havoc upstairs in the bedroom. The next day I took the family home as they decided they would like to get back to their Christmas presents. I then turned around and headed down to Nottingham for an overnight stay prior to my big day, the induction into the top flight. This was absolute heaven to me, travelling the country, mixing with professional footballers and managers and being paid for it. It was as if I was in a dream world.

The morning of 2 January 1989 dawned. This was the most important day of my footballing life so far. I had been used to dealing with Divisions Four, Three and Two but what lay in store for me were these people I had only seen on TV. Going into the Directors' lounge for refreshments before the game and seeing all the trophies on display was a great experience. The home of the twice European Cup winners, and I was going to be out there in the middle refereeing. The pitch was in wonderful condition and generally this was a superb setting.

As kick-off time approached, Liam O'Kane for Forest and Colin Harvey for Everton brought the team sheets in. They both knew it was my first Division One game so I again grasped the nettle and told them how much I was looking forward to the match. I think they were a bit taken aback and the response was something like, 'Well yeah, right, yeah sure, right, well said, have a good game.' My colleagues looked at me, astounded that I had the confidence and temerity to take the initiative in this way.

I found the game a bit of a culture shock. The pace and skilful control was outstanding. Things were going well for me till about the sixty minute mark when Neville Southall held onto the ball for what appeared to be forever. This meant that I had to penalise him with an indirect free kick inside the penalty area. I was surrounded by Everton players and was feeling quite intimidated. My unlikely saviour was Peter Reid, who dragged his players away from me. In the event, the free kick was saved and as we ran back into position Reid ran alongside me and shouted in a Scouse accent, 'Hey you ****, you owe me big time, remember that.'

The game ended 2-0 to Forest and to his credit Reid came to me and shook my hand and was gracious enough to say well done. Neville Southall, however, was not so affable and I think the best I can say is that we disagreed in a friendly fashion. The best moment was when Brian Clough came in and passed a typical Cloughie comment; 'Young man, I thought you controlled the game very well, safe journey home, God bless.' With this he turned and left. Before Cloughie retired I was involved with his teams in a total of eight matches. I have to say that he never gave me any real trouble, apart from the odd lecture. He never went into tantrums like some managers but gave me the benefit of his 'advice' in a more school-masterly way. I remember one game, between Forest and Spurs, when the ball went out of play and ended up in Cloughie's arms. He wouldn't give me the ball back until he had given me a lecture on how I was not doing very well on the day. This in front of a crowd of 30,000. A unique character.

The season continued and I had every reason to be happy with my performance so far. There were one or two other memorable games before the end of the season, but memorable for very different reasons. Firstly, my very first visit to Walsall for the visit of Chelsea in the old Second Division. I was really excited and looking forward to this one; this was a big match for Walsall and it was going to be a full house. Tickets had been sold out for some time and the expectations were huge for little Walsall to create an upset. Sadly, someone forgot to tell Chelsea and they proceeded to demolish the opposition 7-0. Five goals came from a very sprightly Gordon Durie. Bobby Campbell, the Chelsea manager, came into my dressing room after the game looking for the ball to give to Gordon. He was shocked when I said, 'Sorry Bobby, but Walsall took it from me at the end.' He stormed out shouting 'I'll find it and I'll buy the ******* thing if I have to.'

Another highlight would be my appointment to referee the local derby between Bolton Wanderers and Preston North End. Upon arrival, I reported as usual to Des McBain, the club secretary, who always organised the guest tickets and sorted out the expenses book. There was an air of excitement around the place as games between these famous old clubs, particularly with them being neighbours, always generate a lot of tension and expectancy.

When I left the Secretary's office I bumped into the chairman, none other than the legendary Nat Lofthouse, the 'Lion of Vienna'. Nat introduced himself to me but he didn't really need to. I told him, whilst trying not to sound sycophantic, that it was my pleasure to meet him. He then promptly invited me into his office for a cup of tea and a chat. Even then, in 1989, he was aware that players were becoming more and more restricted by referee interpretation. He went on to mention the Manchester United v Bolton Wanderers FA Cup Final when he had infamously bundled the goalkeeper into the net and how he 'wouldn't get away with it now.' His enthusiasm for the game, even in his sixties, was truly outstanding. He outlined his plans for his beloved club, which included, among other things, a new ground; a vision now realised with the impressive Reebok stadium.

A DIFFERENT LEAGUE

As I was about to leave Nat's office, who should turn up at the door but his old adversary and England colleague Tom Finney. I could scarcely believe it, here was the great Tom Finney introducing himself to me and apologising for interrupting my chat with Nat Lofthouse. It's the stuff dreams are made of. As I left them to it, I could almost taste the nostalgia as they set about reliving their great moments in history. Much later in my career I was to enjoy Tom's company when he was guest of honour at the 1994 Charity Shield and after the game both he and his wife joined us for dinner.

The day of 15 April 1989 will live in the memory of football fans forever. This was the day of the Hillsborough disaster and I was at Leeds refereeing their game against Brighton. My two colleagues that day were Bob Ingham and Dave Nolan, both of whom had family going to the match at Hillsborough. When we met up, the talk was all about the traffic going down the road to Sheffield and how exciting it would be to be involved in a semi-final.

Half-way through the first half of the Leeds game I noticed a feeling of indifference in the crowd. The cheers were muted and in general people appeared to be talking and not watching. When I blew for half time and we made our way off the pitch, I said to Bob, 'Strange atmosphere out there.' When we got to the dressing room Dave looked at Bob and I and said, 'There's been an incident at Hillsborough, reports say many injured.' I could see the panic in the eyes of these two men who had children at the match.

News soon came through that the Hillsborough game had been abandoned and at that time there were reports of thirteen dead. I told Bob and Dave to go straight into the Secretary's office and insisted that I wasn't interested in them coming back to do their job until they had established that their children were safe. After about sixteen minutes Howard Wilkinson came in to enquire what was causing the delay. I outlined the situation and Howard was very supportive, merely asking to be given a couple of minutes notice before having to take to the pitch. We eventually resumed after a twenty-four minute delay by which time Bob and Dave had established that their families were safe. The game became a virtual nonentity as everyone knew about the horrors of Hillsborough. At the end of the match we left for home quickly and quietly, the game of football seeming inconsequential in such circumstances.

ONE NIGHT AT THE PALACE

The season concluded with me having completed twenty-two games in the Football League and receiving no adverse criticism of any consequence. On reflection, it might have been better had I received more pointed comment and advice as I now realise that I was again starting to believe people when they were saying how well I was doing. With the benefit of hindsight I can see that at that time I was starting to become a bit on the 'cocky' side. Referees need to be self-confident but there is a fine dividing line between confidence and over-confidence.

I had continued with my Northern League obligations when I was not on League duty. This was my last season with them and I was pleased to be presented again with the Silver Whistle award as the top referee on the merit list. It had been a splendid season topped off by the European assignment.

So, my first season as a Football League referee had passed by. I had learned a great deal, and had the urge to learn a great deal more. At the end of the season I was 21st out of 92 in the merit table. A commendable performance and one I could not fail to be proud of.

4

HOME AND AWAY

SEASON 1989-90 WOULD turn out to be a real test and my fortunes at home would be very different to those abroad. After the previous season, expectations were now high and there would be more than the eyes of the Football League upon me. The next step up from this level is appointment to the list of FIFA referees. To achieve this would be the ultimate accolade and would involve games all over the world.

As I was now an established Football League referee I was restricted to League games and had to give up the lesser leagues. Gaps therefore began to appear in my calendar and I would sometimes have two weeks between appointments. I didn't see the warning signs that this might just take the edge off my concentration.

The season started with a game at Rochdale against Burnley. I always try to do my homework to establish whether there are any 'leftovers' from previous games and there was nothing to indicate any bad blood for this particular fixture. It was obvious right from the start, however, that this was a grudge match. I had to produce the first of five yellow cards after just 24 seconds for a nasty late challenge.

Among all the nastiness an amusing incident happened halfway through the second half. As the ball was played upfield I automatically looked towards my linesman to see if there was an offside. I saw straight away a flash of yellow above his head. Automatically, I blew the whistle and awarded a free kick. My linesman looked at me incredulously and couldn't understand what I was doing. I then realised that in fact the flash of yellow was an inflatable banana being waved by a fan behind him! I am pleased to say that the players had a bit of a laugh when I told them what had happened and we re-started with a dropped ball. The assessor was not amused, however.

As winter approached, I was involved in a most unusual situation at Blackburn when they were due to play Watford on 21 October. The

ONE NIGHT AT THE PALACE

Blackburn manager, Don Mackay, came in at the appointed time of 2.15 p.m. with the team sheet. There was no sign though of the Watford manager Graham Taylor, or anyone else from the Watford club for that matter. When I asked Don about this he said, 'They're not here.' 'I'll go and get them,' I said. 'No, I mean they're not here,' said Don. 'If you're going for them you'd better get your helicopter out.' It turned out that the weather conditions had unfortunately caused a series of serious road accidents on the M6 and the road was completely closed. This meant that the Watford team coach had been unable to get anywhere near Blackburn. Unbelievably, even for those days, they did not have a mobile phone between them on the bus and couldn't get in contact with anyone at the club.

Eventually the police located the Watford wanderers and gave them an escort up the hard shoulder to Preston and back down to Blackburn. They arrived at the ground at 3.40, forty minutes after the scheduled kick-off time. The players had got changed on the bus, which was commendable, but it would not have been reasonable to ask them to get straight off the bus and into a kick-off situation. We agreed a kick-off time of 4 p.m. to allow the team to warm up properly. The crowd, by this time, were probably in need of a warm-up more than anyone.

The Blackburn secretary John Howarth seemed a bit perturbed by the delay and I asked him why he was concerned, as I wasn't aware of any problems with the floodlights. 'It's not that,' he said, 'It's just that if we have to keep any police back after 6 p.m. they go on to double time!' The police Inspector, in the meantime, was telling me to take all the time in the world.

The game got under way and ended up a two-all draw with Simon Garner scoring twice for Blackburn and Luther Blissett returning the compliment for Watford. I sent off a player from each side, the game finished at 5.45 and everyone went home happy, apart, perhaps, from the two dismissed players and the police who missed out on their overtime.

November brought with it the thought of turning out on freezing cold Saturday afternoons and, more depressingly, winter nights. I soon received my first invitation to referee a Leyland-Daf Cup game. This was an evening game in Doncaster. If refereeing seems in any way glamorous I would ask anyone just to consider for a moment how they would fancy Doncaster v Grimsby on a dark cold night in November. Having said that, this was a local derby and there was sure to be a lot of rivalry and local pride at stake.

HOME AND AWAY

I turned up at Belle Vue and to my amazement found nobody to greet me, not a cup of tea to be had to warm me up and raise my spirits. Eventually everyone turned up and a crowd of 1,900 streamed in. When we were ready to kick off I looked across to check that my linesmen were ready. I didn't worry too much about the fact that I couldn't see my colleague on my left flank, as the floodlights were so bad I thought he would be hiding in the shadows somewhere. I signalled the kick-off and the game got under way. Suddenly, out of the corner of my eye, I caught a glimpse of this figure in black rushing across the pitch from the goal area and realised that he had in fact been checking the nets when I kicked off. It was a source of great hilarity to the crowd and I have to confess that I had to smile a little myself at the panic-stricken linesman. I don't suppose I could complain when the match observer docked me a full point for the incident. Never mind, I still got nine out of ten, which was the only consolation for having my extremities frozen for an hour and a half.

I learned an interesting lesson on the last day of the season when I refereed Mansfield against Crewe. This was never going to be a good game to referee as it was going to be a typical end of season game, nothing to win or lose but the referee still needing to keep his concentration. The only redeeming feature that I could see was that you know that with Crewe you are assured of a good footballing team with Dario Gradi coaching the side.

Sure enough the game was dying from the start and there were no real problems and no real challenges until suddenly, after 44 minutes, Mansfield launched an attack. The ball was knocked out for a Mansfield throw-in and Trevor Christie, their centre forward, took a quick throw to a colleague who was then viciously brought down from behind by Winston White of Crewe.

As I was about to dismiss White, Christie rushed in and flattened him with a left hook. White then jumped up and retaliated. The outcome was straightforward: I had to dismiss both White and Christie. I therefore sent them off, one straight after the other. What a mistake. Christie, being the second to be dismissed, ran as fast as he had done all day to catch up to White in the tunnel. He then landed another punch on White, banging his head against the wall. Before I had the chance to react in any way he was apprehended by the policeman on duty at the player's tunnel and taken away to the local police station under caution. I used to think that the tunnel policeman was there to protect the players from opposing fans but I now realise they get more business from the players themselves than anyone else. In the end no criminal action was brought as White refused to press charges. That incident made me very careful about dismissing two players at the same time. I decided that if it happened again I would keep the second player talking for a while!

I thought the season had gone reasonably well but I had in fact slipped to 56th in the merit table. I think I was guilty of ignoring tell-tale signs in the assessment reports, such as 'should have', 'did not', and 'could have done better'. I think all these comments should have been summarised as 'not working hard enough.'

I found myself very much caught up in my new lifestyle, the responsibility and all that went with it. I had failed to realise that my assessments were actually slipping and the reports were becoming more critical. It seemed that I was establishing control earlier in the game but then had a tendency to drift. This was reflected in a number of reports.

The 1990-91 season was to be one of peaks and troughs, with emotions running from sublime pleasure to utter despair. In view of the slip in my ratings after my very promising opening season, I had decided I would make a real effort to improve, or at least consolidate my standing. Although I was aware of my shortcomings, colleagues were telling me all the time of how well I was doing and of high expectations surrounding my progress. This became increasingly difficult for me to handle as flattery is not something that I find easy to refuse!

On the playing front I found myself giving quite a number of cautions and dismissals, which didn't go down too well with the clubs. I seemed to be losing the confidence of the players and this in turn led me into taking the easy option and showing the yellow or red card, which I might not have done previously.

One of the highlights, if that is the correct term, was operating on Oldham's plastic pitch. It seems difficult now, looking back, to think that we actually allowed matches to take place on these surfaces. Although Oldham's was generally regarded to be the best plastic pitch around, it was awful. The game was different, the players had burns on their arms and legs from the plastic surface, and it would take two days to recover from an aching back because of the lack of give in the surface. On the plus side the Oldham public could use the facilities every day of the week without damaging anything. That is fine from the community perspective but what about our game of football? How on earth did the Football League permit clubs to prostitute our national game in this way? In my mind it is not football unless you have grass and mud and everything that goes with it.

The FA Cup came around again and this was to bring my first visit to Shrewsbury. What a beautiful place I found it to be. The ground nestles on the banks of the River Severn and provides a fitting setting for this friendly little club. As I walked down the corridor towards the referee's dressing room I was puzzled by an object leaning against the wall. It was a black circular affair covered in pitch and was approximately four feet in diameter. I could see it was a boat of some sort and, when I enquired, I was advised that it was 'Jimmy's coracle' - for fishing the ball out of the river. Somehow, this seemed so appropriate for the image of the club.

It was here that I sustained what must be one of the most unusual injuries in the competition. It was the replay between Shrewsbury and Bradford City in the second round. We were well into the game when I gave a free kick to Bradford. As I was running into position to restart the next phase of play, Paul Jewell (later to become manager of Sheffield Wednesday but then playing for Bradford), 'accidentally' collided with me and knocked a tooth out of the side of my mouth. Momentarily stunned, I spat the tooth out and chased after Paul, warning him it would cost him £200 for a false one. I wonder if the 'collision' had anything to do with the fact that Paul had been bending my ear continuously (no change there), as he felt, mistakenly of course, that I had not been giving anything Bradford's way. Perhaps it was also something to do with the fact that his team were losing, and indeed did lose the game, to the minnows from the Welsh Borders.

Of all the lessons I learned around this time the one which taught me most occurred on 26 January 1991. I was at Turf Moor for Burnley against Stockport. As usual I had done my homework on recent games between the teams and I was therefore aware of the feeling between the clubs. I had established that the two teams had played on the previous Wednesday in the Leyland Daf Cup and within the previous fortnight the two teams had met in the FA Cup. It was apparent that I would be in for a busy and noisy afternoon, judging by press reports and enquiries with the referees involved in the previous games. The biggest issue though was to be the weather.

ONE NIGHT AT THE PALACE

When I arrived at the ground I looked at the pitch and saw that one side was basking in sunshine and the other half was in shade. Around about 12.30 p.m. Stockport sent a representative to ask me to look at the pitch and asked me to consider a postponement. I half laughed in surprise and immediately thought that because they had played each other recently they wanted to cool off, or perhaps they had injuries, or there could be a million other reasons. Perhaps in my suspicion I didn't consider the true reason i.e. they were genuinely concerned about the safety of their players. So, armed with a pair of moulded boots, I decided to show how suitable the playing surface was. The Stockport players were all moaning and having a snipe as I ran past. At the same time, the Burnley players were saying there was nothing wrong and that it was just that the Stockport players always moan. This sort of situation is difficult enough to deal with on a Sunday morning in the local league but at this level there is much more to consider, not least the supporters.

I decided the game would go ahead and, not unexpectedly, given the conditions, it turned out to be a lively encounter. In the first half the players were brilliant, committed but fair, and I in turn made allowances for the pitch. In the second half, frustrations started to come to the surface and I started to notice niggles going on. I awarded a couple of yellow cards before the balloon went up big time.

In the 80th minute a corner was awarded to Stockport. As the ball came in, the Burnley keeper collected the ball and fell to the ground. David Frain, the Stockport captain, lunged in and committed a late challenge on the now prostrate goalkeeper. I immediately blew my whistle but at the same time the goalkeeper jumped up and swung a punch. Frain retaliated and with it being a corner there were an awful lot of bodies in the box. The effect was mayhem and resembled a Friday night in Newcastle Bigg Market. With the help of a number of players who were still in control of themselves, calm was eventually restored. I ended up dismissing two players but, learning from my previous experience at Mansfield, I ensured there was a healthy gap between the two players leaving the field. Adopting my usual tactic for double sendings off, I despatched the home player first, to a chorus of boos for me and cheers for him. I followed by then dismissing the away player, to a chorus of resounding cheers, thus leaving the crowd in a positive frame of mind. The game ended with a 3-2 win to Burnley but the

Stockport contingency were far from happy and pointed the finger at me for starting the game. I did a lot of reflecting about this and came to the conclusion that the safety of the players should have been paramount and that the lack of opportunity to express themselves had caused frustration that in turn led to trouble. The game left me sad and confused. I thought I had been correct at the time but it was obvious to me that this was not the case.

When the assessment came it made quite good reading with only slight criticisms in minor areas. I should have been delighted. However, the comment at the end read something like, 'This was a severe test of your ability, you are certainly well capable of dealing with these confrontations. You only made one error in the whole game and that was to start it in the first place!' I was deeply embarrassed by the final comment, embarrassed because I knew it was correct.

It was at this point that I decided to seek advice to find out what was going wrong, and, more importantly, to get guidance on how to put it right.

I spoke to the League referees' officer John Goggins and asked him why he thought I was slipping downwards in the rankings. His response was startling but exactly what was required. 'Your slide started the moment you forgot that man-management is the most important part of the referee's game. You've stopped working. Simply sticking your card up a player's nose is not quality refereeing. If you do not improve you are in danger of losing your place, I wish you luck.'

I was feeling desperate. Determined to end the bad run I decided to start concentrating on working hard again. My first opportunity to do so was at the Yorkshire derby match between Huddersfield and Rotherham. I decided to use the game as a platform, mentally preparing from the Thursday and focusing on the game from that point. I also increased my physical preparation. In the midst of all this intensity came a bolt from the blue, a phone call from the FA asking if I was available to run the line at the European Cup semi-final in Marseilles! What a strange game this is. On the one hand I am in danger of dropping off the end of the League list and, on the other, I am being offered the second most prestigious game in Europe. Still, it was a great boost and, I hoped, could only do me good.

Arriving at the Huddersfield match on the Saturday I felt refreshed and ready for anything. I had regained the sense of urgency that I had been missing. The Marseilles appointment had given me a new surge of confidence.

The first half hour of the match was superb and I was everywhere. The player reaction was great and I felt it was all coming back. In the 33rd minute, however, a chap called Iffy Onuora playing for Huddersfield made a quick dash and as things were going so well I tried to keep up. A bad mistake. After about 15 yards I tore my hamstring and went down like a pack of cards. I limped off and I received treatment from the club doctor who suggested I would be out for six to eight weeks. This filled me with horror as I needed to be fit again in four weeks, at the very latest, in order to get a game or two in before the European match.

In desperation, I attended a private hospital every day for two weeks and, as soon as possible, I started stretching. At one stage I was doing so much stretching that I thought I would end up six inches longer than when I started off. It all seemed to be worthwhile, though, as I was able to carry out light jogging after three weeks and, under the direction of my physio, stretched and strained my way through the pain barrier. It's amazing what you can do with an incentive such as the one I had. After four weeks I was up to running and I decided I must take charge of the game I had been offered between Sheffield Wednesday and Blackburn Rovers, otherwise I would have to withdraw from the semi-final.

I found myself in a strange dilemma: what was more important, the physical aspects of my own body or controlling the game in the correct manner? There was only one answer, it had to be done correctly. Fortunately, I managed to get through the game even though I felt the pace after only eighteen minutes. Here I was, just five weeks from the muscle tear, and I had carried out ninety minutes of first class football. Marseilles beckoned in ten days. I had made it.

I increased the training daily until I was feeling really good. There was much local interest in my appointment because Chris Waddle, another North Easterner, was playing for Marseilles at the time. Newspaper and radio interest was immense and this was to prepare me for the level of exposure that would come with the introduction of the Premier League in later days.

The excitement and anticipation reached a peak when the tickets dropped through the letter box. The itinerary looked really impressive and exciting. Flying out to Marseilles from Heathrow, first class, was going to be quite an experience for me, a simple bloke with simple tastes. All this attention and first class treatment was a slight embarrassment but I would be less than truthful if I said I didn't enjoy it. I flew from Newcastle on the Tuesday evening to Heathrow and met up with the other linesman, Alan Gunn, whom I had worked with at Dundee, at the Radisson Hotel. The third member of the party, Keith Hackett, who was to referee the game, was to join us the next morning.

The flight was very pleasant, if brief. With hospitality as it was I would quite happily have settled for a longer flight. Approaching Marseilles I looked down upon devastated woodland, destroyed by a horrendous forest fire which had been whipped up by the Mistral wind a few days earlier. The smouldering terrain looked like something out of a disaster movie. The flight path took us out over the sea and then the plane seemed to nose-dive down the side of the mountains to land on the runway which stretched way out into the sea. A dramatic entrance and the start of three fabulous days.

I was given a taste of things to come when we were met at the airport by a Marseilles representative in a gleaming black stretch Mercedes limousine with blacked-out windows. I jumped in the back seat and started to fiddle with the buttons like a kid with a new toy. Electric seats were moving about and windows were opening and closing, I was having great fun, much to the annoyance of the others.

There was a second person in the car from Marseilles and I assumed he was also a club representative. It wasn't until the following year, when he turned up at a totally different venue, that I discovered he was in fact an agent hired to provide 'corporate hospitality'. He suddenly said in a barely understandable English accent, 'Do you have your kit with you?' 'What a plonker,' I thought, this was the European Cup semi-final, we'd known about the game for six weeks and this guy was asking if we have our kit. Perhaps it was something he had pieced together from his English phrase book. Rather than give him a sarcastic reply I responded politely, 'Yes, why do you ask?' He then asked if our kit was made by Adidas, which it wasn't. When he was given this information we were whizzed off to an Adidas shop and we were kitted out from head to foot in Adidas boots, trainers, tracksuit and kit bag. This was turning out to be a good trip. I wondered whether to feel uncomfortable about this generosity but I reassured myself with the knowledge that Adidas was official FIFA gear.

47

ONE NIGHT AT THE PALACE

We had a look around Marseilles, taking in the sights, and were then taken into a magnificent hotel which was carved into the hillside and which extended out into the sea. We had lunch at the hotel and decided on sea bass. The waiter brought out a three foot long salmon-like fish and asked if it was acceptable. I'm not sure what the French sense of humour is like but I got a rather blank look when I asked if he could cook it first.

After sight-seeing in the afternoon, I experienced what was the biggest treat of all in the evening. We were driven along the motorway towards Nice and in the pitch-black we turned down a country lane. Suddenly in the middle of nowhere the driver sounded the horn and flashed the lights. To our utter amazement wrought iron gates were lit up and started to open. At the same time a beautiful château became illuminated by floodlights and we moved into the grounds. The gates closed behind us and we parked under the trees. The sight was breathtaking and when we got out of the car and entered the building I felt like visiting royalty. Inside, the fittings were as impressive as the exterior. Not being a connoisseur I don't suppose I was fully able to appreciate all the fine furnishings, paintings and fabrics but they looked pretty expensive to me.

We were offered pink champagne as an aperitif and the meal took about three hours in all, the many courses being delivered spot on time and covered in silver domes. The service was like an exercise in synchronisation. For an everyday Telecom engineer from Chester-le-Street this was out of this world. I suppose it would be showing my ignorance if I mentioned that the portions were tiny.

I never did find out who the chateau belonged to; our questions tended to be answered in rather vague fashion. If I'd known about the corruption scandal which was to hit the club the following year I might have looked at things with a rather more cynical eye.

On the day of the game a security brief took place and we were then taken for lunch by the sea. This was followed by a browse through the exclusive Lacoste shop. Whenever we looked at something one of our hosts would say, 'You like that?' At first we would politely reply, 'Yes it's very nice', until we realised that this would result in the item being bagged up and presented to us. I'm certain we could have walked out with the entire contents of the shop if we'd wanted to.

The kick-off was scheduled for 8 p.m. but we had been warned that the traffic would be horrendous and that it would take us at least half an hour to travel the two miles to the stadium. We made arrangements to be picked up at 5.30 and were informed that we would have a police escort. This was just as well because the traffic was at a complete standstill. We needn't have worried, as the police escort had a very effective method of fighting its way through the crowds. The outriders simply took out their batons and started banging on the roof of any car which was impeding progress. Needless to say we arrived in good time for the match.

When we reached the stadium, the Stade de Velodrome, I looked up in admiration at the impressive oval structure which was built in quasi-Victorian style, or whatever the French equivalent might be. We were whisked inside the stadium gates and down into a labyrinthian underworld of buildings and roads. The changing rooms were located in this underground complex as were all the support services. The place was alive with ambulances, catering units and refuse wagons.

Unlike my colleagues, who didn't subscribe to my pre-match theories, I asked if I could use the pitch to warm up. I was refused permission but decided this would not stop me from loosening up. I therefore got changed and, to the amazement of the local delivery men and officials, used the underground circular road as a running track. As there were cameras everywhere this provided the TV people with a wonderful pre-match cameo for their viewers. Personally I didn't give a toss who was watching, I was just intent on making sure I got the warm-up I wanted.

When it came to time for the game the excitement started with the march along the tunnel. This was an underground structure about sixty yards long. At the end of the tunnel there were about twenty steps and, as we ascended these, the roof of the tunnel lifted up and we emerged into the arena. The stadium was packed to the rafters and to accompany our arrival the incredible sound system exploded into a rendition of 'Jump' by Van Halen. This was my first introduction to the stage-managed entrance and what a fantastic build-up it was. Paparazzi lined the route from the tunnel to the halfway line and we were almost blinded by the flashlights.

The game started and, before I knew it, it was all over. The likes of Abede Pele, the Ghanaian international striker, Jean Pierre Papin, the

French superstar of the moment, and Chris Waddle, from the Tow Law sausage factory, were too strong for Spartak Moscow. The result was 2-1 but could have been much more convincing. Marseilles were going to the final and they could party.

We were whisked back to the hotel for a meal, only to find Marseilles were in fact holding their celebrations there. I have wondered since whether there was anything sinister in this as they knew we were staying there. Perhaps it's just my imagination running wild again. In any event, tempting as it was at the time, I thought it would not have been correct to join in so I decided to take room service and end a spectacular day in a simple but relaxing style.

On the third and final day of our adventure we received further gifts from the club: a doll representing the area, a hamper of produce from Provence and an inscribed bronze football boot as a memento. Then it was back to the airport and home.

What had puzzled me throughout these three days was the fact that our driver always carried a black flight bag whenever we went anywhere. During the last hours of the trip we called at the club shop and when we made the mistake of agreeing there was something we liked, I spotted, for the first time, the bag being inconspicuously opened. I managed to get a quick peek inside and I saw that it was full of money, bundles of it.

I like to think that everything was above board during our trip but when the club president Bernard Tapie was convicted of match-rigging the following year my head was swimming as I tried to recall all the aspects of 'hospitality' we had received. Tapie ended up with a jail sentence and the club was punished by relegation and a ban from the European Cup. I used this experience as a learning process and I was very guarded on my future trips abroad.

I was soon back to reality and my season concluded with a game between Wigan and Bradford. This was dull by comparison, as most things would be. It was interesting in as much as the game was dubbed by the Football League as a family-friendly game. This meant that there was no crowd segregation between fans of the different teams.

This was an experiment and I am pleased to say that on the day it worked well. The Wigan players weren't in such a congenial mood however as they ran up a 3-0 win. It was a good day and it was nice to see such well behaved fans. Unfortunately the scheme mustn't have been a success everywhere as it seemed to die a quiet death and I never heard of it again.

HOME AND AWAY

I wondered what would happen to me now that I had received a warning about the standard of my performance deteriorating. How ironic it would be if I was removed from the Football League list having just officiated at a European semi-final. As it turned out, the warning, and my reaction to it, did the trick. I had arrested the downward spiral and my immediate assessments indicated rapid improvement.

Because of the problems, though, I finished at my lowest position of 71 out of 92 in the merit list. I consoled myself with the thought that it could have been worse.

During the summer months leading up to the 1991/92 season, speculation abounded about the possible formation of a so-called Premier League. There was also talk of reducing the FIFA referees retirement age to 45 years. This would create five vacancies and my name was being mentioned by various people as a possible candidate. I decided to activate my defence mechanism and not to build up my hopes in view of everything that had happened recently.

When the 1991/92 season arrived neither of these two initiatives had materialised, although they would come to fruition at a later date. The season was, however, to turn out to be a good one for me. In all I was to referee 29 games, which at this level was quite a schedule. It provided me with a wealth of experience and I was conscious that people were starting to talk about greater things to come. Throughout the season I refused to listen to rumours and decided to keep a fairly low profile and to concentrate on my performances. It was true that I wanted to be admired, like most people who are passionate about their job, but I was not prepared to be lulled into a false sense of security again.

It is impossible as a referee to stay out of the limelight and a brush with controversy was never far away. It therefore didn't surprise me when, very early in the new season, I found myself embroiled in an altercation with two of the most famous managers in the game. This arose out of a well meaning gesture by myself. The game was between Sheffield Wednesday and Nottingham Forest and it was a very warm day. I decided to allow both teams to place water bottles alongside the pitch. Nothing could go wrong with that, I thought, and the tactic had been well received at previous games. However, as the ball was played towards the Sheffield goal it appeared to be going out for a goal-kick. Carlton Palmer, who was playing for Sheffield Wednesday at the time, went to take a drink. Kevin Pressman, the Wednesday goalkeeper, surprisingly managed to retrieve the ball before it went out. Play therefore continued, with the ball finding its way to Carlton, who to my mind had left the pitch and had then come back on to deliberately seek advantage. I decided to caution him as he had not sought permission to leave or re-enter the field of play.

After the game both Brian Clough and Lawrie McMenemy said that they did not think Carlton had actually gone off the pitch. I promised to review the video and promised them that if their view was correct I would rescind the caution, which is exactly what I did do. This is the only time I have ever changed a decision after watching video evidence. I suppose in some ways I was lucky. Rescinding a caution means that a poor decision doesn't have any lasting effect. It would have been a different matter if Carlton had already been on a yellow card as I would have sent him off and that could well have affected the result of the match. That would really have made me Mr Popular.

Ten days later I took charge of an incredible match at Bradford, against Bolton. The score ended up at 4-4 and I awarded three penalties, cautioned one player for kicking the ball away and then sent off three players, one for an elbow, one for a deliberate kick and one for a horrendous challenge. Apart from that it was a good clean game! John Doherty, the Bradford manager came to see me after the match and complimented me, saying that his two players would be disciplined. This was a responsible attitude from a very professional manager. I was pleasantly surprised with his attitude considering many of the decisions were against his team.

Another game worthy of mention is the match between Birmingham and Exeter. After 80 minutes, one of the linesmen had to be taken off with a muscle injury. The first decision by the replacement official, Malcolm Kendall, who just happened to be from Birmingham, was to award a hotly contested corner kick. This, by the law of Sod, led to a Birmingham goal, which turned out to be the only goal of the game. This in turn led to Alan Ball, the Exeter manager, erupting into a fit of rage. As we left the pitch at the end of the game I could see he was seriously wound up and I decided to alert a nearby policeman. Bally continued to rant and rave as we made our way down the tunnel, to the extent that the officer of the law felt it necessary to remove him under caution. I don't think anything came of it but it can't have done a lot for Bally's blood pressure. Who said it's only a game?

On 8 February 1992 something happened in English football that was to affect lots of people in different ways, me in particular. On the face of it the game appeared to be fairly insignificant in that it was a run-of-the-mill game (if there is such a thing at this level) between Oldham and Leeds. On entering the ground I became aware of the presence of the French TV station Canal Plus. Strategically placed around the pitch was an array of seven camera crews. All this for a match which was not even being covered by English TV.

Apparently there was to be a debut of an 'enfant terrible' virtually unknown to English fans. When Howard Wilkinson brought in the Leeds team sheet I was to see that the individual concerned was not in the starting line up but was on the subs' bench. When I mentioned this to Howard he replied, 'I ******* decide who plays for ******* Leeds and no-one ******* else', giving a clear indication that he was pretty cheesed off with being put under pressure to bow to media and public demand.

And so it was that Mr Cantona's arrival in the UK got off to a less than auspicious start. When he did come on after 75 minutes, with Oldham by then 2-0 up, he was stuck on the right wing where, to be honest, he looked like a duck (or should I say a seagull) out of water. However, in view of the frenzy created when he came on it was clear that this was not going to be the last we would hear of him.

I moved on to referee the Rotherham v Barnet game which was decorated by the irrepressible Barry Fry, the Barnet manager. Watching this man run up and down the touchline like a screaming banshee raises some interesting questions about his mental state. This was his norm apparently, and I nearly caused him a heart attack when the ball struck me and was diverted on to the Barnet post, the closest I have come to getting on the scoresheet in senior football.

What really got Barry going though was a decision by the linesman closest to him not to give an offside decision. After receiving various renditions of 'Get your ******* flag up' the linesman called me over and I had no choice but to banish Barry to the stand. As he completed his ignominious journey it was quite amusing to watch him orchestrate the booing around the ground. You have to laugh sometimes.

ONE NIGHT AT THE PALACE

A rather nice but sad sight in footballing terms was witnessed at the Blackpool v Aldershot game at the back end of February. Aldershot were in real financial difficulties and a collection took place around the ground, whilst the game was in progress, to try to save them from insolvency.

The game had nearly been called off, owing to lack of funds for transport, and the decision to go ahead had only been received the day before. The people of Blackpool were very generous and one of the Aldershot players was heard to say afterwards, 'That's good, we've got enough to get home now!' The collection did, in fact, pay the players' wages for that week but sadly the club folded within a matter of weeks.

At the other end of the scale I was in charge of the Sheffield United v Liverpool game on 28 March 1992. There was an incident which I thought nothing of at the time but which assumed greater significance in years to come. After 40 minutes Bruce Grobbelaar came well out of his area and proceeded to lose the ball. Seizing an unexpected opportunity, Brian Deane, the Sheffield United centre-forward, scored a gift goal from the halfway line. The game was re-visited, as they say, six years later when Grobbelaar, Hans Segers and John Fashanu were accused of match-fixing. I was at that stage asked to discreetly provide the FA with a copy of the match video, with the situation being so delicate they didn't want to make the respective clubs aware of the investigations into this match. I didn't play any further part in the investigations which, in the end, came to nothing.

The big game for me in this 1991/92 season came on the very last day when I was put in charge of the Tranmere v Oxford game at Prenton Park. Normally this wouldn't spring to mind as a particularly exciting game but the significance for me was that it could have a very considerable impact on the team I have supported all my life, Newcastle United. It's perfectly reasonable that the football authorities tend not to put officials in charge of their home town clubs, for obvious reasons. However, it would be logistically impossible to avoid all conflicts of interest. So here I was refereeing in a situation where it was generally considered that if Oxford won at Tranmere then Newcastle would go down into the Third Division for the first time in their history. It was a brilliant day, the weather was beautiful, there was a sell-out crowd and the Oxford fans came in party mood dressed as Egyptians, Pharaohs and Mummies. I'm still not sure why, but it did create a mood of fun and a carnival atmosphere which added to the occasion for both them and me.

The match ended with a 2-1 victory for Oxford and this caused me utter dismay. I had upheld my integrity, however, and I felt as if I'd had a pretty good game. I was sitting dejected in the dressing room when Brian Horton, the Oxford manager, came in and asked what was wrong, seeing as I'd 'had a pretty good match' as he put it. When I explained to him the cause of my misery he said, 'But Newcastle have won at Leicester.' 'Doesn't make any difference,' I said miserably. However, we went on to work out that, unexpectedly, Plymouth Argyle had come into the frame and because they had lost, it was they who went down. What a relief, who knows what would have happened to the Toon if they had sunk into the Third. As it turned out this was a massive turning point for them, Keegan had just been appointed and they were promoted the following season. They went on to be runners-up, the year after, in the Premiership with a wonderfully entertaining side including Ginola, Beardsley and Ferdinand. As they say, 'It's a funny old game.'

5

A PREMIER APPOINTMENT

IN THE SUMMER MONTHS following the 1991/92 season there was more frenetic discussion about the possibility of a Premier League. This had been debated for some time and negotiations were at an advanced stage. It was all sorted out and the Premiership did come into being for the 1992/93 season. The Football Association had correctly seen the marketing opportunities for a Premier League and subsequent events have endorsed this initiative, with an explosion in all aspects of the game including money, media profile, advertising and the influx of world stars.

Selection of referees for the Premiership was clearly going to be a bone of contention. In the past the Football League had total control of allocation of officials. Now the Premier League had the obvious advantage in being able to hand-pick their desired referees. They decided to start off with thirty, with the expectation that this might be reduced to twenty-five in mid-season when the situation was a little clearer.

Although my name had been bandied about as a likely candidate, I was not surprised to find out that I had not been selected. There was a glimmer of hope for those referees not handed the coveted green jersey, however, when it was stated that there would be further opportunities at a later date for those not appointed initially. I undertook to work as hard as necessary to achieve my previous standards and reckoned that if I displayed the right attitude and level of performance then one day I might end up in the Premiership.

I therefore trained particularly hard during the close season and even entered the Great North Run, finishing in a personal best time of 1 hour 34 minutes.

Unfortunately, the best laid plans can always be thrown into confusion by the unexpected. When the season got under way I felt I was doing well, into September, when in a match at Rotherham I pulled a hamstring again.

A PREMIER APPOINTMENT

I guess it's always a source of amusement when a ref gets injured but when you think about it we're as liable as the rest of the population to get injuries, particularly when you're in such finely honed condition as I was at the time. That's my argument anyway! I have to say though that I was impressed with my powers of recovery and I was back in action only two weeks later.

I was flattered to be asked to host an Italian referee for three days when he was appointed to referee an Anglo-Italian Cup game between Newcastle and Ascoli. His name was Robert Boggi and my job was to pick him up at the airport, escort him everywhere, and generally look after him. Pretty much in the way I had been looked after in Marseilles. The difference was that I didn't have a holdall full of bank notes and instead of dining in a mansion in the mountains we had to settle for a town centre pizzeria. Never mind, he was a nice chap and we got on well.

Regrettably, I was less than impressed by Robert's performance on the pitch. He didn't seem to be able to handle the heat and the passion generated in games at St James' Park. He ended up sending off David Kelly of Newcastle for retaliation, a decision which in itself was correct. However, David had been given no protection from the typically Italian cynical tactics and he had been kicked on most parts of his anatomy by the time he was dismissed.

At this point of the season I was feeling pretty good. I was fit and I was pleased with my performances.

I was soon to referee a game that would catapult me into the realms of the Premiership. The game in question was Derby County versus West Ham at the Baseball Ground. Before the game I was surprised to see Reg Leafe, who I knew was the League's top assessor. He spoke to me before the game and wished me well.

The game was entertaining, I managed to play lots of advantage and West Ham went two up within thirty minutes with goals from Tony Cottee. The ball was then played out to the Derby right winger Ted McMinn. Ted controlled the ball and then, out of the blue, was sent into orbit by a bone-crunching tackle from Julian Dicks. As the ball had gone in the direction of the West Ham box I decided to play on, shouting at the same time to Dicks, 'I`m coming back for you.' Of course, Sod's Law again prevailed, the attack came to nothing and the ball then stayed in play for about five minutes, which seemed like an eternity. I got the opportunity to stop play when

Colin Foster, the West Ham centre-half, pushed Marco Gabbiadini in the back. I called Dicks across and he tried to express astonishment saying he hadn`t done anything. Anyway, I gave him the yellow card which had been burning a hole in my pocket for the last five minutes and warned him about his future conduct. His bulging eyes and aggressive demeanour bothered me.

After 41 minutes the Derby keeper threw the ball out to McMinn who seemed to be almost shaking in his boots. My first reaction was to look for Dicks and my radar soon picked him up in mid-air, just about to make impact with his target. This time McMinn ended up in the dugout sprawled across the substitute's knee. Moaning sounds encouraged me that he was still alive. Dicks in the meantime was nonchanantly moving back into position as if nothing had happened. As I gave him the red card he was still protesting his innocence but he eventually left the pitch. Not for long though, as when he reached the tunnel he decided he wanted some more. As he headed back towards the pitch I wasn't sure whether he was coming for me or for poor Ted, who was still on a different planet. Fortunately, Harry Redknapp and Frank Lampard were brilliant and they stopped Dicks' advance and personally escorted him down the tunnel. I've heard Julian called psychopathic at times and on this performance I wouldn't have been in a position to defend him against such suggestions!

Within a week of the Derby game I received a letter advising that I had been promoted to the Premier League. This was what I was waiting for and it was a dream come true. They had decided to reduce the list to the required number of twenty-five Premiership refs by axing eight of the original team and bringing in three new. The letter of notification was complete with the treasured green shirt. The elation and excitement was difficult to contain.

Regrettably, on 26 January, my father died and he was never given the chance to see me in the Premiership. This was a source of great sadness to me and at the time I wasn't sure whether I was going to be able to continue refereeing. Fortunately my mother was very supportive and she encouraged me to carry on, saying it was what Dad would have wanted. I decided to continue in his memory and during difficult moments after that I always thought of what he would say, 'Get on with the job and bugger what they think.'

A PREMIER APPOINTMENT

After receiving the good news about the Premiership, my next appointment was an FA Cup tie between Crewe Alexandra and Blackburn Rovers. This was the first time I had come across Martin Tyler, an extremely knowledgeable man and very sensitive to the difficulties faced by referees. I have a lot of time for Martin and I consider that he speaks a great deal of common sense, which is more than can be said for some of his colleagues.

The other memorable thing about this day was that I met Kenny Dalglish for the first time. I have to say that Kenny is not the man you see on the television. He is pleasant, witty, and has a good sense of mischief! In later days I once spent three hours on the train with him whilst travelling from Durham to London and he never shut up. He was amusing, entertaining and, most of all, very knowledgeable about the game. If I was to try to put my finger on why things didn't work out for him at Newcastle it would probably require a book of its own.

Into February, and it was Bolton versus Huddersfield: a pretty unmemorable match apart from one thing. I gave a first-half penalty to Huddersfield and, like many penalty decisions, it didn't make the referee the most popular person around. As the ball was being put on the spot I received a push from behind and when I turned round I saw that the culprit was Tony Kelly of Bolton. Without any hesitation I did the only thing I could and showed him the red card.

At half-time I discovered that the Football League referees' officer was in the crowd and he in fact came to see me and asked if I was OK. I told him I was fine and he then stated that the player's actions represented a technical assault and that he should be reported to the FA. In the event I didn't need to as they contacted me when they heard what had happened. On confirmation of the incident they immediately suspended Kelly and three weeks later a formal hearing took place. As a result of this, Kelly received a six game suspension and a fine. I can't say how much the fine was as I was asked to leave the room whilst it was discussed.

Although the incident did not cause me any physical harm I think it is right that physical contact with referees must be seen to be treated firmly otherwise the situation could soon get completely out of hand. As it was, I believe the level of punishment handed out to Kelly was probably about right. Having refereed Tony several times since, he grudgingly accepted that he was wrong but he made a point of staying well away from me.

ONE NIGHT AT THE PALACE

Since being appointed to the Premiership I was yet to referee my first game and I was therefore very pleasantly surprised to receive an appointment for an FA Cup 6th round game, normally reserved for established higher echelon officials. The tie was between Ipswich and Arsenal at Portman Road. This was my first encounter with Ian Wright. Now you can say what you like about 'Wrighty', foul-mouthed, aggressive, big-headed, show-off etc. But I tell you what, he was a magnificent footballer. I was privileged to watch at close quarters as he gave John Wark a torrid time and helped himself to a wonderful hat-trick. John did his best but there was no way he could restrain this man in this sort of mood and I ended up putting him in the book. Fortunately we managed to contain it to a yellow card. This was also my first encounter with George Graham, an individual I shall come back to later.

It was at this same fixture that I first met the 'sheepskin coat', the one and only John Motson. What is it about this quiet and unassuming man which has made him a household name? Not just here, but all over the world. I was in America recently, somewhere fairly remote, and I thought, 'That voice sounds familiar.' I looked at the TV and there was a computer soccer game, with Motty's voice doing the commentary. My guess is that he must be in the world's top ten recognised voices, probably somewhere between the Pope and Bill Clinton. Quite an achievement for somebody who only wanted to commentate on a football match!

When he came to interview me, I could not believe how well informed Mottie was; he had certainly done his homework and more. It was quite unnerving really, he seemed to know everything about me and had a clipboard from which he kept unearthing all sorts of facts. I nicknamed him 'the mole' after this encounter. John came over as a real professional, even in that first meeting, and he is a genuine nice guy, shy and polite. People love him to the extent that they want to play practical jokes at his expense, not out of maliciousness but because of the lovable character that he is. I remember an FA cup-tie at Wycombe Wanderers, who at the time were a non-League side. A blizzard had been raging for about an hour and the snow was knee-deep. There was obviously no way the match could go ahead so the TV crew asked John if he would just do a thirty second slot to demonstrate the weather conditions. It was a set-up, of course, and they kept spinning it out until after about twenty minutes John was a dead ringer for the abominable snowman. His repeated cries to be relieved were answered with, 'Sorry, John, the links gone down, we'll have to try again.' A true professional.

24 March 1993. It had arrived at long last! My Premiership debut. I was sent to Elland Road to referee the match between Leeds and Chelsea, a nice easy one to start with! There was no love lost in those days between these two teams or for that matter their respective fans. The enmity apparently goes all the way back to the 1970 FA Cup final when 'Chopper Harris' attempted at every opportunity to remove the Leeds centre forward Mick Jones from the game.

There were 42,000 in the ground and the atmosphere was white hot. The crowd were going bananas and the noise level was incredible. I didn't have to wait long for my first taste of real action. After fourteen minutes I caught Tony Cascarino of Chelsea trying to re-arrange David Wetherall's nose. To a certain extent he succeeded as Wetherall's nose was well broken. The only problem for me was that, once again, no-one else had seen the incident as the ball had long since left the scene of the crime. Here I was, not fifteen minutes into my first Premiership game and I was involved in a major incident. As I dismissed Cascarino I was surrounded by the inevitable snarling wolf-pack led by the Chelsea captain Andy Townsend and ably supported by Dennis Wise and Frank Sinclair. What a baptism!

Having dealt with this contretemps, the match got under way and everything went reasonably well for the rest of the first half. As the teams went off the pitch I hung back in the usual fashion to allow the players off the pitch first. When it was my turn to disappear down the tunnel I found myself confronted by a fearsome figure in a black full-length overcoat. This character had a large black beard and long black hair and his physical presence created a shadow around my comparatively minute frame.

This Rasputin lookalike in fact turned out to be the then Chelsea manager David Webb. He looked me in the eye and said, 'Tell me, ref, why did you send my player off?' I replied by telling him what had happened and he then went off down the tunnel. When we came back after half-time Webb approached me and said, 'Thanks very much, ref, I've confirmed what you said and the player will be disciplined.' A refreshing attitude indeed and a great confidence booster for me to start the second half.

ONE NIGHT AT THE PALACE

The game ended with honours even, a 1-1 draw with goals from Lee Chapman and Andy Townsend. I had no more problems and thought at the end that I'd done a pretty decent job.

So, I'd done it, my first Premiership match and it was everything I expected. The emotion and atmosphere was so intense at this level that to be involved gave me a real buzz. When the assessment came in it made excellent reading and talked in glowing terms about my movement and match control. I was highly delighted.

My next appointment knocked me off my feet. I had never refereed further south than Nottingham and now I was being invited to take a trip to the capital. What's more, it was to referee a London derby match between Crystal Palace and Queen's Park Rangers. This was to be the first of many visits to Selhurst Park and I have to say that it never got any easier to get to. Every time I got an appointment to go to Palace or, in later years, Wimbledon, when they started sharing the ground, the instructions seemed to be different. No matter which way I went it always seemed a problem.

The game was fairly dour with typical derby-match spoiling tactics but it was all worthwhile when I got my assessment which again made quite nice reading. The game ended 1-1 with no cautions, which, for a local derby, was unusual. Gerry Francis suggested I had done well, a highly unusual statement from Gerry. I was starting to grow in confidence and instead of feeling apprehensive I was now in a position to enjoy what I was doing and to start building a reputation as a leading Premiership ref.

My next game was to be Nottingham Forest v Tottenham. Now, any Premiership match is going to have an element of rivalry in it but recent events had given this one extra flavour. Teddy Sheringham had just been signed by Tottenham from Forest and there was quite a bit of bad feeling floating around. Cloughie didn't want Sheringham to leave but Teddy had decided he wanted to move back to the bright lights. The whole episode had generated a lot of acrimony. In the Forest side was a certain Roy Keane and among the opposition lurked Neil 'Razor' Ruddock. A lethal cocktail indeed. The three of them didn't disappoint and by the end of the game they all featured in my little black book. Forest won the match 2-1 and at the end of the game I knew I'd been in a tough encounter. The Premier League was certainly proving interesting.

A PREMIER APPOINTMENT

The season finished for me with Leicester City versus Bristol City. The game ended in a 0-0 draw and was mind-boggingly boring. How can an hour and a half pass by without anything at all happening? The only memorable thing was that this was the last game before demolition of the Filbert Street stand. The bits and pieces were being auctioned the next day and I remember thinking that perhaps the auction should be extended to the teams as well.

Although the game signalled a poor end to the season, the bare walls around me in the condemned changing room reminded me of my days in the North West Durham Combination when I got changed in that cupboard on the stage. It then dawned on me just how far I had come. Little was I to know what lay ahead.

It turned out that the season was, in fact, not quite over for me as I received a letter appointing me to referee two promotion play-off games. The first was Stockport County v Port Vale, the second York City v Bury. In the first match it was clear just how much these games mean to the fans of both sides. To a supporter of a Premiership team these type of matches probably appear inconsequential but to the loyal supporter at this level this is the chance for their team to get to Wembley. The contests are therefore always highly charged.

In the first match I gave a penalty against the home side after three minutes. This was promptly missed by Vale's Neil Aspin, much to the relief of the County supporters. As I took up position for the resultant goal-kick the crowd settled down, having expressed their derision to the unfortunate Aspin. During this brief lull I heard a voice from the crowd shout, 'Taxi for Wilkie, waiting outside right now'. I couldn't help smiling; football fans take a lot of stick but the humour of the average supporter is first class. I'll always remember some of the little gems thrown my way from the terraces.

At the end of the season I was feeling pretty confident that as I'd been asked to take two play-off semi-finals then I had every chance of being retained on the Premiership list. I wasn't about to take anything for granted, however, following my previous episode of being somewhat presumptuous. I had learned my lesson.

6

INCE RETURNS

IT WAS WITH SOME relief that I received confirmation during the close season that I had been re-appointed. When the fixture list for 1993/94 was issued I saw with some excitement that I was off again to London, this time for my first visit to Highbury. The sacrificial lambs being offered to the mighty Gunners, on the first day of the season, turned out to be Coventry City who had as usual just avoided relegation the previous season. What the form book did not take into account was the heavyweight threat of the prodigious Mickey Quinn. Here was a man who didn't exactly look like your model footballer and it wasn't hard to see why the fans called him Sumo. I think every ground he played at must have rejoiced at some stage in a rousing rendition of 'Who ate all the pies!'

Apart from being a real character Michael had a wonderful eye for goal and the fact that he was about as quick as a three-legged tortoise didn't seem to bother him. He decided to make history that day and registered the first Premiership hat-trick, in the process consigning Arsenal to an ignominious 3-0 defeat. Quite what George Graham made of it I'm not sure.

The next few games were largely uneventful and included matches between Ipswich and Southampton and Sheffield United versus Wimbledon. This run of mediocrity was ended when I had the privilege of the Sheffield Wednesday and Norwich City game. This wonderful match ended 3-3 and was particularly memorable for a Mark Bowen goal from 35 yards. The game was at fever pitch with the score 3-2 to Wednesday and time running out. Bowen collected the ball outside his own penalty area and played the ball down the right of midfield, running into an advanced position on the left of the pitch. When he was about 40 yards out he received the ball on his chest; moving forward he took a couple of paces and sent an unstoppable left foot half-volley into the top corner past the outstretched arms of Chris Woods, the Wednesday and ex-Norwich keeper, to level the score. A fitting end to a tremendous game.

Soon afterwards I was 'awarded' an Anglo-Italian Cup tie. This, on the face of it, might sound exciting but when you consider the tie was between Barnsley and Grimsby it starts to lose some of its attraction. Not that I mean any offence to the loyal fans of those two teams but refereeing a virtual friendly in front of just 1,200 people doesn't get the adrenalin flowing like standing under the Kop at Liverpool.

Now, that was an experience. Not long after the Barnsley game I was in charge of the Liverpool v Oldham game at Anfield. Oldham had a strong team at the time including players like Darren Beckford, Mike Milligan, Andy Ritchie and Richard Jobson. After just six minutes Oldham took the lead through Beckford and then proceeded to show that they had a bit of the Italian about them. They started time-wasting straight away. For my part I delighted in stopping my watch at every relevant opportunity. In the second half Oldham hung on and on, taking advantage of every time-wasting trick in the book. With just two minutes left, and three Oldham players in the book for procrastination, Ian Rush made the breakthrough. Receiving the ball on the edge of the area with his back to goal, he turned and shot into the bottom corner of the net, in typical Rush style. I thought to myself, 'Here we go.'

There was still lots of time to be added on and I awarded Liverpool a corner in the 95th minute. I took up position by the goal immediately in front of the Kop. This was the Kop as it used to be, all standing and a sea of red and white. The noise was deafening and I would go so far as to say actually painful, so much so that I had to move further infield to enable me to retain any semblance of concentration.

When I hear the armchair pundits in the studio criticising decisions, they should remember, if they've ever been there, what it's like to be in the middle of a red hot cauldron such as this. As players it must spur you on tremendously. As a ref it's a wonderful experience but it certainly puts you under a lot of pressure. The corner was hoisted into a now packed penalty area, there was an aerial challenge and the ball dropped to Rush again who did what he did best, poking it home from three yards for a dramatic last gasp winner.

As we left the field of play I saw Joe Royle standing at the top of the steps with arms outstretched, looking at me and shouting in a not very friendly tone, 'Is it personal Alan? Do you have something against me? Where the hell did you get that extra time from?' As he was obviously pretty hot under the collar I decided not to make light of it and tried to explain to him that his team had been time-wasting for the whole of the second half and it was therefore only right that time should be added on. I'm not really sure he believed me but he left it at that.

In his playing days Joe was a great competitor, hard and fair, and I think that referees do need to accept that people who are competitive and passionate about the game are bound to be upset when things don't go their way. So you're OK, Joe, don't lose any sleep over it.

In November 1993 I received an invitation from the Football League to referee again in the Anglo-Italian cup. Not necessarily an attractive proposition, it might seem, based on previous experience. However, this was to be a little more exciting than the Barnsley v Grimsby match at Oakwell. I was scheduled to referee Ancona against Charlton Athletic in Northern Italy. The arrangement for the Anglo-Italian was that matches in England against Italian opposition would be refereed by Italian officials whilst it would be the other way round for games in Italy. I therefore flew off from Heathrow to Rome on 8 November.

On reaching Rome, however, it soon became clear that economy measures were well in place for this tournament. To save money I was asked to travel to a town called Pescara on the Birmingham City team coach. Birmingham were one of the four English teams left in the tournament after the earlier rounds. When I got to Pescara I was picked up by a driver to be taken to Ancona, which was situated 100 miles north on the Adriatic coast. Unfortunately, the driver spoke no English at all and my Italian at the time didn't extend much beyond Lamborghini, ravioli or Chianti depending on the circumstances. The next two hours then were somewhat difficult and, all in all, I would rather have been on the Birmingham City bus.

I didn't need to worry for too long as I discovered when I arrived at the hotel that I was staying alongside the Charlton Athletic team. This was very pleasant as it was Alan Curbishley's 40th birthday and we were able to have a few beers, later on to celebrate the occasion.

The local media had picked up our presence and to my amazement I found that they were allowed in to televise the evening meal. Cameras were everywhere. Although the attention was flattering it does put you on edge when you're trying to negotiate a plate of spaghetti in front of tens of thousands of people!

Ancona turned out to be a typical little port with all the dubious attractions you would expect to find in such places. It did have a quaint little centre but there was little else to recommend it.

When I arrived at the ground I found it to be a purpose-built modern stadium just outside the town. The facilities were tremendous and, much as we might criticise the Italian soccer fraternity for their volatility, cynicism and gamesmanship, they certainly know how to look after their officials. The referee and linesmen had separate changing rooms and mine was luxuriously appointed with a three-piece suite, television and bar. This seemed a long way from the changing rooms at Filbert Street. 'Who needs a hotel?' I asked myself.

The game itself was uninspirational and ended 1-1. During the match one of the Charlton players sustained a cut knee, for which I cautioned an Italian player. He protested vehemently but I couldn't understand a word he was saying. I simply looked at him and said, 'This is no time for apologies', and after booking him walked away smiling to myself.

The Charlton players obviously felt that the offending challenge was deliberately intended to injure the player and although I didn't have any problem during the game things blew up in the tunnel after the final whistle. This was met with an interesting response from the police who simply prevented me from going into the tunnel and as far as I could tell let things take their course.

By the time I was allowed down the tunnel it was as if nothing had happened. As I was getting changed there was a knock on the door and in came Alan Curbishley, who generously offered me a lift back to the UK on the privately chartered Charlton plane which was flying out of Venice immediately after the game. I turned this down as I didn't want to offend our hosts who I thought were expecting the officials to participate in the usual post-match hospitality at the hotel. This turned out to be a mistake. When I got back to the hotel it was almost midnight as the match had not kicked off till 9 p.m. owing to the heat. The hotel was in darkness with only a night porter on duty and no other sign of life. As I hadn't eaten since lunchtime I was desperate for some food. The porter advised me that I could go down to the harbour below but he wouldn't recommend it as a good idea. I went to bed hungry.

ONE NIGHT AT THE PALACE

The next morning I had breakfast early and was then picked up by the same driver with whom I had spent a riveting two hours the previous day. He took me to join the Birmingham City bus at Pescara from where we made our way to Rome for the flight home. During the flight, all the referees who had been on duty in the competition compared stories and number of cautions. As I had only issued one yellow card, no one won the sweepstake as I had been widely tipped to issue the largest number of bookings owing to my 'dedication to duty on my way up the ladder'.

It was soon back to domestic duties and the first game back was a real experience for me. I was appointed to the Liverpool v Aston Villa game at Anfield. This was to be televised live on Sky on Sunday afternoon. I am not sure whether this filled me with anticipation or trepidation as I had seen some of my colleagues savaged at the hands of people like Andy Gray. Whilst you need to be thick-skinned to be a ref in the first place, it is not a nice feeling to have your ability questioned in front of a huge audience which quite likely involves lots of friends and family.

The day arrived and I took to the field, impressed as usual by the typical Anfield atmosphere. It's wonderful that football presents an outlet for the frustrations of people who tend not to have the luxury of high employment rates and the comforts that go with it. Like my native Newcastle, 'The Match' has incredible significance and can change the mood of the whole city. In the shipyard days on Tyneside it was well known that productivity was much higher on a Monday following a Newcastle win than it was after they had lost. Similarly the Scouse attitude is, 'We don`t have a lot but what we have we're going to enjoy.' I think this is why the Newcastle and Liverpool fans seem to get on so well, a rare but pleasant occurrence in the world of English football.

Getting back to the match, the game got under way and it wasn't too long before I noticed that the Aston Villa away strip, consisting largely of green and black stripes, appeared to clash with my Premiership jersey containing the same two colours. Despite the fact that the Premiership had cleared the respective strips I felt there was a little hesitation in the players when looking around for colleagues or opponents whenever I was in close proximity.

This was confirmed when Bruce Grobbelaar got the ball and was looking to find Jan Molby. Bruce seemed to be momentarily distracted by a glimpse of my shirt and proceeded to drop the ball. I then received a fairly sharp sentence or two from Bruce, who was never slow at letting you know his feelings. He said something along the lines of me needing to get out of the way. Delivered in Bruce's quaint Zimbabwean accent this was something that still makes me smile when I think about it.

More seriously, it wasn't long before Graeme Souness, the Liverpool manager, caught my attention and, although this might surprise many people, mentioned in a very courteous way the problem his players were having. I suggested he should find me an alternative top and he soon reappeared with a white rugby jersey which I wore for the rest of the half. I can't say I was too comfortable in this as it was heavy and obviously designed for someone with a bit more meat on them than me. As I always wore a short-sleeve shirt for matches I was anxious to get changed into something else. At half-time the Liverpool staff found three white T shirts for myself and the linesmen and we went on to control the game without any further incident. Liverpool's Robbie Fowler was as usual the scourge of Villa and scored both goals in a 2-1 victory.

Whilst I thought the action we had taken on the shirts was sensible, and demonstrated our commitment to working with the teams to avoid conflict, I'm afraid the Premier League bosses didn't see it the same way. All three officials received a letter the following week enclosing a photograph (as if we needed one) of us wearing unofficial gear, with a rebuke saying that the team colours had been checked and no clash existed. I suppose it's easy for someone sitting behind a desk to look at the niceties of the situation but I would like to think that if the roles were reversed I would try to understand what goes on in a highly charged and competitive situation. Never mind, my knuckles were rapped and that was it.

Despite such frustrations I wouldn't wish to complain about the Premiership as I was very happy at the more relaxed travelling arrangements, including the flexibility to operate all over the country. This was totally different to the restrictions which applied in the Football League. I guess it all comes down to money and big business in the end. In the Premiership I was allowed to fly to London for matches and this reduced the journey time immensely. This meant that on a Saturday evening my family might get the chance to see me before midnight, which wasn't often the case if I was on the train.

ONE NIGHT AT THE PALACE

One of the drawbacks of being a 'part-time' referee is that you have a full-time job during the week, in my case as a power technician with British Telecom, and then football commitments at weekends. It goes without saying that it requires a very understanding and patient family to put up with this. This is particularly so at those times when they have to put up with you being slagged off in the papers or on TV.

The family disruption isn't restricted to weekends, however. There are many mid-week appointments to cope with and also matches during public holidays. For instance, I was appointed to the Sheffield United versus Liverpool game on Boxing Day 1993. I wouldn't normally travel overnight to Sheffield but as the weather was bad this seemed a sensible thing to do. I therefore left the family at 5.30 p.m. on Christmas Day, the first, but not the last, time that the most important family day of the year would be affected by my 'hobby'.

I drove down the M1, checked into the Swallow hotel in Rotherham and spent Christmas evening watching everyone enjoy themselves at their Christmas functions. In fairness, I should mention that by this stage the financial considerations had become much more compensatory with the match fee at that time being £200 compared to £95 in the Football League, a welcome development.

The next morning, conditions were still freezing so I went to Bramall Lane at 7 a.m. and carried out a pitch inspection. It was touch and go whether the pitch was going to be suitable or not and I found myself once again being in the hot seat. A hot seat would have been very welcome actually as I hung around the ground all morning whilst the valiant ground staff endeavoured to get the pitch into playable condition. There was no under-soil heating and they had worked hard with straw, mats and covers to protect the pitch. It is always difficult to call a game off because there are so many factors to consider, not least the travelling fans. There are also the caterers, police, public transport staff, turnstile operators, traffic wardens and others to consider. Not to mention the possible fixture difficulties a club may face later in the season. None of these are as important, however, as the safety of the players. I wanted to ensure that I didn't repeat my mistake of the earlier Burnley and Stockport game and I wasn't going to allow the game to go ahead unless I was absolutely convinced that the pitch did not represent a danger to anyone.

INCE RETURNS

Somehow the ground staff got the pitch into suitable condition and, after I confirmed that the state of the playing area was consistent in all areas, the game kicked off at twelve noon as scheduled. Everything went well and although it ended in a goalless draw the game itself was entertaining and exciting. No injuries of note were sustained and this fortunately confirmed my judgement that the pitch was safe. In such circumstances, however, it only takes one nasty incident to instigate a retrospective witch-hunt and, who knows, in today's litigious society, to the referee being sued. On the other hand, if everything goes well, not many people congratulate the referee for getting it right.

I returned home at 6 p.m. and joined the family for Boxing Day tea. I felt really good and healthy as there is nothing like a hard run around in cold weather to give you a great feeling of well-being once you get showered and changed, and sit down for something to eat. The bottle of Valpolicella doubtless played its part.

Another example of the dilemma facing referees in deciding whether games should go ahead occurred soon afterwards at Blackburn when Rovers were due to play Wimbledon. The Ewood Park pitch had been waterlogged the week before and their game against Middlesbrough had been postponed. They were particularly hoping that this game would go ahead, for a number of reasons. Not least of these was the fact that the advertised intention was to hand out vouchers for a forthcoming major cup tie. This in effect would ensure a maximum crowd for this fairly run-of-the-mill Premiership match.

On the day of the match I awoke to torrential rain and was expecting to receive a phone call at my Preston Hotel from John Howarth, the Blackburn secretary. When this did not materialise I decided to go to the ground earlier than usual in view of the uncertainty. I arrived to the sight of groundsman Steve Gardener driving around the pitch on a 'Warthog' machine. This was a wonderful contraption, borrowed from Old Trafford cricket ground, which sucked up all the water and threw it into the area in front of the stands. It was proving very effective and Steve was confident that the pitch would be playable. I therefore retired to the '100 Club' and took advantage of the Blackburn hospitality in the shape of a few pre-match sandwiches. I then went to the referee's changing room to prepare my kit.

ONE NIGHT AT THE PALACE

At 1.50 there was a knock on the door and in walked Kenny Dalglish. Kenny promptly advised me that I had better come and have a look at the weather. It was raining 'stair-rods', as they say, and the pitch, which was slightly undulating at the time, was collecting puddles in the dips. As kick-off time got nearer I informed the police officer in charge that there was some doubt about the match and he put himself at my disposal and await-ed further instructions. I advised Kenny, who simply said that he was happy to leave it to me, and then I spoke to Joe Kinnear, the Wimbledon manag-er, who replied a little more passionately. 'It's your ******* job not mine,' would probably summarise Joe's articulate response.

By this time, 2.30 p.m., there was a capacity crowd of 29,000 in the ground. This really piled on the pressure and a tough decision needed to be taken. Considering the distance some fans travel to get to games you can't help feeling that you don't want to disappoint them. On the other hand the standard arrangement is for clubs to refund admission money if a game is cancelled before the kick-off. This does not apply if the game is abandoned once it has started.

It was apparent to me that with the passage of time and the continuing rain there was no way this game was going to get under way. I therefore told the respective managers of my decision and decided that before the official announcement to the crowd I would go out with a ball and look as though I was weighing up the situation. I made a bit of a show of this to the crowd, making sure I kicked the ball into the deepest puddles. I then left the pitch and soon afterwards the decision was communicated. Blackburn accepted the situation equably, as did the crowd. Wimbledon, being Wimbledon, felt obliged to show their opinion of things and to the groundsman's dismay proceeded to get changed, take to the pitch and dive around in the puddles!

By far the biggest game of the season for me was the next Premiership match which was West Ham against Manchester United. This was Paul Ince's first return to Upton Park since his transfer to Manchester. This par-ticular transfer had been very acrimonious, not only because Ince had been a great favourite at West Ham but also because he allowed himself to be photographed in a Manchester United strip whilst transfer negotiations were going on.

I arrived at the ground and was looking at the pitch when the West Ham security officer approached me and said, 'See you later out here for the security briefing.' I informed him that I always do the security briefing in the dressing room and not on the pitch. He replied, 'That's not the way we do it at West Ham.' 'Well, today is different then, see you in the changing room at 1.45,' I said.

When the appointed time came, the door suddenly burst open and here was this character expecting to take part in a briefing. I asked where was the police representative and he advised me that it was not practice to invite them. Amazed by this, I suggested he retrace his steps and come back again with the police and perhaps he might have the courtesy to knock next time. He soon returned, this time with a gigantic police Inspector who immediately expressed his gratitude at being invited. The Inspector went on to explain that it wasn't so much crowd control that he was concerned about but more the fact that information had been received suggesting three different death threats against Paul Ince.

He informed me that they had been warned to expect an armed intruder from the East Stand - armed with what he was unsure. This attack was expected within the first half. He then explained that they were also expecting an attack from the Bobby Moore Stand from someone who might have an automatic weapon. Finally they were expecting some sort of attack from the West Stand during the second half from the area where the two sets of supporters are close together. 'Don't worry,' he said, 'We have plans in place to make sure nothing untoward happens. And don't get concerned when, with ten minutes to go, you see all the police horses and dogs around the pitch.' Trying to stay cool I said, 'No problem, myself and my colleagues will do everything we can to make sure things go well.' At that I turned round to look at my fellow officials to find that they had disappeared to the toilet!

When we took to the pitch the noise levels were high and I could almost taste the tension. Manchester took the field with only ten players, there being no sign of Paul Ince. I didn't need to look to confirm when he did appear, as the noise immediately told me. The atmosphere was vitriolic and menacing. Ince came over to me and said, 'Will you tell me when there is ten minutes left, ref, as I need to be off and away.'

Only five minutes into the game I awarded West Ham a free kick and Ince, true to form even in these circumstances, started remonstrating enthusiastically with my decision. He calmed down a little when I suggested he might not need to worry about being told when there were ten minutes left as he might not be around at the time. I also suggested that I could see a very inviting way to make myself a hero with the West Ham crowd. This appeared to do the trick and he behaved himself for the rest of the match.

With ten minutes left Ince was substituted and left the ground immediately. As I had expected, there were no major incidents and all I had to report was the distasteful racial abuse, which included the throwing of bananas. Unfortunately, there are a number of grounds in this country where this sort of mentality is par for the course and West Ham is one of them. It is sad for the genuine supporters that they get tainted by the behaviour of racist morons.

There were two more games of note this season. Firstly, there was Arsenal v Chelsea, a needle match of considerable standing. As everyone knows, if you are going to referee a match in London the big ones are Arsenal v Tottenham or Arsenal v Chelsea. Arsenal won this one 1-0, with only one caution issued in the whole game. This went, not unusually, to Dennis 'The Menace' Wise. Only one yellow card was a pretty incredible statistic for this fixture. Although it was a good game, the main feature for me was just how nice it is to referee at Highbury. Mind you, the dressing rooms are miniscule and there is hardly room to get your cards out of your pocket. The thing that makes it really pleasurable is the general ambience. The people are very friendly, the marble halls memorable and the pitch is of the highest quality. No running around in mud and puddles here. I always looked forward to my visits to Arsenal after this.

The other memorable game was Oldham v Sheffield United. This was an extremely intense game, with the occasion matching the importance for both teams. If either team won they would stay in the Premiership; if Oldham only got one point, or were to lose, they would go down. Sheffield could perhaps stay up with one point. The evening started off badly when the fourth official hadn't turned up by 6 p.m.

I had taken a friend, Stuart Loudon, a regular companion and retired Football League linesman, along to the match and he went to the bar while I went to get changed. Wondering what I could do for a fourth official I decided to ask the Oldham representative who was looking after me to go to the bar and see whether Stuart had taken a drink yet and, if not, then to ask him to come to see me with a view to helping me out as fourth official. Stuart had ordered a whisky but fortunately hadn't touched it , or so he tells me, and he agreed to do the job.

The Oldham support team scraped around to find some gear for Stuart to wear and he eventually came out for his big time performance in a pair of the old-time rough leather boots with leather studs and ankle-high uppers. They looked as if they had been modelled by Hughie Gallagher in the 1930s and quite what they did to Stuart's feet over the next 90 minutes I'm not sure.

Oldham took the lead in the first half with a goal by Sean McCarthy. Sheffield equalised in the second half and the game became more and more frenetic as both sides struggled against the drop. In the midst of all this a ball was played over the United defence for the Oldham centre-forward McCarthy. Simon Tracey, the United keeper, came rushing out of his area and promptly flattened him. This was not a good atmosphere to be sending someone off, particularly a goalkeeper, but it had to be done.

The intimidatory protests were as you might expect but I managed to show just one yellow card before order was restored. Meanwhile, Stuart was coming into his own on the touchline where Dave Bassett, the United manager, and his assistant Geoff Thomson were insisting on sending on a substitute for the dismissed keeper. Stuart was having some difficulty getting through to them that to do this you must take off an outfield player. Fortunately they eventually clicked and they did the necessary to allow the reserve keeper onto the field. Stuart had done his bit and I was grateful for his assistance and professionalism.

Handling substitutions can be a difficult business in the hurly-burly of a fiery match and a great deal of concentration is required. You only have to look at the Tranmere v Sunderland FA Cup fiasco in 1999 to see what can happen if substitutions aren't handled correctly. In that case Tranmere had eleven men on the field when they should have had only had ten following the sending-off of Clint Hill. Although this was only for a few minutes the eleventh player, brought on inadvertently as a substitute for the player sent off, was involved in defending the free-kick that was awarded for the dismissal. Sunderland's belief was that this extra player was instrumental in them being knocked out of the Cup. In the subsequent inquiry the fourth official and one of the assistants were exonerated, but the referee and the other assistant were disciplined and suspended for two games. On appeal, the assistant was given a reprieve, leaving the unfortunate Rob Harris to take the rap. None of this was much use to Sunderland, however, as they lost their subsequent appeal to have the match replayed or Tranmere disqualified.

Fortunately, thanks to Stuart, any such mishaps were avoided on this occasion. As it happened Oldham were relegated on the night and they were eventually joined by United, who went down to Chelsea on the last day of the season.

During this 1993/94 season I was privileged to be again invited to take part in a European Cup tie, this time as a linesman for a second round, first leg match in the Basque region of Spain. The match was between a club called Osasuna, who are based in Pamplona, and Stuttgart from the German Bundesliga.

This would turn out to be one of the poorer experiences on my trips abroad. We flew from Heathrow to Bilbao, the brevity of the flight not allowing us to enjoy British Airways hospitality to the full extent. We were met by a very nice chap who was to drive us the one hundred and twenty miles to Pamplona, in an Opel Kadett (Vauxhall Astra). Oh, where is my stretch Mercedes now when I need it most?

During the trip we were very fortunate to accidentally bump into Michael Robinson, the former Liverpool, Manchester City and Queen's Park Rangers player. Michael had taken to life in Spain like a duck to water and he showed us round one of his many fine furnishing stores in Pamplona. Michael became a hero in Pamplona after first helping to get them out of the Spanish Second Division and then, when he had to retire through injury, he tore up his contract because he knew the Pamplona club could ill afford his salary for the eighteen months remaining. Michael now commentates on Spanish soccer for TV and radio as well as running his furnishing business.

It was on this trip that I discovered that for some reason the Basque football fans absolutely loathe English officials. As we took the field we were greeted by a cacophony of catcalls, jeers and boos. This continued for most of the match whenever a decision was made. By the end of the game, which was a soporific 0-0 draw, I was knee-deep in rubbish which had been thrown over the six-foot fence. The evidence of all of this garbage along the touchline was enough for the match delegate to report the misconduct of the Osasuna fans to UEFA and a fine of the equivalent of £18,000 would soon follow.

We were taken from the game to a restaurant for a very nice meal, returning to the hotel at about 2 a.m. to be greeted by a representative of Stuttgart, who had been waiting there since the conclusion of the game! He had missed us in the changing room where any gifts would normally be distributed and had diligently stood guard (no pun intended) in the hotel foyer until our return. Among the offerings that night was a Stuttgart shirt, club memorabilia and, strangely, a hairdryer (for which I was immensely grateful, of course!).

During this season I had felt very good emotionally about refereeing, feeling strong and confident. I also worked hard on my fitness and on doing things correctly. I had cut down my alcohol intake, which was difficult as I do enjoy a bottle or two of good red wine. Increasing my daily training hadn't been difficult as I have always enjoyed the physical rigours that go with refereeing. I felt I was in good shape and undertook to maintain this during the close season.

7

'GO ON, TISS, SHOOT!'

IT WAS NOW THE SUMMER OF 1994 and because of the World Cup there were wagonloads of directives from FIFA floating around. Referees were now instructed to take a hard line on certain aspects of the game. The areas where more stringent attention was to be given included yellow cards for kicking the ball away, encroaching at free kicks and tackles from behind. This was obviously going to lead to a very difficult time for referees as it would, in the short term at least, lead to more criticism and abuse from players, fans and managers.

It was also the season when the Premiership would break away from the Football League and for the first time referees performing in the Premiership would not be eligible to referee Football League games. This breakaway caused something of a rift between the two organisations and there was a degree of animosity owing to the development of a 'them and us' attitude. Fortunately, this situation did not cause any serious problems and matters improved as time went on.

As the new season opened I was greatly honoured to receive an invitation to go to Wembley as reserve referee for the traditional curtain raiser of the Charity Shield match. This was between Manchester United, the FA Cup winners and title holders, and Blackburn Rovers, who were runners-up in the Premiership.

The new FIFA edicts were demonstrated for the first time in this game and this resulted in Philip Don issuing seven yellow cards, five of these to Blackburn and two to United. After the match Alex Ferguson was quite phlegmatic about the new rule. This was perhaps not wholly unrelated to the fact that only two of his players were booked and his team won the game. Kenny Dalglish on the other hand was in orbit having gone berserk at the five bookings. Whether his reaction would have been the same had he been in the same position as Alex, I can only hazard a guess.

'GO ON, TISS, SHOOT!'

The game itself was a typical Charity Shield game, something of a practice match, with Brian McClair scoring the first and Paul Ince scoring with a spectacular overhead kick. After the game Philip was invited to explain to Sky viewers the reasoning behind the yellow cards. This he promptly did, with me alongside him lending moral support.

My first game as referee this season turned out to be Nottingham Forest v Manchester United. This was on a Monday evening, televised on Sky, and it wasn't long before I realised that I was going to become something of a Monday night specialist. I was appointed to so many Monday games that a phrase was coined by the Sky commentator: 'It's Monday night, it's Sky night, so it must be Alan Wilkie as referee.' I quite enjoyed this brief brush with fame, though on reflection should I have listened more closely to the intonation used? As the old saying goes, 'It's not what you say, it's the way that you say it!'

The Forest game was memorable for two fantastic bits of footballing skill which both led to goals. But first I had been forced to implement the new yellow card regime very early on in the game. Firstly Ryan Giggs was brought down from behind by Des Lyttle and Des became the first entrant in my 94/95 book after just twenty-five seconds. He was followed approximately five seconds later by Bryan Roy for dissent, having a go at me for what he thought was an even earlier foul against himself by Gary Pallister. This was proving to be an interesting start to the season. Never mind, only another 89 minutes 30 seconds to go.

Under the new regime there was no room for common sense to prevail or discretion to be used. The directives were quite clear and my own performance would be marked down if I didn't implement the new rules. Thus I had booked two players in the first thirty seconds and I began to wonder if I should have paid a visit to the stationers on the way to the ground. Fortunately, things settled down and the players concentrated on their football, which after all is what they were there for.

The game was adorned, as I suggested, by two wonderful goals. The first was when Lee Sharpe crossed from the left and Andrei Kanchelskis, who was running in from the right, hit a volley into the opposite corner of the goal, nearly ripping the roof off the net in the process. This was countered, perhaps even surpassed, by a magnificent effort from the emerging Stan Collymore. Stan picked the ball up just inside the United half and beat three players before unleashing an unstoppable shot past Peter Schmeichel from thirty yards. Not many people beat the great Dane from this distance and I expected to see a lot more from Stan in the years to come. Unfortunately he went on to make the headlines for mainly the wrong reasons.

The next match of note was at White Hart Lane between Tottenham and Southampton. This was notable for the dismissal of Sol Campbell, a genuine player who is excellent to deal with. Matt Le Tissier had played an excellent ball through for a really fast wing-back called Neil Heaney, who I never saw again after this match. Neil was racing for the goal confronted only by Ian Walker when he was brought down from behind by Campbell, who tried unsuccessfully to win the ball. I was 100 per cent certain that the offence had taken place in the penalty area and without hesitation awarded a penalty. I have no doubt that Sol was trying to win the ball but as he had clearly denied a goal-scoring opportunity he had to go.

Le Tissier duly obliged from the spot, as you would expect from someone with a penalty-taking record like his. This led to Southampton winning 2-1. The penalty had been hotly disputed and I had booked Mickey Hazard, a fellow Geordie, for enthusiastic protests. After the game Jeff Shreeves, a Sky representative, came to see me to ask if I would talk them through the penalty decision. In case I was being set up I asked what the camera showed and he advised me that it looked like a penalty. So off I went to the Sky TV room where Nick Collins, the presenter, asked me to talk through the incident. I did this without seeing the video first, a very naive thing to do.

I explained that to me it appeared the offence had taken place about a yard inside the area. I then watched as they showed the video re-run to the whole nation. I felt sick inside when I saw that the tackle appeared to take place on the edge or just outside the penalty area. I had a feeling of horror at the thought that I had been stitched up by the Sky people. However, when it was played at slow motion it was apparent that contact was made inches inside the box. What a sigh of relief (and what a great decision)!

It taught me a lesson, though, not to comment in front of millions of people without asking to see the video first. It brought home to me what a difference angles can make, as my estimation of where the offence had taken place was adrift by a considerable margin. Apologies to my friends at Sky for even dreaming that they might have set me up.

On the subject of Sky, I have to mention my opinions on the indomitable Andy Gray. I have nothing against Andy as a person, and as a player he was superb, being very brave and direct. However, I sometimes get the feeling that he relishes the opportunity to ridicule the officials. I happen to know that Andy was once offered a refereeing course to help his overall appreciation of the game. His reaction was apparently, 'No chance, wouldn't go near that sort of thing for a pension.' Here's an offer Andy - give me a call and I'll give you some personal coaching as a referee and then we'll put you into a game. Better still, get it televised on Sky and if you would like me to do the commentary I'll be happy to oblige!

The Tottenham game was part of a double-header for me as I was going on to Paris the next day. I had flown down to London on the Monday morning and checked into the Hospitality Inn on Bayswater Road as I had to report to Heathrow the next day to meet David Elleray, Paul Rejer and Dennis Madgwick. We were off to run the European Cup match between Paris St Germain and Bayern Munich, where I would be fourth official.

Being a match official can be painful at times but it does have its brighter points. We had a superb trip, staying at a hotel on the Champs Elyseé and having dinner in the world-famous Lido nightclub. There were hundreds of people waiting in the queue to gain entry to the Lido but our host simply waved his magic wand, we flashed our FA blazer badges and we were in. We were given VIP treatment, with the best seats and quality champagne to add to the occasion. The best was yet to come as the show to follow was a stunning success. I was enthralled by the technical splendour of the show which, among other things, included a submarine appearing from underneath the stage, and being pursued by a helicopter which appeared from the darkness above. This was definitely a night to remember.

The next morning we went to the magnificent Parc des Princes for the safety meeting and began to savour the surroundings. This started the build-up to the match and generated the feeling of anticipation always present before such occasions. We were then taken on a whistle-stop tour of the main sights of Paris before returning to the hotel to relax before the game.

The journey to the stadium brought back memories of the Marseilles trip as we were again accompanied by motorcycle out-riders who performed heroics to get us through the traffic-laden capital. As we approached the stadium it was dark and the illuminated view against the Parisian skyline was dramatic and filled us with excitement. When we stepped into the stadium I found myself in a huge foyer which, with its enormous glass partition, separated the pitch from the changing areas. The retracting glass doors opened to allow us to proceed for our pre-match walk around the pitch. By now the noise level was increasing as the Bayern Munich supporters had been allowed into the ground an hour early to keep them off the streets.

When kick-off time came the stadium was alive and fans of both teams ensured it was a spectacle of noise and colour. When the teams appeared they were littered with people who over the next few years were to become household names in England. David Ginola, Frank Leboeuf and Jurgen Klinsmann were all in the starting line-up.

A classy, chess-like, game ensued and PSG won 2-1. It was an exciting, as well as tactical, game but under the new rules eight yellow cards were produced. Lothar Matthäus was not happy with the refereeing and I noticed him muttering something derogatory about the 'English something or others'. Why he felt it necessary to do this in English I'm not sure. I would have thought he would have been safer to do it in his own language. A touch of arrogance perhaps.

Back on the domestic front, my next match was Sheffield Wednesday v Leeds. Again this was a Monday night match, televised live on Sky. It also happened to be my wife's birthday. In view of the fact that I was away from home on such an occasion it prompted me to have a word with the Sky commentator Ian Darke. He kindly changed the usual greeting to 'It's Sky football on a Monday night so the referee must be Alan Wilkie and happy birthday to his wife Margaret!' As my greatest supporter Margaret would always watch the teams come out and observe the pre-match preliminaries but would switch off as soon as the adverts came on prior to the kick-off. It's not that she isn't interested in football but she didn't like to see me embroiled in possible controversy, she was simply happy to watch me get things underway. She therefore caught her birthday greeting and this earned me a few plus points to make up for the fact that I was away for the occasion.

The match began and I was aware that these Yorkshire derby matches always had potential to be fiery affairs. I wasn't wrong. After three minutes

'GO ON, TISS, SHOOT!'

Gordon Watson of Wednesday hit Mark Tinkler of Leeds in the midriff with what can only be described as a drop-kick. The red card was therefore out of my pocket before it had even got the chance to get warm. In his post-match report Howard Wilkinson, the Leeds manager, stated that the referee started well and that no-one could argue with the sending off after three minutes, an unsurprising comment, as it was an opposition player that was dismissed. He went on to say that my control diminished after that. I do wonder if this might have something to do with the fact that I disallowed what would have been the Leeds winning goal in the last five minutes. Carlton Palmer had run clear in the penalty area and planted the ball in the bottom corner of Kevin Pressman's net, only for the goal to be ruled out by a linesman's raised flag indicating offside. I have to say that on viewing the incident later I have some sympathy with Howard as I believe the linesman's decision was incorrect. Unfortunately I had not been in a position to arrive at a different conclusion and had readily accepted my colleague's judgment. I believe, however, that Howard allowed this one decision to cloud his judgment of the whole match. Unfortunately he is not the only manager to allow a small-minded and biased attitude to affect their assessment of the referee's performance over the game as a whole.

David Pleat, on the other hand, was much more even-handed. When I sent off Watson and called on the Leeds physio to treat the unfortunate Tinkler I could see, on the Wednesday bench, a very agitated manager. He was clearly unhappy at the decision and I was expecting a rough ride at half-time. Watson, when he had left the field, had apparently said to David something like, 'It's a ******* joke, I never touched him.' Understandably David, who had been a long way from the incident, believed his player and was furious at being down to ten men so early in the game.

As I was leaving the field at half-time David was waiting for me. 'Shit,' I thought as I awaited a tirade from him. It came as a very pleasant surprise when he said to me, 'I've seen the video of the sending-off Alan, excellent decision, Watson said he never touched him - the video shows he nearly ******* decapitated him.' He added, before heading off to his team's dressing room, 'Just keep up the performance for the second half.' I would not have wished to be Gordon Watson at the half-time team talk. Ironically, this is the same Gordon Watson who a few years later sued a Huddersfield player for a reckless challenge on him. He won the court case and was awarded substantial damages against the player and also vicarious liability against the Huddersfield club.

When the Coca-Cola Cup second round came along I was appointed to take the game at Old Trafford between Manchester United and Port Vale. United tended to use these matches to blood their youngsters and, sure enough, standing in the tunnel waiting to make his debut was a young eighteen year old called David Beckham. I took the trouble to ask him if he was nervous and he replied, 'Not me ref, just watch tonight and you'll see something special,' very much in the way that the young Paul Gascoigne had done all those years ago. Well, I have to say that whilst he was not exactly modest, he was certainly accurate! For a young lad he displayed great maturity (an area of his game which was to be questioned at a later date on a World Cup stage) and his talent was there to be seen by all. The most appealing thing about David's performance that night was the amount of happiness he was going through, which was evident from the almost constant smile on his face. He was definitely an outstanding talent, as his progress since then confirms.

Soon after this game I was asked to go to another European Cup tie, this time as fourth official. The game was between Real Zaragoza and Dukla Prague but was in fact being played in the lovely city of Valencia, owing to the Zaragoza ground being closed because of previous crowd trouble. Dermot Gallagher was the appointed referee with Mark Warren and Phil (Jossie) Joslin as linesmen.

Again I found myself having to endure the trauma of the first class treatment in the BA lounge, loving every minute of it. Soon it was arrival time in Valencia and as it had been an early flight we were taken for lunch to what we thought was a pleasant little restaurant, before going on to the hotel. On arrival at the hotel we found that our rooms had not been booked. Apparently they had got the dates wrong. As we stood there in all our FIFA finery, laden with our luggage, Dermot said, 'Now I know how the baby Jesus felt - no room at the inn.' As we fell about laughing, the chap on the reception desk seemed less amused, not suprising considering his predicament. We then sat in reception whilst the matter was being resolved. The resolution appeared in the form of a procession of four glum-faced Spanish businessmen who it seemed were being shown to another hotel.

We were then shown to our recently vacated rooms and with perhaps the slightest tinge of guilt we settled into our very nice accommodation.

In the evening we were taken to the Valencia training complex, which turned out to be one of the most interesting excursions I was to encounter on my footballing travels. The complex contained a miniature stadium that could house up to 5,000 spectators and was for the sole use of the reserve and youth teams. Incorporated in the stadium were living quarters for the young players, aged fourteen years upwards, hoping to a make a career at the club. These boys lived, trained, and were educated here. Adjacent to this was an area of fifteen full size floodlit football pitches which, we were informed, were used every evening to train youngsters from the age of six upwards. Each pitch had its own dedicated coach. It was a wonderful sight and I am pleased that many British clubs have followed the continental example and invested in similar facilities.

The next day was spent sight-seeing and we were taken to the ground at 7 p.m. for a 9 p.m. kick-off. An interesting feature of the officials' changing room was that it had its own mini-chapel, the only time I had come across this on my travels.

When we took to the pitch our worst fears were confirmed: only 150 people had turned up! This was not what we had travelled 2,000 miles for and there was a huge feeling of anti-climax. The reason for the crowd being so sparse was that there is a lot of rivalry and ill-feeling between the followers of Zaragoza and those of Valencia. The Zaragossans could not bring themselves to go to Valencia, much in the same way, I suppose, as Newcastle supporters might feel about Sunderland and vice versa.

The game itself was like a training session; there seemed to be no motivation due to the surreal atmosphere surrounding the match. Any noise made by the few fans who were present simply echoed around the empty stadium. Zaragoza won 2-0 but Dukla had missed a chance to capitalise on what was effectively a neutral ground.

As is usual with these games, the late finish meant that the night was over by the time we left the ground and we simply had a meal and went back to the hotel.

We were about to head for the airport the following day when we were asked by our host if we would like to go to lunch. We agreed it would be a good idea and, after three quarters of an hour stuck in a traffic jam, we found the little restaurant we had been to on our arrival two days before. This being Spain, and particularly the Valencia region, the menu seemed to consist of paella, paella or paella. Although I'm not a great fan of this concoction, it seemed very pleasant at the time and, after a very relaxing interlude, we headed back to the airport for the flight home.

I had expressed for some reason the wish to be the last person on the aeroplane before take-off. We had been called to the boarding gate when we realised that no one knew where 'Jossie' was. We guessed where he might be as he loves, on these trips, to spend all his match fee before even leaving the airport. He would therefore be hunting for presents for his wife and kids. We got the airport official to put out a call for him and as the Tannoy announcement boomed out Jossie came into view as fast as his legs would carry him, carrying an enormous floppy Spanish donkey like you see on the comedy sketches of British holidaymakers abroad. This had me in stitches and will be an undying memory of my trips to Europe.

The game had been on the Thursday evening and I was due to referee Crystal Palace against Ipswich Town on the Saturday. It had therefore made sense to head straight for London having negotiated annual leave from work. I arrived in London on Friday evening and booked in at yet another hotel, feeling rather tired but otherwise fine.

The match at Palace went well (once I had found the ground) and although Palace won 3-0 it was a lot tighter than the score suggests, with all three goals coming in the last five minutes. I can never understand those spectators who leave five or ten minutes from the end just to miss the rush. Don't they know that twenty-two per cent of goals are scored in the last five minutes of a game? What's the point in getting home thinking you've watched a 0-0 draw for an hour and a half and then when the results come on the radio or television you see a completely different scoreline!

Towards the end of this match, although I don't think it was instrumental in the three goals, I had started to feel unwell and I only just managed to hang on till the end. When I got back into the dressing room I was suffering from stomach cramps and sweating. I was shipped off to King's Cross station as soon as possible. When I got on the train I mentioned it to the guard, asking him to ensure I didn't pass my stop at Durham if I fell asleep as I felt unwell. He ensured I got off at the right stop and I made it home without any accidents. I was ill and off work for a week however.

'GO ON, TISS, SHOOT!'

It appears the paella had been reheated as it had been ordered somewhat earlier and we then got stuck in traffic on the way to the restaurant. It was apparently a rabbit paella, which is a local delicacy of the Valencia region, but I'm afraid my stomach wasn't up to such delights, particularly when re-heated. I later learned that Dermot and Jossie had also been quite ill. Mark survived unscathed but there again he will eat anything and would be a strong contender for the gold medal if they extended the Olympics to food-tasting.

After recovering from this little set-back I had a memorable day on 10 December 1994 when Blackburn Rovers were playing Southampton. All my Southampton games seemed to be interesting and exciting and this was no exception. It was end-to-end stuff with Blackburn eventually running out 3-2 winners. The highlight, however, was a Matt Le Tissier goal which apart from anything else defied the laws of physics. He picked the ball up around the half-way line and moved forward with me running directly behind him. I could see exactly what Matt could see. Tim Flowers was standing to one side of his goal. I found myself shouting, 'Go on Tiss, shoot!' I don't suppose I was supposed to do this but if you're a true football fan it's difficult to resist the temptation. In fact, one of the pleasures of refereeing is that you're out there, part of the sport you love, among the most talented and famous people in the game and getting a player's eye view at the same time.

So here I was, standing directly behind the enigmatic hero of Southampton, with the best view in the world of what he would do next. He took another two or three steps forward and then from 35 yards he took my 'advice'. The ball seemed to be flighted to head for the goalkeeper's top left hand corner, where Tim Flowers was standing, but, in the air, it changed direction and ended up nestling neatly in his top right hand corner, to the astonishment of the England keeper. It was an absolutely phenomenal shot and one which won the goal of the season competition. It was a privilege to be there and an even greater privilege to be standing right behind Matt when he conjured up this piece of magic. He never did tell me whether I had encouraged him to shoot. I don't think I want to know, I'll just bask in the glory, in my mind, of having played some small part in a piece of football wizardry.

I had a dream appointment on New Year's Eve 1994 when I took the Leeds United v Liverpool game at Elland Road. This is always a mega-fixture with the rivalry still simmering from the days of the 1970s when they both dominated English football with magnificent teams. Confrontations spring to mind like Norman Hunter versus Tommy Smith and Ron Yeats trying to outdo Jack Charlton in the battle of the centre-halves.

This appointment boosted my confidence immensely as they don't come any bigger than this. I was feeling good, happy with my performances and generally well up for games such as this. Liverpool won the match 2-0 and the strange thing about this game was that on this occasion the home team were so bad that they were booed by their own fans every time they touched the ball and the opposition were so brilliant they were cheered for every pass. A very unusual occurrence.

When I got home I received a phone call from the FA asking if I was free on 2 January. When I replied positively I was stunned to be advised to report to St James' Park to referee the game between Newcastle United and Manchester City. This was most unusual as, due to my proximity to Newcastle, not to mention being a life-long fan, I was exempt from such fixtures. However, the appointed referee, Peter Jones, was ill. As it wasn't in my character to turn anything down, I agreed on impulse to take the game. It wasn't until I put the phone down that I realised the enormity of what I had agreed to. It was no secret that I was an avid Newcastle fan and my appointment to this game was hardly going to go unnoticed even though the programme showed Peter as the ref.

I tried to get used to the idea over the next thirty-six hours although I have to admit that all sorts of things were going through my mind. On the day of the match my usual preparation was immediately knocked out of sync, I set off for the ground at 11.45 a.m., whereas I am usually arriving at my remote destination around this time. I enjoy listening to music whilst I drive and choose the type of music very carefully to offer mental stimulation before I arrive. On this occasion I had such a short journey that I had no time to do this. All of which heightened the awareness that this was a different fixture for me.

The heady Keegan days were in full swing at St James' and the usual capacity 36,000 fans packed the ground well before kick-off. I decided to have a good warm-up before the game and went out onto the pitch. Here I was on the treasured St James' turf, which was in beautiful condition, the same pitch where as a youngster I had watched my heroes Len White and Ivor Allchurch.

The Smiling Referee in relaxed pose
away from all the pressure.

Me, aged 8, with no idea what's to come.

My first cup final - yes, it really is me!
- at Durham University, 1978.

My first Football League game in charge, Mansfield Town
v Northampton Town on 19 August 1988. On the left is
Fred Hackett, with Paul Rejer on the right.

Community service - An important part of the job of a referee is visiting schools. I like to think these visits help to change the youngsters' views on referees.

At close quarters - Julian Dicks and I
not quite seeing eye to eye.

Emmanuel Petit decides that I'm the one
who should be leaving the field.

Above: Controversy - I'm escorted off the Valley Parade pitch after awarding three penalties to visitors Derby County.
Below: Danny Granville of Leeds, hidden by Lee Bowyer, is given his marching orders.

A Galaxy of stars look on as I send off Frank Sinclair.

Typically Gallic celebrations.
Frank Leboeuf with Graeme Le Saux.

Travels in Europe: Above, in the trophy room at Valencia, and below, Paris St. Germain v Bayern Munich, enjoying the delights of the Paris Lido.

Above: History in the making as Wendy Toms becomes the first lady to assist in a Worthington Final, Tranmere v Leicester City at Wembley, February 2000.
Below: a little tête-à-tête with Emile Heskey in the Final.

What a way to make history! I'm carried off at that 2000 Worthington Cup Final.

Feeling as strained as I look, I hobble up the 39 steps to collect my medal.

Left: My last game at Old Trafford, where, below, Albert Morgan, United's kit man, presented me with a Ryan Giggs shirt signed by the players.

My family: Above with my wife Margaret,
and below, my two sons - Carl (left) and Ben.

Times up - end of an era.

'GO ON, TISS, SHOOT!'

It seemed as if everyone from the North East who remotely knows me was in the crowd that day as I heard lots of shouts to the effect of 'Hello Alan, what the **** are you doing here?' from the crowd while I was warming up.

Brian Horton, the ex-Oxford manager who had cheered me up that day at Tranmere and who was now in charge at Manchester City, appeared and his initial comment was something like, 'Hello again, have you walked to the ground or did you take the bus!' I wasn't sure whether this was a barbed comment from the away manager or just a joke. I was probably feeling over-sensitive about the situation but I was very conscious of the scrutiny every decision would be subject to. I was also aware that there would be a subconscious possibility of me being too fair to the visitors and making Newcastle suffer as a result.

The processional march onto the pitch took on greater significance than usual; this was my ground, my people, my team. I had to stop thinking like this as my future might depend on being able to control my feelings of support for my beloved Black and Whites. The meeting of captains for the formal toss-up brought Garry Flitcroft and Peter Beardsley together and the resulting photograph still adorns my study wall.

After 35 minutes Peter Beardsley ran across Alan Kernaghan and ended up on the ground. As the crowd howled their disapproval I decided that Peter had simply fallen over. However, my assistant was waving his flag and I stopped play and went over to speak to him. 'He was tripped,' he said. 'Who by?' was my response. 'The Blonde one,' said my assistant. Well, as Alan Kernaghan, Garry Flitcroft and the Brightwell brothers all had fair hair, this was not particularly helpful. I decided to put him on the spot and asked for a better description of the offender in the knowledge that if it was a deliberate trip it was a bookable offence. 'He's about six foot,' I was informed. Not a lot of help this as all of the aforementioned fall into that category. I decided to just beckon in the general direction of the players and fortunately Kernaghan came across and didn't argue when I told him he had been seen tripping Beardsley. I then gave him the yellow card.

The game went on and after 42 minutes I awarded a penalty to Newcastle for a trip on Beardsley by one of the Brightwell boys. Beardsley went to pick up the ball but to everyone's surprise Ruel Fox got there first and took it to the spot. To everyone's dismay, including mine, Fox proceeded to hit the kick wide of the post. I was in two minds whether to run after him and hit him or to award a re-take and let Beardsley have a go. I couldn't do either of course and had to suffer in silence as the game ended in a 0-0 draw.

After the match Kevin Keegan came in and wished me all the best and a safe journey home. I wasn't sure if his mind was still tied up with the game or whether he didn't actually realise where I had come from. I subsequently asked to be excluded altogether from Newcastle games as the emotional factors were too much for me to be able to concentrate fully and do the teams justice.

The games over the Christmas period went well and then there were some early FA Cup games before I refereed the Aston Villa v QPR game. This game was notable for the duel between John Fashanu - the Villa centre forward - and Alan McDonald, the QPR centre half. Fashanu was renowned as a robust and aggressive player but he met his match in McDonald. After one particularly tough aerial battle Fashanu ended up in a crumpled heap on the ground. The ball was kicked out of play and I signalled for the Villa physio to come on. I went across to see what the damage was and saw that Fashanu's teeth appeared to be all over the place. Jim Walker, the physio, was trying to spray water in Fashanu's mouth and John wasn't liking it one bit. Walker then told him to sort it out himself and left the field. Fashanu also left the field and went running down the touchline holding his face. When the game ended I asked how he was and was told that he would be at his Harley Street dentist by now, having dashed straight off to the airport. Such is the life of a superstar. Still it kept his smile in good shape for his television appearances.

8

CANTONA SEES RED

THE FOLLOWING WEEKEND I drove to London as I was due to referee the Spurs v Manchester City game on 21 January. I had to call the game off because of a waterlogged pitch and I then drove up to Birmingham for the remainder of the weekend to make arrangements for a conference of the Association of Premier League and Football League Match Officials. I did this in my capacity as a member of the governing body, an appointment of which I was very proud.

I had no idea that in three days time I would be involved in an event which would have an impact on the image of football all over the world.

On Sunday 22nd January Manchester United were playing Blackburn Rovers. This was not only a grudge match but was also crucial in terms of league standing as both teams were in contention for the championship. Manchester won the game 1-0 and that set them up nicely for the forthcoming mid-week game at Crystal Palace, which I had been appointed to referee.

I took the train to London on Tuesday morning and booked into the Eccleston Square Hotel in preparation for the Palace match. On the evening of the game I made the usual tortuous journey to Selhurst Park.

On arrival, I was met by the assistant referees, Eddie Walsh and Grant Hegley, and the fourth official Bob Hintz. Bob, surprisingly, was an American. He was on secondment to IBM in Portsmouth for two years and, as a reputable referee in the States, was gaining valuable experience with the Premiership.

He would not have expected, however, to become embroiled in an episode which was to make international headlines. Before the game George Crawford, the Palace security man - an ex-policeman and international rugby referee - came to see me, accompanied by the match police commander. We inspected the ground and had a chat about which fans would be sitting in the various sections.

ONE NIGHT AT THE PALACE

Since the demolition of pitch-side fences, following the Hillsborough disaster, the seating in the stands in this compact little stadium came very close to the pitch itself. However, there was no history to suggest this would be a problem. As is always the case, whenever and wherever Manchester United play, there was a sell-out crowd and a full house of 26,000 would soon fill the stadium.

Alex Ferguson brought in his team-sheet at 6.45 as did Steve Coppell, the Palace manager. Alex was in unusually fine form and was obviously on a high following the victory over Blackburn. I got the impression that he was particularly satisfied that Alan Shearer for Blackburn had had a goal disallowed. Shearer was the source of some acrimony between Rovers and United over abortive transfer discussions, something which Alan is reminded of every time he visits Old Trafford. Ferguson was beaming from ear to ear and said to me and my colleagues, 'Wasn't it a good decision to disallow the goal?' When I told him I hadn't seen the game he seemed surprised and good-humouredly passed comment on what referees do in their spare time.

When the time came to take to the pitch I met the teams in the tunnel. The two teams formed up and the difference in the attitude was apparent. Manchester United's players were imperious whilst the Palace team looked tension-filled and worried. This gave me an extra spur and put me even more on my toes, thinking about what might lie ahead. I led the teams out to the usual resounding cheers and boos which accompany every Manchester United game. The atmosphere at all their matches is electric and it is something the players have to learn to live with. To the opposition players and fans alike, this is always a Cup Final match.

The game started quietly enough and I found myself under-employed in terms of enforcing the new FIFA yellow card directives. However, I was starting to become more and more aware of the constant complaining by United's star player Eric Cantona, who seemed to be getting himself rather steamed up. I put this down to the frustration of being man-marked by Palace's Darren Patterson.

The first half came and went without any bookings or incidents of note, apart from when Cantona went to ground and stayed there moaning about his close marking. Following a moment's cursory treatment he was fit to carry on. This was the only tangible sign in the first half of any problems to come but it was enough to make me aware that there might be recriminations later. I was beginning to feel that apart from this isolated incident the evening might turn out to be something of an anti-climax.

I started to get an uncomfortable feeling when comments were made to me whilst waiting to take the field for the second half. In the tunnel, Cantona looked across at me with a blazing stare and in his inimitable Gallic accent offered the comment, 'No cautions first half.' As there was a certain tone in his voice I replied, with a little edge myself, to the effect, 'Well observed Eric, no cautions.' He then, even more enigmatically, offered another comment, 'No cautions second half.' At this point I wondered what was going on and started to become uneasy. Alex Ferguson then came past and with a dark look on his face said in my direction, 'Just do your ******* job you, just do your job.'

We took the field and I got the second half under way, completely oblivious of what was to come. After six minutes Gary Pallister played the ball back to Peter Schmeichel in the United goal who promptly launched one of his huge kicks upfield. As the ball landed in the Palace half Richard Shaw, the Palace central defender, turned to run after it. Before he could complete his turn Cantona kicked out at him and Shaw ended up on the ground looking very bemused. As I had witnessed the kick at close quarters I had no hesitation in my mind that this was a red card offence. I believe Cantona made contact with Shaw, but even if he had missed, as suggested by some, it would still be a sending-off under law 12 of the game, 'kicks or attempted kicks'. As I ran to the scene, where Shaw was prostrate on the ground, I took the red card out of my pocket. As usual with Manchester United, I found myself surrounded by a host of snarling players, the protests being led by Andy Cole and Paul Ince. There was lots of posturing going on with players of both teams squaring up to each other, more a matter of threat than intent, I felt.

Trying to calm the situation, I was one minute engaged in meaningful discussion with Cole and Denis Irwin and the next I was talking to myself as they had run off to join in a fracas taking place on the touchline some 40 yards away. I immediately took off in the same direction and when I got there I attempted to drag players back on to the field of play, not quite sure of what was going on. I decided the best thing I could do to restore order would be to get the game under way, a view supported by Brian McClair, who was shouting to me to do just that. I looked up the field to Gareth

Southgate, who had the ball at his feet and indicated that he should take the free kick without delay. The commotion appeared to die down and the game was played out without further incident, ending in a 1-1 draw with goals by first David May and then Chris Armstrong. At the end of the match the first two players to shake my hand were Brian McClair and Paul Ince. The gesture from the latter was particularly appreciated in view of his fiery reputation and constant bad press.

Back in the changing room I was still oblivious to what had happened, as was Eddie Walsh, my assistant. My other assistant, Grant Hegley, however, had witnessed events clearly and gave us a vivid account of the incident. He explained that as Cantona was walking to the tunnel after being dismissed, he was suffering a lot of abuse by the home fans. This had come to a head with one particular youth running down the aisle between the seats and hurling insults at Cantona. The Frenchman had responded by leaping into the crowd and directing a karate kick at the fan concerned, slightly injuring nearby spectators in the process. Eddie and I could not believe what we were hearing and were completely taken aback. Just as we were trying to take all this in, George Crawford came in with the duty police commander. They had begun to regale me with their account of the incident when the door burst open and in steamed a furious and red-faced Alex Ferguson. 'It's all your ******* fault, if you'd done your ******* job this wouldn't have happened.' His demeanour was such that I was extremely pleased to have a 6'6" policeman in the room with me. The police officer told Ferguson in no uncertain terms to leave and go back to his room where he would be questioned later.

George Crawford and I realised we needed to hold an immediate meeting to look at the sequence of events and to make recommendations to prevent similar occurrences in the future. This was not an easy task as my stomach was churning, I felt sick and my head seemed ready to burst. However, with the help of George, the police match commander, the official match observer and my three assistants we were able to put together a plan which would later dictate future arrangements for match stewards, refereeing and policing at football matches throughout the country. We didn't realise it at the time but our recommendations would form the basis of a blueprint for match day security procedures in the future.

CANTONA SEES RED

The problem had been that Cantona was a long way from the tunnel when I sent him off and there was very close proximity to the spectators. Our recommendations suggested that, in future, players would stay on the pitch until a steward came to escort them off the field. There would also be a 'match team' of stewards dedicated to looking after officials. By the time we had sorted this out it was 11.30 p.m. and I was still in my wet match strip which was becoming somewhat anti-social by now. I went to have a shower while the match observer went to check out what was happening elsewhere. The bars and restaurants had long since been cleared but the media were still around in droves. A Palace official invited me to the boardroom and I willingly took up his offer.

It was there, at approximately midnight, that I saw for the first time what had happened earlier. I was able to watch in horror the Sky TV and CNN World News coverage of the incident. I felt sick to the pit of my stomach. Here was an incident in my match that I hadn't even seen and it had been reported around the world while I was still in the changing room.

An ironic aspect of all this was that when I decided to get back to the hotel I had to join a taxi queue. I had been told there was a rank right outside the ground but when I got there found dozens of people milling around. When I tried to get back into the ground to make a phone call I found everything locked up. Here I was, my picture being shown all around the world, and me standing forlornly in a taxi queue in the middle of South London!

When I got to the hotel I sat in the room and had a drink while I played over events again and again in my mind. I eventually went to bed at 3.30 a.m. and managed to get a few hours sleep before getting up to make my way back to the North East. As my train ticket was an open return I decided to take a cab to FA Headquarters to file my report. As the driver turned into Lancaster Gate I was horrified to see the world's media camped outside. I immediately told the driver not to stop but to carry on to King's Cross.

Three hours later the train drew into Durham station and I immediately started to feel more relaxed. I was looking forward to reaching the refuge of my house and family. I was ready to enjoy some peace and quiet.

I took a cab from Durham station to Chester-le-Street, the time being around 1 p.m. I had only been away one day but I couldn't get back soon enough. As the cab approached my house I was once again shocked when I saw the house was surrounded by reporters and TV cameras. My first reaction was to tell the driver to go straight past and this we did. However, I realised that I had to brave the media at some stage and, once I had gained my composure, I got out of the cab and approached the front drive.

With all the flash bulbs going off, and everyone talking at once, my head was spinning. I muttered something about having made a statement to the police and any further comment would be sub-judice. This and a few photographs seemed to placate the majority of the press and I managed to get into the house where my family were waiting anxiously to see me. 'Quiet trip,' I said as I entered the front door. 'How's everyone here?'

Subsequently I had two interviews with Croydon police but I am afraid I wasn't able to help them too much as I really didn't see the assault with which they were charging Cantona.

I spent quite a bit of time thinking about what made Cantona snap. I will never forget the expression in his dark eyes as I showed him the red card. He had a hollow look on his face and a vacant expression, as if he was somewhere else. He had obviously been frustrated by the man-marking tactics and Palace's spoiling approach to the game. This sort of situation makes it difficult for a play-maker such as Cantona and he had shown previously a tendency to react. He had been dismissed for stamping on the chest of Swindon's John Moncur and on another occasion had nastily flicked out a 'back-heel' in the face of John Polson of Norwich City. This had gone unnoticed by the referee but was vividly picked up by the TV cameras.

I also believe there is a factor arising from playing two games in a short period of time. In this case United had played a critical match on the Sunday, followed by the Palace match on Tuesday. The physical problems associated with this are well recognised but I don't think much thought has been given to the emotional side of things. I know from refereeing experience that it can take two to three days to get a big match out of your system.

High profile stars have to learn to close their ears to the mindless utterings from the terraces. Whilst this is not easy, it must be done. A referee, for instance, has to adopt a philosophical mental attitude for every match no matter what level it is played at. In the Cantona case it seems that the final straw was an insult about his mother. Hard as it might be, there is no justification for assaulting a spectator, even if that person did run down the aisle with aggression and hatred on his face. You only have to look at the stunned faces of the innocent people in the crowd, including women and children, as Cantona leapt among them, to realise what damage he had done to the game. Quite what affect it has on the future behaviour of those youngsters for whom he was a role model remains to be seen.

As for Alex Ferguson, his reaction was disappointing to say the least and was just one more episode in his tempestuous relationship with life. This wasn't to be my last encounter with Alex.

9

'THERE'S A BULLET WAITING...'

AFTER THE CANTONA INCIDENT, I was feeling shell-shocked and not a little drained. My feelings were, 'If I'm to have another game, please let it be somewhere quiet and out of the limelight.' I knew I had done nothing wrong yet somehow I felt tainted by the actions of Cantona. Now that the legal side of things, with the court case and his suspension, was receiving massive coverage in the press there was no escape. True to form my next game, far from being out of the limelight, was a 'live' FA Cup tie between Sheffield Wednesday and Wolves.

No matter how hard I tried to avoid being the centre of attention it just appeared to follow me around. Despite all attempts to play down my previous game it was all the Sky people wanted to talk about in the build-up to kick-off. My wife cringed as the camera played on me and the commentator debated at length the goings on at the 'Palace'.

The game itself was a bit of a bore and was heading for a nil-nil draw when, in the second or third minute of injury time, I awarded a penalty to Wednesday for what I perceived to be a trip from behind. The kick was taken and missed and the game ended scoreless.

No one had made any comment about the award of the kick until Jeff Shreeves, the Sky manager, came and told me to come and listen to the transmission going on at the moment. It was an interview with Graham Taylor, who was then manager of Wolves, and he was berating the standard of Premiership referees and me in particular. As if to support his argument Sky were running a shot of the penalty decision from a camera behind the goal which showed I was incorrect in awarding the penalty kick. I thought to myself - 'Must remember to stand behind the goal to give decisions in future!'

It was at this point I realised just how fragile my emotions had become. I began to wonder whether it was all worth it, but Taylor's words were all I needed to encourage me to show them what I could do. The replay was held a week later and I paid my first visit to Molineux. With Taylor's words ringing in my ears I performed as well as any referee could hope to do. This game also ended in a draw, but as it was a replay it went to penalties. As required, I went to the respective managers to get the details of the penalty takers. Trevor Francis politely gave me the shirt numbers and I then approached Graham Taylor. I asked if his players were ready to take the penalties and the response was something along the lines of, 'My players are always prepared and know exactly what to do.' This was delivered with a sneering grin and a clearly sarcastic tone.

The vital missed penalty for Wednesday was taken by a reluctant Chris Waddle. I shall always remember the haunted look on his face when he turned to me as if to say, 'Can I have another go, please?' Chris, of course, had already suffered the embarrassment of missing a penalty for England in Italy in the 1990 World Cup. I couldn't help but feel sorry for him.

The games came thick and fast now, including a Liverpool v Wimbledon Cup tie which Liverpool finally won after a replay. Then Blackburn beat Arsenal 3-1, this being the season that Blackburn were pressing for the championship. This was followed by a draw between West Ham and Norwich and a game between Sheffield Wednesday and Nottingham Forest, not the first time I had refereed a match between these two sides.

This was a game with a difference, however, with Forest winning 7-1, a fantastic performance for an away side. They were driven on by their inspirational leader Stuart Pearce who, as well as possessing a bone-crunching tackle, packs a thunderous shot. He used this to good effect on this afternoon, crashing in two unstoppable strikes. He gave a wonderful performance all round.

Just before the Wednesday v Forest game I received a notification from the FA appointing me as fourth official to the FA cup semi-final between Spurs and Everton. This was to be held at Elland Road on 9 April 1995. This represented a real highlight for me and I was particularly pleased to be involved.

As Elland Road was only a matter of 80 miles away I didn't travel on the previous evening but set off at 8.30 a.m., needing to be there by 10.30 for a 12 noon kick-off. This was a big mistake as the match traffic was horrendous. I made good time right up to three-quarters of a mile from Elland

Road. Travelling with me were my son and his friend, who had come along as he was an Everton supporter (for some reason). I asked them to get out and find a police officer to see if I could get some sort of escort to the ground. They duly returned with a policeman and I wound the window down and explained my predicament. 'Nothing I can do I'm afraid, the traffic is completely solid,' he advised me. I therefore asked him if he could do a damage limitation exercise by phoning ahead and letting them know where I was and why I was delayed. A pretty embarrassing moment and one I took care never to repeat.

I eventually got to the ground and regained my composure by kick-off. By 11.30 I was refereeing a penalty shoot-out for youngsters for the John Charles trophy. The great man himself was there to present the trophy. I don't suppose too many youngsters remember the name of John Charles but people of my era will know that the 'Gentle Giant' was the trend-setter in terms of British footballers going to Italy when he was head-hunted by Juventus in 1957 for what was then a record transfer fee. He went on to become a folk-hero in Italy as well as in Leeds and his native Wales.

As we lined up in the tunnel I had a great feeling of pride at being involved at this level. It was an honour to know that the FA had confidence in me taking over if anything happened to the referee.

Everton had the upper hand in the early stages and went into a two-goal lead. Spurs then started playing with a new sense of urgency and were given a life-line when they were awarded a penalty which was expertly despatched by Jurgen Klinsmann. With twelve minutes left, Paul Rideout sustained an injury and was taken to the far side of the pitch where the Everton physio tried to establish how serious it was. At this point Joe Royle called to Daniel Amokachi to get himself ready and warm up. The signals coming across from Paul Rideout were that he had damaged his leg and would not be able to carry on. I went across to Amokachi and suggested that he took off his jewellery in preparation for coming on.

I was waiting for a stoppage in play to make the substitution and when this occurred I held up the number board to indicate 'Rideout off, Amokachi on'. While this was going on I noticed that the signals coming from Rideout had changed somewhat and he was becoming animated, indicating he wanted to carry on. As Amokachi took the field Joe Royle came running up in a state of panic shouting, 'No, I said not yet.' 'Too late,' I replied. 'He's on, I can't do anything about it now.'

The next few minutes were memorable for the steam coming out of Joe's ears. Quite what would have happened had Amokachi made a mess of things I'm not sure. In the event, Joe's ranting calmed down a little as Daniel scored the goal which put his team 3-1 up and a step closer to Wembley. When the same player scored his second goal in the 89th minute to finally kill off the Tottenham fightback I was feeling mightily relieved.

At the end of the game Joe Royle was now my big pal and came across and jokingly offered me a job, saying I was obviously a better tactician than himself. Joe might be fiery and outspoken at times but he is extremely honest and everything comes from the heart. He also has a sense of humour, which cannot be said for all Premiership managers, and I have a great deal of respect for the man.

There were two more extremely important games left among the half dozen remaining before the end of the season. The first of these was Leeds United v Norwich City. The latter were perilously close to going down and had two more games, following this one, to save themselves. However, they needed to win all three games to be sure of safety. Everything was going well for City after an hour of play, having gone into a 1-0 lead. However, Leeds equalised and then with eight minutes to go Tony Yeboah was brought down by John Newman. It had to be a penalty and Yeboah scored from the spot to give Leeds a 2-1 win.

On the full-time whistle my colleagues, as usual, came to join me at the halfway line. In next to no time we found ourselves surrounded by furious Norwich players and their very angry manager Gary Megson, all blaming me for their relegation. It didn't seem to occur to them that the fact that they hadn't won any of their previous sixteen matches might have something to do with their predicament. I gently pointed this out to them and made my way off the pitch.

One of the consequences of this little scene was the introduction by Leeds, for all future matches, of a squad of 'bouncers' to come on at the end of the game to surround the officals. Not a very desirable thing to have to happen but quite a sensible one. For someone refereeing a contentious game Elland Road is now as good a place to be as any.

ONE NIGHT AT THE PALACE

The biggest game of the season for me took place on Sunday 14 May 1995. This was to be a title decider no matter what the result. Games just don't come any bigger than this. I had been appointed to referee the last game of the season between West Ham and Manchester United at Upton Park. At the same time Blackburn Rovers would be playing Liverpool at Anfield, a game to be refereed by David Elleray.

The position from Manchester United's point of view was quite simple: they had to win to have any chance of the championship. Blackburn only needed to draw to be champions. This appointment was a massive boost to my confidence, which had only recently recovered from the Cantona incident and its aftermath. To be appointed to such a prestigious and important game and to be in the company of 'Lord' Elleray for the joint appointment was indeed a huge honour.

The Premier League had become neurotic about issues of timing in order to avoid giving either side the advantage and they therefore appointed officials to be present at both grounds. These were to be in constant telephone contact and the games would only kick off with signals to the referees from these 'timekeepers'.

The game at Upton Park turned out to be a fantastic occasion and chances fell thick and fast to United. They were frenetic in their attempts to put the ball in the net in order to seal their third consecutive Premiership title. Unfortunately for poor Andy Cole, most of the chances fell to him and he wasn't having one of his most inspired days. To be fair, the opportunities all seemed to be half-chances rather than clear-cut sitters. However, when half-chances build up they accumulate to the point where the person concerned can begin to look the villain. On one of his better days, or if he had been given more 'difficult' chances, I am sure a player of Andy's calibre would have scored the vital goal.

As it was, West Ham took the lead through Trevor Morley and this put United under even more pressure. There was even greater excitement when Brian McClair equalised in the second half. The West Ham penalty area was now the subject of a siege and bodies were flying everywhere. Ludo Miklosko was having the game of his life turning shots round the post and over the bar. The game was now at fever pitch and to add even greater pressure Alex Ferguson brought on the battering-ram figure of Mark Hughes. Despite Hughes' famed physical presence all United's efforts were in vain and they could only manage a draw.

One point was not going to be enough for United, even though Blackburn were in the process of losing at Liverpool. The final whistle went and the Manchester players were stunned. I must confess to having more than a degree of sympathy for them, particularly in view of the way they had played: hard but fair and with a tremendous level of skill. For all their determination and talent, a combination of circumstances on the pitch had conspired to lose them the title. At the end I saw a very disappointed Alex Ferguson waving at his players and telling them to get off the pitch and not to bother with the formalities of shaking hands. He obviously was not in the mood for hanging around and wanted to make as quick an exit as possible. To their credit the United players ignored their fearsome boss and went ahead with the handshakes. A sporting gesture to complete a memorable sporting occasion.

Somehow, I'm still not sure how it happened. I managed to be presented with the Sky Man of the Match champagne. I decided that it would be a fitting end to the day if I was to consume this with my colleague Stuart Loudon on the way home.

We were on the train back to the North East accompanied by Stuart's son Chris. Stuart went off to get some glasses from the buffet car and in the meantime I decided to open the bottle, as inconspicuously as it is possible to do on an Inter-City train. The next thing I knew, Chris went running off to the buffet car, horrified, shouting, 'Dad, you'd better come quick with those glasses, there's champagne all over the ceiling and I've no idea where the cork's gone.' Stuart, with visions of an irate passenger sporting a black eye, came running through lurching all over the aisle with the movement of the train. At this point we all disintegrated into laughter, which was a great release from the tension of the afternoon's pressures.

The journey was a memorable one and we managed to consume a whole magnum of champagne between us. The Manchester United players would not have been having a good night but I think we made up for them. I was feeling very happy with life at this time, very happy indeed. I was not bothered who won the championship; if it couldn't be Newcastle then I was quite happy for Blackburn to give their fans the pleasure. It was nice to see Jack Walker rewarded for all the effort he had put into making his hometown club a major force in English soccer again after a long period in the wilderness.

ONE NIGHT AT THE PALACE

The summer months passed as usual with preparation for the new season. The gap in between the seasons was becoming very brief and my involvement with the Association of Premier League and Football Match Officials was quite demanding on my time. As it was approaching the time when I would be president I was much more involved in such issues as organising the annual conference. This takes place at the end of June/beginning of July and makes the summer break very short.

Allied with training and other Premier League meetings, which we were obliged to attend, there wasn't a great deal of time left for anything else. Somehow I managed to fit in a family holiday in Menorca.

The time soon came round for the first appointments of the new season and I was particularly pleased to have as my first game the newly-crowned champions Blackburn Rovers, who were at home to Queen's Park Rangers. The game was memorable for one reason only and that was an indiscretion by Tim Flowers. Trevor Sinclair was bearing down on goal and Tim came charging out and up-ended him. I immediately knew that I had no alternative but to send him off for denying a goal-scoring opportunity. However, Tim being the old pro that he is stayed down injured. A number of QPR players came to me individually while Tim was receiving treatment and asked what action I was going to take. I informed them that the offence was a dismissable one and that as soon as Tim recovered I would be showing him the red card. They each then went over to Tim and enquired about his condition, safe in the knowledge that he would be leaving the field as soon as he recovered.

When the trainer managed to get Tim to his feet Rovers immediately tried to substitute him before I could get the chance to send him off. Full marks to them for trying everything they knew but I'm afraid it was to no avail and I wasn't going to be conned. As Tim left the field after the red card he looked at me and winked, as if to say, 'You can't blame me for trying.' I couldn't help smiling and I was particularly pleased at Tim's response, which effectively endorsed my decision to send him off.

My next big event was to be the return to the capital of Eric the Terrible for the first time since his sending off at Palace. In fact, he had only just returned from suspension at the game with Liverpool the week before. The game was at Stamford Bridge against Chelsea, and someone at the FA obviously had a sense of humour as I found myself appointed to this game. In addition, the other officials were the same with Eddie Walsh and Grant Hegley my assistants. Even the match observer was the same. To add to the intrigue of the event BBC had the same match crew, with Clive Tyldesley commentating.

An abiding memory of this particular game was of the number of interruptions I had in my changing room. I ended up feeling like a monkey in London Zoo. Having gone to my changing room early, at 1 p.m., in what I thought was a good ploy to keep a low profile, I must have had what seemed like a hundred knocks at the door over the next hour or so. If I am exaggerating slightly it is only minimal and the true number was certainly in the many dozens.

A man came in to check the telephone, another the lights, then the shower. Then an officer from Fulham planning department turned up, to be followed shortly afterwards by a representative from Hammersmith Planning Department and ten minutes later an Environmental Health Officer. And so it went on. I had this feeling that there was a huge curiosity factor and everyone wanted to see the ref who had sent off Cantona at Palace.

When the time came to ring the bell to tell the teams to leave their respective dressing rooms, I was amazed by what greeted me as I left my own room. The tunnel at Stamford Bridge is about thirty-five yards long. The away team are allocated the changing room at the far end of the tunnel, a psychological ploy, I guess. The home team have the changing room nearer the front and finally the refs cupboard is nearest to the pitch. When I entered the tunnel I looked around and to my astonishment saw a line of security guards all the way from the Manchester dressing room to the end of the tunnel. There must have been twenty 'gorillas' in the space of that thirty-five yards.

As I passed certain United players they were very generous in their greeting, incuding Brian McClair and Denis Irwin, two players of whom I had come to expect such behaviour. I have to add that Peter Schmeichel came into this category also and acted like a complete gentleman. When I saw Cantona I looked at him but he just looked straight through me. 'Fair enough,' I thought, 'I won't let his attitude affect my judgement or decisions on the pitch.' As we lined up there was much hilarity among the Chelsea players about the 'bouncers' and many comments were directed my way about whether we were expecting trouble.

ONE NIGHT AT THE PALACE

The Manchester United Head of Security was a chap called Ned Kelly. Actually, I think Ned would put the original infamous outlaw to shame. He is a giant of a man and his pedigree is apparently ex-SAS. In fact, if you believe everything said about him, he was the first man into the Iranian embassy during the siege in London. I for one was not going to argue with this assertion.

As Cantona took the field, who was alongside him but big Ned Kelly. 'This is a new one,' I thought, 'a bodyguard alongside a player on the pitch.' What happens if someone fouls Cantona, I found myself wondering, does he get a knuckle-duster in the teeth? Perhaps I was getting carried away. Anyway, I instructed one of my assistants to remove Ned from the field. 'Piss off,' was the reply, 'tell him yourself.' We decided we'd perhaps mention it to him at half-time but fortunately Ned chose to take a seat in the stand about three minutes before kick-off.

The game got under way and United were magnificent. They strolled through the game with Cantona running the show and showing why he was the superstar. Paul Scholes was also brilliant and, apart from a great all-round performance, scored two goals to contribute to the 4-1 scoreline.

As Chelsea got more and more frustrated Frank Sinclair flew in with a reckless challenge on Brian McClair. It had to be a red card, and not just because I thought Brian was a nice guy who deserved better. Ironically, the first person to go over to Sinclair to commiserate was Cantona. I suppose there was a feeling of comradeship at both having been 'victims' of my decisions. At the end of the game there were many handshakes from the players. It did not escape my notice, however, that there was one missing. I didn't let it lose me any sleep.

My next appointment was again as big as they come, particularly in London. I was to ref the game between Tottenham and Arsenal on 18 November. I had been feeling that I was having a really good season and I felt full of confidence and physically very fit. This appointment only served to boost this feeling further and I was also pleased, in view of the magnitude of the match, to have Lord Elleray as my reserve official. It's nice to know that, in the event of anything unexpected happening, you have a man of that sort of calibre standing by.

I always enjoyed training but fixtures such as this give you added incentive and I stepped up my efforts a gear prior to the game. I travelled down to London on the Friday afternoon, earlier than usual, as the Middlesex branch of the Referees' Association had arranged for me to give a speech that evening. I was picked up by a branch member and whisked off to Enfield to give my address. I was suitably fed and watered - well, you know what I mean - and it was back to the hotel for about 10.30 p.m.

Games such as this one take on a greater importance as no matter who Spurs or Arsenal are playing they want to win, but in games against each other defeat is simply out of the question. In these games you can cut the tension with a knife.

The players lining up in the tunnel brought back memories of that night at the Palace; there was fear and tension etched on the faces of both teams. I was going to have to work hard at this one, that's for sure.

In the first half of an intense and passionate struggle I was surprised that I had only recorded eight free kicks and had not had to brandish a card of any description. In the second half the count was six free kicks but surprisingly they resulted in five yellow cards!

I suppose someone wanting to be critical of referees might possibly see this sort of statistic as an indication that referees want to get themselves noticed. I can assure them that this is not the case and that the yellow cards issued were not discretionary but were due to the nature of the offences as the game began to hot up. All I can say is that for such a game, with such intense rivalry, this was a remarkably low count of fouls and full credit must go to the players involved. Spurs thoroughly deserved their 2-1 win.

A particularly memorable thing from this game, at least for myself, was that in the match observer's report I was given a full 10 out of 10. This confirmed my view that everything I had done was in the spirit of the rules as they stood at this time.

On the subject of referee's discretion, or the lack of facility for this, there was a good example in my next game which was between QPR and Aston Villa. It also reflects on the approach of some youngsters to the game. It was a sad introduction to the big-time for a youngster with considerable talent. Lee Hendrie was making his debut for Villa as a second-half substitute and almost the first thing he did was to kick the ball away. I am not just talking about a token gesture with a little tap but a big wallop. This had to be a booking under the laws of the game and I would have been disciplined myself if I had not taken the appropriate action. As Lee was a mere seventeen years old I suppose you could put it down to youthful exhuberance. On the other hand, it wouldn't take a lot of intelligence from someone who earns his living every day from playing football to know that this would not be tolerated. Fair enough, a minor indiscretion. However, later in the game, Rufus Brevitt of Rangers was running away from Lee with the ball when Lee stupidly tripped him from behind. Again I had no choice and it had to be a yellow card. This second yellow meant that Lee's dream debut ended in ignominy and the sad thing was that it was completely avoidable.

At the end of the game the Villa physio Jim Walker, a very nice individual, asked me if I could not have shown some leniency. After I explained the circumstances to Jim he said, 'You know he did something similar on Wednesday night playing for the reserves and we had to take him off as a precaution.' This led me to think two things: firstly, does this young man have a problem? And secondly, if Villa knew he was susceptible to this why did they not substitute him again? I don't know the answer but I like to think that Lee has matured now that he has more experience under his belt.

My next match was Wimbledon v Everton on New Year's Day 1996. I decided that, as New Year celebrations were obviously going to be out of the question, I would treat my wife and family to a trip to London. We booked an apartment in Dolphin Square near to the Houses of Parliament. Unfortunately my eldest son Ben, who was seventeen at the time, was poorly and unable to come. On arriving at the rather swish apartments I received a phone call from Wimbledon asking whether I would come down to the ground to do a pitch inspection at 7 a.m. the following morning, New Year's Day. I agreed of course and took my youngest son Carl with me. The Wimbledon officials and I agreed that with a bit of work and a bit of sunshine the pitch would probably be playable. This was a good assessment and the game did go ahead as planned. It was memorable for two fantastic goals from Duncan Ferguson. The first came when, with his back to goal, he spun and crashed a shot into the net from 20 yards; the second being a trademark Ferguson goal when he rose magnificently above two defenders and powered home a bullet-like header from 15 yards

The score was 3-2 to Everton and the game represented a fantastic start to the year. This was a year, it turned out, which brought back to me something which I believed had gone. I thought my involvement in European matches had ended now that I had reached the age of forty-five but I was to be pleasantly surprised.

At the end of January it was FA Cup 4th round weekend and my involvement was a match, televised live, between Sheffield United and Aston Villa. There had been a sharp snow fall over Sheffield the night before the match and whilst it appeared that the pitch would be playable, the main discussion points revolved around getting the streets clear enough for supporters to actually reach the ground safely, having the snow removed from the pitch and, finally, removing the quite substantial snow from the terraces. This discussion took place at 7 a.m. and the club called for an army of volunteers to come and clear the terraces. It was only at mid-day that the police finally gave the go-ahead. This was only made possible by the efforts of the Sheffield United fans and the local council employees who all did a sterling job.

The game was a cagey affair and it was 0-0 with ten minutes left when Savo Milosevic burst into the penalty area only to be brought down by the outstretched arm of Alan Kelly, the Sheffield goalkeeper. I awarded a penalty and cautioned Kelly. He remained on the field, however, as the ball was going away from the goal and he therefore did not deny 'an obvious goal scoring opportunity'. In the midst of a barrage of snowballs, Dwight Yorke stepped up and cheekily chipped the ball over Kelly, who had made a despairing dive to his left. This was the only goal of the game and was scant reward for the efforts of the United fans who were sent home disappointed.

After a shower I made my way to the club lounge where I knew the draw for the next round would be shown on television. I got there just in time to see a re-run of the penalty incident and Alan Hansen supporting the award of the kick. This was immediately followed by the 5th round draw. Like every other referee I watched these draws with excitement and anticipation. Which tie would I get? Would I get a match at all? As the draw was made I was looking for the plum ties and then, as Manchester United came out of the bag followed by Manchester City, I thought to myself, 'Yes, that's the one for me.' Of course I realised that the likelihood was that I would probably get something much more mundane and I did not allow myself to get too excited.

ONE NIGHT AT THE PALACE

On the following Friday a letter dropped through my door from the FA. I opened it with excitement but no great expectation. I jumped straight to the important bit of the letter, by-passing all the preliminaries. I couldn't believe my eyes, there it was staring out at me: 'Fixture number eight, 18 February, Manchester United versus Manchester City'. A shiver ran down my spine. Yes, it was to be Alan Wilkie to referee the biggest tie of the round!

As the date for the match drew near I tried to suppress my mounting excitement and attempted to retain my detached professionalism. As a football fanatic myself this is not a particularly easy thing to do. It is often easier to take your mind off a forthcoming big event by diverting your attention to other games but through no fault of my own I would only have one fixture between the 4th and 5th round ties. Try as I might this game was going to be at the forefront of my mind for quite some time and, to add even more spice, the game was to be shown live on BBC1 with half the nation watching.

The big weekend arrived. I had decided to travel down to Manchester the day before, which was my usual practice for games of over one hundred miles travel. This was probably a silly thing to do as everyone in the hotel was either going to the game or at least talking about it. Was there no escape? I think if I am truly honest I was really enjoying the attention and the status of being associated with such a special occasion.

On the Sunday I made my way through the mounting traffic and the milling fans, the United fans having travelled from all over the country for the game. The television crews were swarming all over Old Trafford like little ants scurrying here and there. I felt such pride at just being there.

Forty-five minutes before the kick-off, I heard a loud knock at my dressing room door and there was Franny Lee, the City chairman, resplendent in his light blue jacket and blue striped shirt. As he strode barrel-chested across the room he said very forcibly, 'Alan Ball tells me you're a good, strong referee. Well you'll need to be today because these games are different.' Whether Alan Ball did say that I'll never know but I'm sure Franny's little introduction was intended to remind me that there were two teams out there. I never did have the pleasure of his comments on how things turned out. Perhaps it's just as well really.

'THERE'S A BULLET WAITING...'

All too soon it was time to meet the players in the tunnel. Talk about an atmosphere; it was hard to comprehend. Here we had players from all over the world, yet the pervading sense of local rivalry and animosity in that tunnel was overwhelming.

The two captains, Keith Curle of City and Steve Bruce of United, made their way to the centre circle and grudgingly offered a half-hearted handshake to each other - a quick pose for a photograph and we were off.

The game started at a hectic pace and in the early stages City were irrepressible. After about five minutes the City danger man Kinkladze was pole-axed by a flying tackle from Keane and the scene was well and truly set. City soon took the lead following a rare mistake by Peter Schmeichel when he raced out of his area in an attempt to close down Uwe Rösler who had beaten the offside trap to run on to a wonderful through-ball from Kinkladze. Rösler comfortably rounded the stranded Schmeichel to stroke the ball into the net.

Soon afterwards there was a flare-up when Michael Brown brought down Denis Irwin and in the ensuing melee there were confrontations between Niall Quinn and Gary Pallister, Keith Curle and Andy Cole and, as you would expect, Roy Keane was in there agitating as well. This resulted in cautions for Curle, Cole and Brown. Keane, who had already been booked, was fortunate that my attention was taken up by Curle and Cole, who had each other by the throat.

The next, and most contentious, flashpoint came soon afterwards when I awarded a corner kick to United. I took up a position which by chance (or was it good judgment) allowed me, and it seems only me, to have a perfect view of an off-the-ball infringement. As the ball came across I could see that Michael Frontzeck had one arm around Cantona's waist and the other arm around his throat. I blew the whistle as Cantona was obviously being prevented from going to the ball. As the offence was punishable by a direct free kick and it took place in the penalty area then, of course, it had to be a penalty kick. After much debate Cantona took the kick and duly equalised for United. This was decisive as United won 2-1 and progressed into the next round. Meanwhile, City were forlorn at losing out on a possible trip to Wembley and even more desperate that it was at the hands of their hated neighbours.

After the game the big discussion point was the penalty award. Alan Ball was interviewed on TV and said that in his view, 'It may have been a penalty and it may not have been a penalty.' He went on to say that his players had not done themselves justice with their second-half performance. I was greatly relieved at his objective and honest opinion which demonstrated great integrity.

The real problem, however, came the following week when I started receiving mail at my home address from City fans making all sorts of threats. None of the letters were addressed correctly and the envelopes carried vague references such as 'A. Wilkie, The Referee, Chester le Street' and some were even addressed through FA Headquarters. The Royal Mail did a great job, or did they?

The letters ranged from one-liners such as 'There's a bullet waiting for you at Maine Road' to the more descriptive dialogue telling me what they were going to do to my family, first of all my wife and then my children. Whatever the threat it would result in a slow and painful death.

The situation was so bad I had to get the police involved, but they had little to go on until there was a breakthrough when one of the City supporters sent a letter to me via the FA. He had not only signed it but had addressed it as well. The letter contained a diatribe describing how I had spoilt his little boy's birthday treat, as it was his intention to take him to Wembley to the Cup Final. He seemed to ignore the fact that this had been only a 5th round game and that there would have been another two rounds before getting to Wembley. The Moss Side police were delighted; this was what they were waiting for. All the letters were despatched to the CID in Manchester, who later informed me that they had located the ringleaders of the hate campaign. Thankfully, after this, the post became worth opening once again.

There was more to making a simple penalty decision than receiving hate mail afterwards. The so-called experts had decided that as they did not agree with my decision then it could not be correct: Alan Hansen, who in the previous round had supported the penalty award at Sheffield United, decided he could not agree with my Manchester United decision. This was reason enough for some of the misguided viewers of Match Of The Day to ridicule my children at school. This, in my view, demonstrates why these 'experts' should be more controlled in their comments.

It wasn't just the letters or the derision though, as the following week I started getting phone calls regularly at 7.05 in the morning. The caller simply said, 'Are you satisfied with what you've done....' I always hung up before he could complete the sentence. I eventually got fed up with this and one particular morning, when I heard the by now familiar voice, I said, 'Hello, BT Intercept service, can I help you?' The caller, somewhat taken aback, said, 'Can I speak to Mr Wilkie please?' I put the phone down for a few moments and then came back saying, 'Can you say who's calling please?' It turned out to be someone who said they were a so-called DJ for a Manchester local radio station with the name of Penk. After another few seconds delay I came back and said, 'I'm sorry, Mr Wilkie doesn't want to take the call, do you wish to take it any further?' The answer was 'No' and I'm pleased to say that after this I never heard from this odious individual again.

If indeed the call was from a DJ, then the whole episode demonstrates what an obnoxious lot these media individuals can be. They seem to take their lead from people like Chris Evans, who think that because of their elevated 'status' they can cause whatever intrusion they like on private individuals. They also, of course, make a great deal of money in the process. I like to think that if I was the owner of a radio station I would respect people's privacy and not allow (or even encourage?) such antics by immature and big-headed 'icons' of the young.

Life had to go on. I was either to quit and let the morons win or I could pull myself together and stand strong against them. The acid test of my resolve would come in my next Premier League fixture. If things were to go wrong here then it could signal the end as far as I was concerned. This was to be the Last Chance Saloon.

The game turned out to be exciting, and as well as the excitement there was an incident, again involving Tim Flowers, which he won't forget in a hurry. It wouldn't have seemed amusing to him at the time but, on recollection, it might just bring a wry smile to his face. Tim had a habit of digging the pitch up with the heel of his boot in order to mark his angles on the edge of the goal area. I warned him in advance not to do this as it could result in a booking. The result of the warning was that Tim waited until the game got under way before carrying out his ritual, reckoning, correctly, that I wouldn't then notice. He was to pay for this by way of a humiliating moment during the first half. Blackburn were 1-0 up and seemed to be in control when Liverpool's Stan Collymore shot weakly from 35 yards. Stan had scuffed the shot and the ball trickled towards the Blackburn goal. As Tim came out to pick up this seemingly innocuous little shot the ball hit the rut which he had dug earlier and bounced over his shoulder and into the net. Collymore's face was a picture - but nothing compared to Tim's. I must one day see if I can obtain a good photograph of this and get it framed for my study wall!

The game continued and it ebbed and flowed with first one side taking the initiative and then the other. Eventually Liverpool got the upper hand and were leading 3-2 with only injury time remaining. I had been really pleased with the way the game had gone and with my performance. I could feel my self-esteem coming back to reasonable levels again. Then, in the fourth minute of injury time, Alan Shearer hit a shot from outside the penalty area which struck John Barnes on the arm. John was well in the penalty box at the time. I adjudged that the ball had struck Barnes and that it was ball to arm and not arm to ball. This being the case it was not deliberate and couldn't be punishable by a penalty. I therefore awarded a corner kick and, to be fair, I didn't notice a lot of complaint from the players, although the crowd had plenty to say about it.

The game ended 3-2 and I left the field pretty content at my performance. I met the referee's assessor, who complimented me on a good performance, and I then suggested that after I got changed we should go to the Directors' Lounge for a drink. 'I don't think that would be a good idea, Alan,' he said, 'I've been up there and the mood is pretty ugly. You're not the most popular man around at the moment.' This felt like a dagger blow and I felt quite sick. Having just convinced myself that the joy of refereeing was worth all the crap that goes with it I was stunned at this setback. I took the assessor's advice and left the ground. What was particularly sad was that there is no more hospitable club than Blackburn and I had always been treated with great respect on my previous visits. It just goes to show how fickle football people can be. Whilst I was very sad I still maintain to this day that Blackburn are a very friendly club. I am also pleased that Jack Walker was not one of the people involved in the 'ugly mood' incident as I had great respect for him and was very sad to learn of his recent death.

I set off for home, accompanied as usual by my trusty friend Stuart Loudon. On the way back I explained to Stuart that I just didn't think it was worth continuing any more. Stuart insisted that I pull over for a pint at the Haynes Arms, just south of Middlesbrough, and over the next half hour he persuaded me that really I had a lot to offer the game and that I would regret any untimely retirement. Having considered the position over the weekend and discussed everything with my family I decided I would continue. It was a close call however and this was not the happiest time of my life.

Life soon picked up again and I saw a funnier side of the game when I was appointed as reserve referee to Keith Cooper, who comes from Wales. Much as I like a laugh and the occasional prank, I'm not in the same class as Keith when it comes to fooling around. The game was Middlesbrough v Sheffield Wednesday and it was time for the pre-match meeting with the police and security staff. I had commented to Keith that whilst these people were invariably very professional and thorough, they tended to be very dry and there wasn't usually a great deal of humour to be found at these meetings. 'We'll see about that, boyo,' said Keith with a mischievous smile on his face.

The meeting got under way, held as usual in the referee's dressing room. As the security brief was in full flow Keith suddenly leapt across the room and pulled out from his kit bag a leopard-skin thong. He then proceeded to invite the Inspector of police to try it on. The place disintegrated into laughter at this and the rest of the meeting was a bit more entertaining than usual (and not because the police officer accepted the invitation, I should add). One thing I never did establish was just what was a leopard-skin thong doing in a referee's kitbag in the first place!

My final appointment of the season was as reserve referee to Paul Durkin at Middlesbrough for the game with Manchester United. This was the game which would see United crowned champions once again with a comfortable 3-0 away victory. After the game there was a knock on the door and who was there but Alex Ferguson with a bottle of champagne in his hand. He handed it to us with a big smile on his face and said he would like us to enjoy the champagne and celebrate the title victory. It was a nice gesture but I couldn't help wondering if it would have happened if I had been the referee rather than Paul.

On the European front I was invited to be fourth official in Bulgaria for an International 'friendly' with Germany. The match was held in Sofia and

I found this a fascinating and enjoyable trip. The city is beautiful and has many impressive and ornate buildings. A slight drawback was that everywhere we went we were pestered by people who wanted to buy sterling or dollars from us. The desirability of both of these currencies making the purchasing power much better than the local currency, the Lev.

On arrival at the hotel I went through my usual ritual of checking my equipment to see if I had forgotten anything important. After going through it the usual fifteen times at home, there shouldn't be much chance of that happening, I thought. I laid out neatly on the bed, two shirts, shorts, two pairs of socks, two pairs of sparkling football boots, two whistles, two watches, pencils and other ancillary bits and pieces. Having satisfied myself that everything was there I started to put the gear away. I had no sooner put away my boots when the phone rang. It was Martin Bodenham, the match referee and leader of our party, telling me to hurry up as we had to leave immediately to meet the head of the Bulgarian FA who had just arrived at the hotel. I left hastily leaving the rest of my gear on the bed. After a pleasant evening, learning all about Bulgaria, I returned to my room around midnight. Being extremely tired I simply moved all the items off the bed, putting them into my holdall and climbed into bed ready for a good night's sleep.

The next day we were taken on a trip to Plovdiv where we were given a guided tour of a vineyard. At the end of the visit we each received a presentation pack of two bottles of red wine and a bottle of Bulgarian brandy. The latter is locally known as rachia and whilst I am sure it has an acquired taste it also has the equivalent strength of domestic paintstripper.

In the evening we arrived at the splendid 70,000 capacity stadium, which was only a few years old. In the changing room everyone was preparing for the game in their own way. When I delved into my bag I was horrified to discover there was no trace of either of my watches or whistles. They had obviously been taken from my hotel room while I was out the previous evening. I could understand someone taking the watches which were worth quite a bit of money but I was somewhat intrigued at the loss of my £3 Acme Thunderer whistles. As for the watches, I commented to my colleagues that I now didn't have the time of day for the Bulgarians.

Panic-stricken, I salvaged the situation by scrounging from the rest of the team. I was pretty unhappy, however, and hoped that no-one would have any problems with their remaining watches as I had deprived them of their spares.

This match was a difficult one for Martin, who ended up, unusually for him, issuing nine yellow cards and two reds, not a modest total for a friendly. For my part, I had an active role to play when it became necessary to remove the Bulgarian coach from the dugout for threatening one of the linesmen. He refused my invitation to leave the technical area and in the end he was only persuaded when I called on a machine-gun-toting policeman who, with a few gestures of his gun, encouraged the necessary action by the coach.

The game finished 1-1 and none of us could say we enjoyed it. We returned to the hotel where we encountered Pierluigi Collina and his team of officials who had been officiating at a European club match in the city that evening. This was my first meeting with Collina, the now world-famous referee with the bald pate and piercing eyes. A very nice chap but not someone I'd like to meet in a dark alley.

This European assignment completed, I was appointed to run the line in the Intertoto Cup at Cardiff, not such an exciting venue but one which I was very pleased to accept. The teams involved were Ton Pentre of Wales and Heerenveen of Holland. This was to be my last match in 'Europe', so just as my Euro career had begun with my driving to Dundee, it ended with me driving to Wales. I believed at first that the match was to be played at Cardiff Arms Park but it was actually held on the practice ground outside! This was just as well as the atmosphere inside the Arms Park with only 400 people would have been somewhat unreal. As it was, everyone had a great time. The Welsh club didn't have great expectations and therefore weren't too disappointed with a 7-0 home defeat by a team who were subsequently involved in the Champions League. They made us feel part of what, for them, was a very special occasion.

At the end of this 1995/96 season I came into conflict with Neil Harman of the Daily Mail. An article had appeared under his name in the Saturday morning edition saying that Paul Danson, Paul Alcock and Alan Wilkie would lose their status as Premier League referees at the end of the season owing to poor performances.

To say I was shocked by this would be an understatement. I knew it to be untrue, certainly in my case. I contacted the others and we agreed we needed to do something about this misrepresentation as soon as the future appointment situation could be clarified. Paul Danson unfortunately wasn't selected for the following season and was 'relegated' to the Football League, but both Paul Alcock and I were retained as expected. We decided after much consideration that legal action would be appropriate unless the Mail offered a retraction of their assertions.

After much to-ing and fro-ing we agreed to accept the Mail's offer of an out-of-court settlement, together with a published apology. The amount in question wasn't significant and the only reason for us accepting was that we didn't think it would be a good idea to proceed with a court case in view of the low profile we as referees were trying to keep.

As is usual in these cases, the amount of text in the retraction was nowhere near as significant or as prominent as the original article. I think the apology appeared in the bottom corner of page 62 on a week-day edition, where as few people as possible would see it. It seems that journalists can make up whatever stories they want without too much fear of subsequent embarrassment. This little incident only served to make me even more determined that the forthcoming 9196/97 season would be a good one for me and I worked especially hard in training to make sure I was ready for it.

10

VINNIE'S PLEA

WHEN THE NEW SEASON came around I found myself, in the first few weeks, at Tottenham for a Sunday afternoon televised game against Leicester City.

Tottenham is a splendid place to visit but in recent years has become a victim of the 'corporate hospitality culture'. All clubs these days need to embrace this concept to a certain extent in order to survive but Tottenham have taken it to extremes. It used to be the case that officials were offered tea and coffee in the main lounge area but this suddenly changed to the point where we would be shepherded to a corner of the room, away from the corporate guests, and offered a couple of flasks of tea and some plastic cups.

The first time this happened to me, I went to take a cup and saucer from the main table, only to be told that as I wasn't a sponsor or sponsor's guest I couldn't have a cup or saucer. I took them anyway, with instructions to the waitress to charge me if she had a problem. I understand that things have since changed and that the officials get invited into the Directors' lounge. It would be nice to think my stance had something to do with this.

For the game against Leicester I had as my fourth official Paul Durkin, who by this time was an up-and-coming FIFA referee who had just made an impact in Euro '96 when he substituted for the injured Dermot Gallagher. During the first half I cautioned Stuart Nethercott of Spurs for a foul on Emile Heskey. Little else of consequence took place in the first 45 minutes but in the second half, with about 20 minutes remaining, Nethercott again gave chase to Heskey. As Heskey cut across him and entered the penalty area he went tumbling to the ground. Nethercott had tripped him, or had he? From my viewpoint it certainly looked that way and I awarded a penalty.

ONE NIGHT AT THE PALACE

As Steve Walsh placed the ball on the spot my mind started racing. Should I have cautioned Nethercott? As Walsh struck the ball comfortably to Ian Walker's right I realised that, under the rules at that time, this would have been the correct course of action, even if a little harsh. But it was too late and Nethercott avoided being dismissed. However, this was not the end of the matter for me as in the stand watching me as match observer, was Philip Don, who had recently retired as a referee. At the summer meeting of Premiership referees we were informed that anyone failing to carry out their duty regarding cautions or dismissals would receive a maximum mark of four out of ten, irrespective of the rest of their performance. I put this thought to the back of my mind and got on with the job in hand and concentrated on the game, which City won 2-1 courtesy of the Heskey 'tumble'.

After the game Philip Don came to see me in my dressing room for the usual post-match de-brief. Unusually for Philip he went into some detail about how well I had done and told me that he might well have considered giving me a mark of nine out of ten had it not been for the fact that I had missed the second Nethercott caution. He went on to say that because of this his 'hands were tied' and that he would have to give me a four. The return home seemed like the longest train journey I have ever endured.

My next game of note was the one which marked the return to Highbury of the disgraced George Graham, now manager of Leeds. There had been much speculation about what sort of reception he would get and what profile he would adopt at the game. His normal routine would have been to sit in the Directors' box for the first half and the dugout for the second. In the event, George appeared in the dugout from the start. To some people's surprise he was given a standing ovation by both sets of fans and this must have been very pleasant for him.

As far as the game goes, I happen to believe that George's game plan for this match, which must have been so important for his personal pride, was to go for a 0-0 draw. However, this plan was thrown into confusion when Arsenal scored in the first minute. After this, Leeds seemed to be in total disarray and appeared to lose all their discipline. By half-time they were 2-0 down and of six yellow cards issued in the first half, five of these were to Leeds players. As we trooped off the field at half-time I was in my usual position at the back of the line, having let the players walk off first.

120

Unfortunately, waiting for me in the tunnel, lurking in a little cubbyhole well-known to George from his Arsenal days, was the man himself. He was waiting to pounce in order to berate me with a tirade about how I was spoiling the game etc. etc. Taken aback by this, I invited George into my dressing room for a discussion. I suggested to my assistants that they should remain outside for a few minutes. The ensuing conversation concluded with me suggesting, in words that George would understand, that we should each get on with our respective jobs and that if he would care to instil some discipline into his players then it wouldn't be necessary for me to get the book out so often.

Leeds eventually lost the match 3-0 but it wasn't necessary to award any yellow cards in the second half so perhaps George had, after all, instilled some discipline into his side. I suppose from his point of view he might also have felt that our little meeting had had the desired effect and that I had changed my approach for the second half. This certainly wasn't the case but if it helps that we both feel we benefitted from the discussion, that's fine by me.

I was particularly upset about the nature of George's 'verbal assault' when I recalled that when he was suffering darker times I had taken the trouble to seek him out and give him some moral support. At the time George had been serving a suspension from football management following the infamous 'bung' allegations. During this suspension I had seen him standing in the tunnel at Stamford Bridge immediately before the Chelsea v Manchester United match which I was refereeing.

He was standing totally alone and didn't look as if he had a friend in the world. I made a point of going across to him, shook his hand and asked him how he was. He replied that he was OK and that he was match commentator for Capital Radio. He appeared grateful that someone had bothered, in the excitement of the build-up, to share the time of day with him.

On reflection, it's amazing how in football someone can be a pariah one minute and a hero the next. Here was George in disgrace and isolation but, not too long afterwards, he was accepted back into the fraternity. Money talks, I guess, and there is no doubt about George's managerial capabilities. If a chairman decides he wants his team to win things he will not let morals or ethics stand in his way.

ONE NIGHT AT THE PALACE

One of the more memorable games I was involved in this season was the Coca-Cola Cup tie between Liverpool and Arsenal. I was delighted to be appointed to this fixture as it usually resulted in an exciting match and this was to be no exception. One of the popular myths in football is that referees don't give penalties against Liverpool when they're defending the Kop. I dispelled this thought pretty quickly, not once but twice, in the first half. After all, here is a man who gave a penalty against Blyth Spartans and lived to tell the tale!

The first incident in the match took place when John Hartson chased a long through-ball into the Liverpool penalty area, David James rushed out and brought him down, conceding a penalty. This was followed by a second penalty when James up-ended Ian Wright. The keeper was clearly not having a good day but he stayed on the field as neither foul prevented an obvious goal-scoring opportunity. Wright duly scored both penalties, slotting both to the goalkeeper's left, to send Arsenal in at half time with a 2-1 advantage.

In the second half Liverpool pressed continuously, finally getting their reward when they equalised. It was shortly after this that I cautioned Steve Bould for an off-the-ball incident and it wasn't many minutes later when Bould challenged Steve McManaman on the half-way line. This was a challenge so late that McManaman had already parted with the ball, having played it into space for a colleague, but I decided to play advantage as Liverpool still had possession in an attacking position. Unfortunately, the advantage didn't come to anything and the move petered out with a goal kick being awarded.

I then went back to Bould and dismissed him as the offence merited a yellow card and he had already been booked. This is something I would have done whatever the outcome of the possession. Steve's reaction I found rather amusing but it was pretty much in keeping with what happens when players are sent off in such circumstances. 'I don't know what you're talking about,' he said. I knew what I was talking about and before long so did Steve as he made his way to the tunnel with the boos of 40,000 people ringing in his ears.

The advantage rule is a good one but it can cause difficulties for the referee. The problem is that when you play advantage the player committing the foul usually thinks they have gotten away with it. They then ham it up when you come back for them, a bit like Julian Dicks at Derby. However, I think the modern interpretation of the rule has been to the benefit of the game and spectators in general.

One of the aspects of refereeing in the League or Premiership is that you need to decide whether to 'close dates off', in other words make yourself unavailable for certain dates. There are times when it would be wise, from a family point of view, to do this but on the other hand no-one likes to turn a game down. I suppose it's almost like a drug and you get withdrawal symptoms if you know games are going on and you're not involved.

Thus I had not closed off New Year's Day 1997. I did feel it highly unlikely that anything would crop up at short notice and I had therefore made arrangements to celebrate the New Year in style. I had booked to take my wife Margaret to see 'Lord of the Dance' at Newcastle Arena on New Year's Eve and then to go on to a hotel where we would enjoy a dinner dance and stay for the night. I might have known, when the phone rang on 30 December, that life wouldn't be that simple.

It was the Premier League asking whether I had still not closed off New Year's Day. I confirmed this was the case and reckoned that if anything was on offer it would be something within striking distance, such as Leeds or Manchester. It didn't bother me that I would have to abstain on New Year's Eve, I could still enjoy myself and simply drive down or across, whatever the case might be, in the morning.

There is a certain excitement and feeling of importance in a late appointment. I suppose it gives you a considerable feeling of being wanted. However, I would find it difficult to explain my feelings when the League representative then said, 'That's good, I'll put you down for the Southampton v Wimbledon game.'

My heart sunk, what a trek, particularly over the holiday period when trains and planes would be limited. And how was I going to explain this to Margaret? Having declared that I hadn't closed the date off I wasn't now in a position to turn anything down as we referees can't pick and choose. But Southampton! They just couldn't have picked anywhere further away.

Having scraped my wife off the ceiling I started to look positively at ways of making the trip and salvaging something of the domestic and social arrangements. I thought I might be able to fly down and still be able to catch 'Lord of the Dance', which was an afternoon performance, before

I left. Unfortunately this would not be possible as the only flight would be on the morning of New Year's Eve and not returning till 2 January. Similarly, if I was to drive I would have to leave incredibly early on New Year's Day. In the end I settled for the train, this being the most practical arrangement, but it meant I would have to travel on New Year's Eve.

To Margaret's disgust I had to leave 'Lord of the Dance' half-way through the performance and head for Newcastle railway station to catch the 4 p.m. train to London. She had not been impressed either by our entrance to the Arena. I had thought there would be somewhere in the reception area where I could leave my luggage. Unfortunately, owing to tight security, I was stopped at the outer doors and told I could not proceed any further. It was only when the Arena manager, Colin Revel, who coincidentally used to be a Northern League referee, recognised me that I was rescued. He and his security colleagues had great fun at my expense before agreeing to put my bags in his office.

At least Margaret had the consolation of still going to the dinner-dance in the evening, the party now being seven people rather than eight. Talk about making yourself popular!

The train on New Year's Eve was never going to be fun but I hadn't reckoned on the company of a drunken Scotsman for three hours of the journey. 'Frankie' continually insisted, in the most friendly way, that I join him in drinking from his by now half-empty bottle of whisky. I didn't like to suggest to him, seeing that it was Hogmanay, that he might have been travelling in the wrong direction.

Relieved at reaching King's Cross, I took a cab to Waterloo, offering a suitable incentive to the driver to get me there within twenty minutes to make my connection to Southampton. Arriving into Southampton at 11 p.m. I made it to the hotel just in time to see in the New Year with a solitary drink to absent friends. I wondered at this point whether I had shown good judgement in making myself available but at the end of the day if you're going to operate at this level of a sport you have to be totally committed. My wife has often suggested I should be 'committed' but in a slightly different sense.

I was awoken the next morning by a telephone call at 7 a.m. from the Southampton secretary asking if I would come down to the ground to carry out a pitch inspection. The weather had turned very cold and they were anxious to stop the Wimbledon fans travelling down if the pitch was frozen. The Wimbledon team had travelled the night before so they were already in town. When I arrived at the ground at 7.45 a.m. I found the pitch covered with tarpaulins as Southampton didn't have underground heating. There seemed to be some give in the ground and I felt that with a little bit of sun on it then it would be OK. I certainly hoped so, given the tortuous journey I had made, not to mention the domestic aggro from my long suffering wife.

I carried out another inspection at 11 a.m. in the knowledge that the Wimbledon buses were due to leave South London at 11.30. The centre of the pitch by this time wasn't too bad and it would take a stud. However, I thought back to my earlier experience a few years ago at the Burnley v Stockport game where the centre was playable but the wings were frozen and all sorts of havoc had ensued. I therefore asked for the wings to be uncovered and sure enough the ground was rock hard. Although it was flat it would have been very difficult for the players to keep their balance. There would also have been tremendous confusion, with some parts of the pitch being soft and other parts solid. I therefore decided to call the game off. Neither team objected to this and I think I was probably more disappointed than anyone. I certainly wasn't looking forward to telling Margaret, although I knew she would be her usual understanding self. I did have a feeling of letting the family down for a football event which never happened.

I caught the 12.30 train to start my journey back home, arriving at 8.45 p.m. It was a pretty miserable Wilkie who trudged through the door that evening. To make matters worse I was extremely tired after the journey so I don't suppose I would have been very good company. Such are the joys of a Premiership referee.

I had the privilege on 29 January 1997 of refereeing a game in which one of my all-time heroes, Stuart Pearce, was playing. If I'd ever had enough talent to play the game at professional level I would have modelled myself on this man despite (or perhaps because of) his fearsome reputation. I just loved his passion and commitment and his 'They shall not pass' attitude. Pearce was at this time acting-manager of Nottingham Forest following the departure of Frank Clark.

The game was a local derby against Coventry City. This fell at a time when Darren Huckerby was terrifying Premiership defences with his speed and not inconsiderable skill. Although he had been popular with the fans during his stay at Newcastle, his previous club, he hadn't been able to make the breakthrough to the first team as Newcastle, under Keegan, had an incredible array of strikers including Ferdinand, Beardsley, Asprilla, and Kitson. However, the Toon Army were sorry to see him go and Darren had set about proving his point to Keegan and the rest of the Premiership in the best way possible. True to his present form he did indeed terrorise Forest and scored an incredible goal. Collecting the ball in his own half, he ran at great pace down the right wing, cutting inside Pearce and entering the penalty area. He then cut back to his right and smashed the ball high into the net past the helpless Mark Crossley to score the only goal of the game. Stuart was not amused.

As the game went on Huckerby continued to give Pearce a torrid time. When Stuart asked me, with four minutes left, how long there was to go I had a premonition of impending doom for young Darren. Sure enough, as he set off down the wing at the speed of light, 'Psycho' went after him. The result was Darren keeping someone company in their seat in the stands about four rows back. Pearce looked at me and said, 'You know how it's spelt, ref, I just had to have a go!'

I think this was an old pro, getting towards the end of his career, who just needed to teach the precocious newcomer what the game can some-times be about. I think Pearce was also very frustrated at the lack of com-mitment and poor performance by his team. This was shown by the way he raced off the field without shaking hands with anyone at the final whistle. I suppose when you are a manager as well as a player it gets to you if you feel that the rest of the team are not putting in as much effort as yourself.

In view of Pearce's mood I was very surprised when I found him wait-ing at the end of the tunnel for me as I left the field. He shook my hand and thanked me for the game. This was a gesture which meant a great deal to me, particularly when he was in such a ferocious frame of mind. This was one occasion when I was glad to be a referee rather than a player. I would not have cared to have been a Forest player in that dressing room for the next half hour or so.

Liverpool v Leeds was looming on the horizon for me and I looked for-ward to it with anticipation. As mentioned earlier, this has always been one of the big fixtures and the rivalry gets no less intense. It was a Wednesday evening match in the middle of February and I made the trip to Merseyside in atrocious conditions but still looking forward to the game. There is somehow an altogether different perspective to games played in midweek in the winter. It helps lift the gloom of winter days and gives the fans something to look forward to during the week.

Unfortunately, on this particular day, it rained and rained and rained. I felt there was every chance of a postponement and when I went to the ground I was greeted by a despondent-looking groundsman. He was definitely struggling against the conditions and there was no sign of a let-up in the weather. Pleading with me not to make an early decision he impassionately declared, 'Twenty four years and I've only had one match postponed - and that was due to a burst water main, not the pitch.' He went away and got a weather print-out and then started to ring friends who were 'weather experts'. When he came back he persuaded me to delay a decision until 7 o'clock, which was the latest point at which I could decide to allow fans into the ground. 'It'll stop raining at 7 and the pitch will be immaculate by 7.30,' he said.

When I returned for the inspection at spot on 7 p.m. it had indeed stopped raining and there was a very happy groundsman standing in the middle of the pitch with his pitchfork. He had kept his promise and the game went ahead on a wet but very playable pitch. I have nothing but admiration for groundsmen, who always take a personal pride in their pitch and regard it as a personal battle against the elements when weather conditions are atrocious.

At the pre-match security briefing I suggested to the police chief, Bernie Swift, that he might like to be on hand in the tunnel at half-time. When he asked why, I told him that he would find out but that basically I wasn't in the mood to be confronted by anyone with a Scottish accent during the interval. The game started in lively fashion with a booking after 24 seconds for Lucas Radebe, who had been assigned to man-mark Steve McManaman, who can often run the show for his team from midfield. Lucas is a great footballer and if it was left to me he wouldn't be wasted as a man-marker but there again I suppose if I was that good tactically I would be a manager myself.

The first half ended with three yellow cards, all to Leeds, and a scoreline of 4-0 in Liverpool's favour, an unheard of score at half-time in such a fixture. Liverpool were rampant and were running Leeds ragged. As I went into the tunnel there was Bernie Swift, complete with swagger-stick tucked imperiously under his arm. As we approached the steps into the dressing room area we were chatting away when I suddenly caught a glimpse of what I had been expecting. The fine shoes, the expensive suit, covered by a very expensive overcoat. 'Ref-a-ree' was the first word to come from this apparition but Bernie didn't let him get any further. With an expert manoeuvre of his swagger-stick Bernie led the fuming Scotsman to his own dressing room without him being able to utter a word of protest. Quite a satisfying moment when I think back.

The game ended at 4-0 and there were no yellow cards in the second half. After the game I had to pass by the infamous Liverpool 'boot room' (for the uninitiated, this is a small room in the corridor housing a cosy little bar) and I overheard George Graham say to the Liverpool lads, 'The referee did well the second half; it's a pity he had to dish out those yellow cards in the first.' This was said with a clear edge to it and, I was convinced, in a manner sufficient for me to hear. It was George's way of getting his point over and as I passed by I simply said, 'Thanks for the compliment George, see you next time.'

The season progressed and my next Premiership game was Derby County versus Chelsea. This was an exciting time for Chelsea fans with the acquisition of foreign stars, not the least being player-manager Ruud Gullit and recent signing Frank Leboeuf. For me, however, the most inspirational player in the Chelsea side was one another of my long-time heroes, Mark Hughes. I had long admired 'Sparky' and appreciated, in particular, his strength, skill and determination.

It's funny how things work out in football but if it wasn't for the fact that Hughes was coming through the ranks at Old Trafford in the early 1980s then Manchester United would probably not have released Peter Beardsley. It would have been interesting to see what sort of career Peter would have had at Old Trafford if he had been given the chance. As it was, I was quite happy at that outcome because otherwise I would have been robbed of the great pleasure of seeing Peter display his skills at Newcastle.

Back to the Chelsea game and it was generally accepted that the 'new' Chelsea would be too strong for middle-of-the-table Derby. They had reckoned, however, without the determination of a Derby side motivated by the ubiquitous Jim Smith. Derby clinched a splendid game by three goals to two and the match was full of incident. In the second half Frank Leboeuf punched the ball off his own goal-line preventing a certain goal. As I walked up to him and showed him the red card he smiled and shook my hand saying, 'Sorry ref, I know there's nothing else you can do.'

This turned out to be Ruud Gullit's last game as a player for Chelsea as he went down injured after a challenge and, although he tried to play on, he was more seriously hurt than he thought. He had in fact broken his ankle and he never really made it back as a player except for one or two cameo appearances. I consider myself fortunate to have refereed a number of games in which Gullit played and I have to say he was a joy to watch. His talent, skill and vision were wondrous to behold and it's only a pity we didn't get to see more of him in England when he was in his prime.

Shortly after the Derby game I was put in charge of the second leg of the Coca-Cola Cup semi-final between Wimbledon and Leicester. The game was to be held at Selhurst Park after the 0-0 draw at Leicester. If the game ended 0-0 it would go to penalties but if it was a score draw then Leicester would go through.

I met up with my colleagues at our London hotel and we headed off to the ground. As was usual when the officials turn up here, the ground was deserted with the exception of a few stewards scurrying around trying to get things ready. We decided to have a look at the pitch and on walking out of the tunnel I saw a figure in the centre circle wearing one yellow boot and one green boot, both with the Lotto logo on them.

'Hello Al,' he shouted, 'come on over, I need to speak to you.' As I approached he put his arm around me, effectively separating me from my colleagues. 'I need your help tonight Al, I'm on one yellow card and I don't want to miss Wembley; you wouldn't want to do that to me, would you Al?' I decided to put on a stern face and a serious tone. 'If you work hard at your game and your behaviour I'm sure you won't have anything to worry about, Vincent,' I said using his Sunday name which I knew he disliked intensely.

So, I explained to Vinny that if he could control himself then we should be OK. The look in those steely blue eyes told me he had received the message. Little did I know that those same eyes would become a tough guy symbol in Hollywood movies. 'Lock Stock and Two Smoking Barrels' was certainly an appropriate title for Vinnie's first starring role.

ONE NIGHT AT THE PALACE

It's funny how being a footballer can lead to becoming a star in other areas as I remember seeing Cantona making an appearance in the film 'Elizabeth' not so long back. And then we have David Ginola strutting his stuff on the catwalk and John Fashanu presenting 'Gladiators'. There are many more, of course, who bite the dust and end up in dire straits when their playing days are over. I guess it all boils down to personality at the end of the day.

I can remember Vinny's performance in the Newcastle v Wimbledon game at St James' Park a few years ago when the Wimbledon goalkeeper was sent off for running outside his box and bringing down Les Ferdinand. Who else should take over in goal but the extrovert Jones. Wimbledon were already 3-0 down and Vinny had to face the most rampant attack in the Premiership. He wasn't able to prevent more goals going in during a 6-1 defeat, but he did strike up a great relationship with the Newcastle fans behind his goal with a performance of witty repartee. This did give a clue that there was something of the showman in his personality. He wasn't a bad goalie either.

After the first few minutes of the Leicester game Vinnie said to me, 'If I can get through this game without a caution I'll give you my shirt.' I wouldn't have put any money on it. This game demonstrated to me what a grip media interests have on the game. Sky TV had just about achieved a stranglehold on important games. When a game was being televised it was as if they owned everything in and around the ground. There would be droves of engineers and floor managers, a couple of interviewers and of course the portable camera. This game would be no different, live on Sky, a draw in the first game and everything to play for. So the scene was set for a mega-battle with every footballer's dream, an appearance at Wembley, as the prize.

There was one little problem however. This was South London and my least favourite ground for getting to, Selhurst Park. I was not the only person to find it the most inaccessible of places and ten coachloads of Leicester fans were apparently gridlocked in Brixton. In an effort to maintain public order the police advised George Crawford and I that the kick-off needed to be delayed. Usually a delay would be fifteen minutes but on this occasion the police wanted thirty minutes. I informed the clubs, who understood the situation but expressed their irritation. I understood their

dissatisfaction as there are pre-match rituals to be followed and good managers put a lot of planning into motivating their players immediately before
the game. A delay at such a critical time can have the effect of reducing the
players' adrenaline flow and affecting their mental state of mind. Joe
Kinnear did make the observation that ten coachloads of fans is more than
Wimbledon would normally expect for a home game in total.

The TV people were now in a dilemma as everything is planned to the
micro-second for television. Being ever-resourceful they decided to use me
as a (no cost) stand-in. They advised me that they would like seven minutes
of my time and explained that they wanted me to talk about the delay and
what it meant to the competitors.

The questions were asked and I gave the answers. I decided to add a bit
on the end, however. I pointed out that the referee and his team are also
affected by such delays, perhaps even more so as the referee has to be
involved in decisions affecting lots of people, not to mention big business
such as Sky TV. Delaying the kick-off could also affect many people's travelling arrangements after the game and I explained that this sort of situation can put the referee under a lot of pressure. Like the players, this can
disturb concentration and mental preparation. A poor decision in the first
few minutes of a game could have serious implications for a club, could
result in the manager's services being dispensed with and could destroy a
player's ambitions as he might never get close to Wembley again.

Perhaps I was laying it on a bit thick but the look of genuine surprise
on Nick Collins' face confirmed my feeling that people did not have much
appreciation of this. Hopefully my few words may have done something to
help an understanding of the officials' position in such circumstances.

It was eventually agreed that kick-off would be 8.15 and there would be
no more delays. In the tunnel the tension could be felt and I could see the
apprehension in everyone's eyes. I have never jumped from an aeroplane
but I would imagine the feeling would be the same: one minute in a safe
place and the next catapulted into the unknown - this was my first semi-
final in the middle. Sam Hamman, a character whom I had become close
to, gave me a good luck hug as I walked past.

Visits to Selhurst Park usually involve crowds of as low as 4,500 with
only the big clubs such as Manchester United, Spurs, Arsenal or Chelsea
filling the ground to its 26,000 capacity. As I took the field on this occasion,

however, I found myself looking out at a heaving mass of people with not a single space to be found.

The scene reminded me of my early visits to St James' Park as a kid when there would be a 60,000 crowd, with youngsters being passed over the heads of the crowd down to the front to sit on the safety of the cinder track.

On reflection, and in the light of tragic developments since, it is amazing that there weren't more major mishaps in those days. I remember the situation getting very close to disaster, though, at the Inter City Fairs Cup semi-final against Glasgow Rangers when thousands of Rangers fans came down to Newcastle from Scotland without tickets. Nothing was going to stop them getting into the ground and they somehow acquired ladders and other climbing aids and clambered over the walls. The official gate that night was 57,000, which was maximum capacity at the time, but it is estimated that there were actually another 8,000 fans in the ground.

I have never been so scared as during the crush that night, both inside and outside the ground. It makes you realise just how close tragedy can be and that, taking all things into account, the all-seater stadiums of today are much more sensible. If there is a loss of tradition and a slightly diluted atmosphere it is a small price to pay for safety.

At Selhurst Park everything was under control and well monitored; it was just a pleasure to experience such an atmosphere at a ground where it is often very sterile. As we prepared for the kick-off the noise reached a crescendo and it was clear this was going to be a special night. Wimbledon versus Leicester wouldn't normally set the pulse racing but I have to give credit to both teams, they both tried to play football the way it should be played. This may surprise some people, given Wimbledon's reputation. They showed on this occasion however that they are capable of playing the 'beautiful game' if they put their mind to it. There was a significant battle going on in midfield with Vinnie battling it out with the combative Neil Lennon, the champion of courageous haircuts. Neil, whom I admire greatly, is also a courageous person generally having battled for a long time against a career-threatening back injury.

In the later stages of the first half, Wimbledon took the lead with a goal scored by Marcus Gayle. The move leading up to the strike was one of precision with a lot of slick passing leaving Marcus with a simple tap-in from about six yards. On the way to the restart Vinny ran past me and said, 'This is when I need you, Al,' a sure sign that things were warming up. I responded by saying, 'Just keep listening to me.' For the next fifteen minutes or so, whenever I was close to Vinnie, I was talking, shouting and cajoling all the time. I'm not sure where this approach stands in the referees' manual but, if I can help a player to keep his head and play the game properly, then that's fine as far as I'm concerned.

In the second half Leicester started to apply considerable pressure and nerves started tightening. Wimbledon only had to avoid conceding a goal and they would be at Wembley. Steve Walsh of Leicester had other ideas and put his side level after about seventy minutes, the goal coming from a free kick on the Leicester right wing. As the ball was hoisted into the penalty area Walsh timed his run to perfection and produced a prodigious leap to tower above two defenders and power a bullet header into the Wimbledon net.

As the game approached extra time the Wimbledon fans were now the more concerned as they had to score again in order to win the match. Joe Kinnear had decided to rattle a few cages by throwing on Mick Harford for the last few minutes of normal time. Unfortunately the first cage he rattled was mine and he became, in the 92nd minute, two minutes after coming on, the only player to be booked on the night. This was for what some would say was a typical Mick Harford attempt to 'unsettle' Kasey Keller, Leicester's American World Cup goalkeeper, by going in with a late challenge. Being generous, perhaps it was just Mick's age catching up with him and the old Norman Hunter adage, 'But I got there as soon as I could ref,' might have been appropriate.

Extra time turned into an end-to-end thriller with both teams spurning chances to settle the tie. Wimbledon failed to make the breakthrough and crashed out at the last hurdle having not lost either of the ties. Leaving the pitch Terry Burton, Kinnear's second-in-command, had the good grace to congratulate me on my performance. This was an act which meant a great deal to me, as having just lost the chance of a Wembley Final, he took the time to speak to me. Top man.

From my point of view I had to be satisfied with my performance and, never being one to reject compliments, I well remember the description by Henry Winter in the next day's Guardian when he described me as 'The excellent Mr Wilkie who had an outstanding game.'

ONE NIGHT AT THE PALACE

So what do referees do after a game of such magnitude? Go out and celebrate, of course. It was therefore with a comfortable, warm feeling that I went out with friends and colleagues to a Chinese restaurant in Shaftesbury Avenue, returning to the hotel for drinks till around 3.30 a.m. This might not sound very exciting compared to the excesses of some players but you can imagine the stories in the daily papers if a Premiership referee was found lying in the gutter in the West End.

'Where is my Vinnie Jones shirt?' I asked myself when I woke up the next morning. Well, Vinnie had been so disappointed at missing out on Wembley that I'm sure the last thing on his mind would have been a shirt for the referee. Never mind, I would see him again soon I was sure.

11

BEARDSLEY IN THE BOOK

I WAS NOW IN MY forty-fifth year and I must confess that from the age of forty-two I had been finding it harder and harder to maintain the level of fitness I demanded of myself in order to participate at the highest level in football. I had always been a naturally fit person but I also worked hard to maintain the sharpness I felt I needed. I decided that as I enjoyed the job so much I was still prepared to go through the pain barrier as I felt that I still had plenty to offer the game. I also knew that if I retired prematurely I would watch big matches and think, 'Why am I not out there?'

The status, or perhaps more accurately the notoriety, of being a referee meant many invitations to Sportsman's Dinners and many other similar functions. The demands grew and grew, with Sky TV inviting me to appear on one of their sports programmes, and local TV asking me to appear on their sports review show. I never achieved the really top accolade of opening supermarkets however!

I did not seek this attention nor did I particularly want it. On the other hand, to reject it would give the wrong message to everyone. I decided I would do anything I could to enhance the reputation of referees as sports-loving human beings rather than arrogant individuals parading throughout the country on a massive ego trip. With the advent of satellite TV and the money-men wanting to cover every angle possible, it was inevitable that the profile of referees in the Premiership would explode beyond recognition.

It is not so long ago that fans would be hard put to name the referee at their most recent match. That is the way most referees would want it, as, like I said earlier, the definition of a good refereeing performance is that the ref doesn't get noticed. Times change, however, and anyone remotely in the public eye has to accept the publicity, good or bad, which goes with it.

ONE NIGHT AT THE PALACE

As the season raced to its conclusion I was to feature yet again as fourth official in an FA Cup semi-final, this time Middlesbrough v Chesterfield at Old Trafford. I have to remind myself that Chesterfield got so close to an FA Cup final. They did, however, and they had chances in the first match to actually get there. In the event they drew 3-3 at Old Trafford and succumbed 3-0 in the replay. The first game was full of incident and Chesterfield will forever maintain that they were deprived of an historic Cup Final place through a refereeing decision.

It was 2-0 to Chesterfield when, still in the first half, they hit the bar and the ball bounced down beyond the goal line. The referee's assistant, Alan Sheffield, ran back towards the half-way line with his flag aloft, the signal that a goal had been scored. Unfortunately for the Spirites, David Elleray saw things otherwise and awarded a free kick to Middlesbrough on the six yard line. Much confusion ensued with no-one except David sure why the goal had been disallowed. I was positioned near the half-way line and from where I was standing I could clearly see that the ball had crossed the line but I had not been able to see any infringement. As I was close to the Sky TV monitors I had a quick look at the incident and still couldn't spot the offence which caused the goal to be ruled out.

After the game David insisted there had been some pushing in the build-up to the move. I can only assume that this was something the cameras did not capture. Whatever the rights or wrongs of the decision I am absolutely certain that this was the turning point of the match. Not only did it stop Chesterfield from going 3-0 up, it also provided the spark for a Middlesbrough recovery.

The second half was equally dramatic with Boro fighting back from a 2-1 half-time deficit, despite the sending off of Vladimir Kinder for a second yellow card very early in the second half. Interestingly, Bryan Robson at the end of the game was furious with David Elleray over the dismissal of Kinder for what he thought was an innocuous offence for the second yellow card. My view is that the decision was correct and that David had no choice in the matter seeing as it was due to shirt pulling. Kinder should have considered the consequences before doing this. I also can't help feeling that Robson conveniently soon forgot about the controversy in the first half where the decision went his team's way.

In the replay, Chesterfield could not repeat their heroics, playing like a team with its heart ripped out. As so often happens in situations like this, the fortune of the club declined dramatically in the wake of their exploits and they ended up being relegated not long afterwards, with manager John Duncan eventually losing his job. Still, what a tremendous achievement for such a small club and it was no disgrace to go out to a Middlesbrough side which at the time included foreign stars such as Juninho, Ravanelli and Emerson.

I went from Old Trafford to refereeing the English County Youth Cup Final which took place at Cambridge United's ground. Although this might sound something of a come-down I did not view it this way and to be appointed to any Cup Final was an honour as far as I was concerned. The game will not go down in the annals as a piece of footballing history, however, as Cambridgeshire beat Lancashire 1-0 in a fairly dour match.

Two years to the day since the Leeds v Norwich game, I would return to Elland Road to referee Leeds and another team in danger of being relegated. This time it was Middlesbrough. The unique thing about this game was that Middlesbrough actually had enough points to ensure their safety, but because of their inability, or unwillingness, to fulfil the fixture at Blackburn earlier in the season, when they had a lot of players ill, they were to be deducted three points. This meant they had to win at Leeds to stay up. I was delighted to receive the appointment as this was sure to be a challenging game and, depending on how it was approached, could get out of hand.

As the title had already been decided, Sky had chosen to concentrate on relegation battles and this was their game for Sunday 11 May 1997. As always with Sky games, I had butterflies in my stomach and tried to hide this nervousness, or excitement as I preferred to think of it, from my colleagues. Leeds had nothing to play for but their pride and I found myself wondering whether they might lie down and do their close neighbours a favour. Not to mention that Middlesbrough's survival would mean one more local match for Leeds the following season instead of a journey to somewhere like Ipswich.

The day was warm and sunny, the pitch was in excellent shape and we took to the corridor six minutes before kick-off, this being the timescale stipulated by Sky. The procedure is that one minute is allocated for the cameras to witness the teams assembling in the tunnel area, a further one minute to carry out a jewellery inspection (if they don't have any, I ask if they want to buy some), three minutes of adverts while the players move on to the pitch and the officials check the goal nets, with the final minute covering the toss-up and kick-off. The whistle does not get blown until the referee receives a thumbs up from the Sky floor manager who is situated on the half-way line.

Once the whistle is blown the commercial and bureaucratic aspects can be forgotten and full concentration can be given to the game itself. The ancillary features can be a tiresome distraction. Once a game was under way, however, I was always in my element, with total control and everything down to me in making the final decision on all that went on. A huge responsibility but one I thrived on.

The game itself was quite a good spectacle, with perhaps the best spectacle of all being a healthy-looking female streaker who ran on to the pitch as we were preparing for kick-off. She was heading in my direction but unfortunately the enhanced security arrangements were very effective and the stewards managed to intercept her first. Apparently, this lady's friends were on holiday in Ibiza and they had phoned her to say that if she could get herself on Sky during the match they would pay her fare to go and join them. Unfortunately for her, she ran on just as Sky switched to the pre-match commercials. I don't know what the temperatures were like in Ibiza but there were certainly a few raised temperatures in Elland Road.

After this diversion, Leeds were the first to regain their composure and they took the lead in the first half. In the second half, Juninho equalised after a typical mazy run and Boro went after the all-important winner. I added six minutes of stoppage time but Boro were unable to make the vital breakthrough and, when the final whistle went, their players were devastated. I felt for the players, some of whom I knew quite well. Robbie Mustoe, Gianluca Festa and Juninho were desolate. I did my best to console them but I had to leave them to it in the end. Bryan Robson had no complaints about the game, just about the Premier League Management Committee and the deduction of three points. From my point of view I think the decision was correct considering that Boro had in excess of twenty professionals on their books. They would have been better served turning out a team for the Blackburn game including youth players, and losing, rather than getting no points and then having three deducted. I know this is a view shared by many Middlesbrough fans. The three deducted points made the difference between survival and relegation.

It's funny how things turn out in football and the Leeds scorer of the goal which sent Boro down was Brian Deane who soon went off to Benfica, in Portugal, only to return to the UK to sign for Boro.

I drove up the A19 and as usual I felt a thirst coming on as I approached the Haynes Arms. I decided I had done enough to earn a drink so I pulled over and parked the car. I hadn't given a thought to the fact that as this was the main road to Teesside it would be full of Middlesbrough supporters. As I walked into the Lounge I was confronted with a mass of red and white.

While I was making my decision on whether to turn around and leave, someone shouted, 'Hey, it's the ref.' To my amazement a round of applause broke out and I was invited to sit with a group of fans. This I did for the next hour or so and it is times like this when you feel that all the abuse referees put up with is worth it in the end. I found it particularly edifying when I considered how distressed the Boro fans were at the implications of the day's events.

The time between seasons was becoming ever more minimal, the break now being down to eight weeks. Following two weeks holiday, I had to prepare for the annual conference of the APLFLMO, more conveniently known as FLYMO, along with preparation for the annual fitness test. Then it would be time for the pre-season friendlies. Where did the summer go?

The fixtures usually arrive in mid July and these cover the months of August and September. I had surprised lots of people by expressing an interest in refereeing at Barnsley on the first day of the season. I liked this idea because it would be a piece of soccer history as it was their first season in the top flight having never been in the Premiership or the old First Division.

As was now the custom, the Premier League called all referees to a meeting in July to outline changes on the laws of the game and to discuss any change of emphasis in the application of the laws. This was held at Keele University in Staffordshire and consisted of video presentations and lectures. Also, around this time, the Premier League Academy took off and the Premier League referees were appointed to control the under 18 games. This was an enjoyable task as the discipline shown was very refreshing. The response of the coaches was also first class. I recall John Carver, the Newcastle coach, asking why I had given a free kick against his captain. When I told him it was for dissent he replied, 'You should have given him the yellow card, that's the only way he'll learn.' He was right and I reflected that by being involved with the cream of the country's young players we were in a position to help and educate them as they progressed through the system.

Some of the youngsters coming through at that time were lads with real potential for the future, some of whom have now made the breakthrough to the top. Among these were Kieron Dyer (Newcastle), Robbie Stockdale (Middlesbrough), Paul Thirlwell (Sunderland), Ledley King and Luke Young (Spurs) and Joe Cole of West Ham. They all have tremendous futures in front of them if they keep their feet on the ground.

There are many more young players out there with lots of talent but, unfortunately, commercial pressures mean that clubs often require a quick fix and tend to go for established stars. This can only be at the expense of up-and-coming youngsters and can destroy their confidence in making the grade. Lots of young players have abundant skill but if their confidence is dissipated they head for obscurity.

I left Keele thinking about the fact that I had three seasons left. I tried to look at this positively and told myself that this was quite a long time and that I would have many more experiences in that time. Well, I was certainly right on that score. I also told myself that I was going to try to enjoy every minute of it. I realised that I was in a privileged position and I wanted to accumulate all the memories I could in the time that I had left.

The fixtures arrived and I was indeed scheduled to take Barnsley's first Premiership game. The Tykes were to start the season at home at Oakwell against Premiership ever-presents West Ham. I also had another five Premiership games scheduled for August and September. My personal preparations were going well and, although another year older, I was managing rather well, I thought. The pre-season fitness test came and went with no problems and the thorough medical checks showed that everything was fine with my health generally.

On 9 August 1997 the Barnsley game arrived and it was a beautiful day, sun blazing and no wind. Probably a bit on the hot side to play football but just right for a carnival atmosphere like this. Oakwell was in pristine condition and, although Barnsley may not seem like the most exciting place to be, this was a very special occasion.

Whilst I was waiting to lead the teams out I was talking to Neil Redfearn, the Barnsley captain, and wished him good luck for the season. On overhearing this, Harry Redknapp shouted over, 'Don't forget there are two teams out there,' a phrase that referees hear with boring regularity. I was a bit concerned about Harry's tone and informed him that I was well aware of this fact. He conceded the point and said, 'I didn't mean anything by it, you've never let us down before,' which I suppose was something of a compliment.

The entrance was as good as anything I had ever encountered before, even at bigger clubs. The colour, the noise and the carnival atmosphere were breathtaking. Unfortunately for Barnsley, the experience of West Ham at this level meant the game ran away from them quite early on and they ended up losing 2-1, a scoreline which demonstrated West Ham's profligacy in front of goal rather than Barnsley's performance.

An amusing incident happened after about 75 minutes when I issued a caution to John Moncur of West Ham for dissent. Firstly he objected to the yellow card and then, realising the futility of his protests, put his arm around me and said, 'Come on Alan, make it for anything else but not dissent. The gaffer will fine me for that, put it down to a trip or something, anything but dissent.' For the remainder of the game it was a case of 'Remember, not dissent' every time he passed me. In the end I couldn't get rid of him and it was as if he was marking me. Eventually I said, 'Go away and I may consider it.' Having done so I found myself with no alternative but to submit my report citing dissent. Sorry, John.

Although they lost that day, the Barnsley fans were fantastic and they did their team proud. I was pleased that they had a goal to cheer and, even when West Ham scored their second goal, they continued chanting for their own team: 'It's just like watching Bra-zil, Bra-zil.' Certainly the atmosphere was very Brazilian and the fans were a credit to the game.

The next fixture to appear on my doormat was a Coca-Cola Cup tie, second round, first leg, Hull v Crystal Palace. Although I have a serious side to my character I also like a good laugh and the occasional piece of mischief. So when the team sheets came in I looked down and saw an oppor-

tunity for a bit of fun. After the respective managers, Steve Coppell and
Terry Dolan, had left the changing room I decided to play a prank on the
Palace kit manager. Hull play in gold and black stripes, the stripes being
about four inches wide, and black shorts. Palace play in deep red shirts with
blue stripes and, on this occasion, white shorts and socks.

I asked the Palace man to bring in a shirt and after examining it I said,
'I don't think we can get away with that. You'll have to wear your second
set,' knowing full well that he had brought only one set of kit. The panic
on his face was a real picture and I almost began to feel sorry for him. I
took him along to the Hull dressing room and I asked to look at one of
their shirts in order to compare. The player involved went along with me
and said, 'They're too close ref, we can't play with these colours' and rounded off by adding, 'I'll try to get our reserve strips for Palace but I think
they're a bit damp as they've just been washed.'

The Palace man was by now apoplectic and was pleading his case. I took
the Hull reserve shirt into the Palace dressing room and the players were
unmerciful in pulling his leg. 'We're not wearing orange,' shouted Bruce
Dyer, 'We'll have to call the game off!' shouted another. At this point Steve
Coppell came into the dressing room and asked if there was a problem with
the kit. 'Not at all,' I replied, out of earshot of the victim, 'we're just having a bit of fun.' Fortunately Steve saw the funny side and himself took part
in the demolition of the kit man's ego.

Ten minutes before the kick off I decided to help the kit man out a little and told him that for his benefit I'd let the game go ahead with the strips
as they were. With a huge sigh of relief he thanked me profusely and
expressed his never-ending gratitude for getting him out of a tight spot.
When the teams went out on to the pitch for the warm-up there was much
laughter and I suddenly saw the kit manager running along the touch line
shouting, 'You bastard, you really had me there.' The players were falling
about laughing and the crowd must have wondered what on earth was
going on. Here was a red-faced character in a track suit threatening his own
team mates as well as a Premier League referee in full view of 6,000 people.

We went back into the changing room to make final preparations and
suddenly the phone rang. I answered, 'Referee's room, referee speaking.' A
broad Yorkshire accent on the other end of the line said gruffly, 'Radio

Humberside here, can you tell me the teams for tonight?' Thinking this might be some sort of revenge by the kit man I replied, 'Hull and Crystal Palace.' This didn't have the expected response so I said, 'Look you're through to the referee's room and I'm on my way to start the game.' His response was priceless. 'If you're the referee you'll have the team sheets and you'll know who's playing.' By this time I was getting to quite like this guy and I admired his persistence. It may have been unorthodox but I decided to take the time to read him the team sheets. It made me a little late for getting out on to the pitch but I couldn't help smiling at his cheek.

The game was poor and half-time arrived with Hull leading 1-0. I was having a drink with my colleagues in the changing room when the phone went again. 'I'm certainly popular tonight,' I said to the others. When I picked the phone up I found myself speaking to a lady who was asking to speak to William Brown. I thought this must be a member of staff so I pointed out that this was the referee's room. She then advised me that William Brown was actually standing on the terraces and that she needed to speak to him urgently.

Thinking that there must be some family emergency I asked her what the problem was. I was somewhat taken aback when she said it was just that they had a car for sale and someone had responded to the newspaper advertisement making an offer! Being ever helpful, and something of a car enthusiast, I asked her what type of vehicle it was and she advised me that it was a Ford Sierra 1.8 LX with 110,000 miles on the clock, no tax but 6 months MOT. 'We asked for £1500 and he's offered £1250,' she volunteered. After enquiring about the body condition and the tread depth of the tyres, I replied, 'I think you should take it.' She then thanked me for my help and said goodbye. By this time it was time to get back on the field. 'That's the quickest half-time I can remember,' I said to the lads, who by now were in a state somewhere between bemusement and hysteria. I thought to myself that perhaps I could take to being a car salesman when my refereeing career ended.

The game finished 1-0 to Hull, not that it mattered after such an eventful evening.

Talking of retirement, at this time I was really enjoying every game and treating each one as if it would be my last. In the next match I would find out what my standing was with one very famous player in the Premiership.

I am talking about Ian Wright, some people's worst nightmare. The man is a great athlete and has an abundance of skill. However, he is disliked by many people for his aggressive and sometimes arrogant approach. The truth is that this is a man with an overload of charisma who, to me, created excitement and, for the most part in his playing days, considerable fun. Before games he would usually come up to me and put his arm around me and say, 'Yo, Wilks, how's things?' and we would pass the time of day for a while. I think he found it strange that a referee could have a sense of humour and I think it was this which made us hit it off.

I was refereeing the Everton v Arsenal game at Goodison Park and the score was 2-2 in the second half when I awarded a corner to Arsenal. I detected Michael Ball jostling at the far post and Wrighty looked at me and said, 'He's after my shirt, Wilks, what you gonna do about it?' I looked at Michael and simply said, 'Leave him alone, will you, that's going to be my shirt after the game and I don't want any damage done.' This had the desired effect and the scuffle ended. After the game I was headed for the lounge Everton used to entertain their guests and, as I crossed the area between the dressing room and lounge, I heard this voice say, 'Yo, Wilks, do you really want my shirt, man?' ' I would be honoured,' I responded. 'I'll send you it in the post,' he said and as we shook hands I thought that would probably be the end of it. However, the following Thursday there was a knock at the front door and there was a parcel for me. Inside was a shirt with an inscription saying, 'Alan, you're not a bad ref, God Bless.' This is one souvenir that will always have a special place in my trophy cabinet.

On the subject of shirts, my next visit to London took me back to Wimbledon, for the match against Sheffield Wednesday. Somehow I did not bump into Vinny until the teams were lining up in the tunnel. When he saw me I got the usual, 'Alright Al?' and I replied, 'You're a right con-man, what happened to the shirt after the Leicester game?' As I turned to lead the teams out I heard Robbie Earle shout out, 'Ref, what have you said to Vinny, he's disappeared.' Then Vinny re-appeared throwing a shirt into my dressing room as he ran past. 'Sorry Al, I forgot, alright now?'

This is not the sort of thing that most people would imagine going on as the teams stand in the tunnel waiting to enter the arena for a top flight match. I have to say that I found Vinny to be a nice guy and a very genuine competitor. Yes, this is the same man who had the distinction of being cautioned after four seconds whilst playing for Chelsea, has numerous sendings off to his name and a pretty bad press over the years. You take people as you find them.

Talking of Vinny and Wimbledon reminds me of an earlier visit to Selhurst Park, where I always found the Dons to be a friendly and peaceful club to visit off the pitch - I stress, off the pitch. The dressing room was very small but always spotless, with fresh fruit and bottled water always available. The lounge area provided tea and coffee pre-match and a chance for the girls to sell match-day lottery tickets. The number drawn gets announced at half-time and the prize money is dictated by the size of the crowd. As I ran on to the pitch for the second half of this particular match, I heard the announcement that ticket number· 1010 had been drawn. Without thinking, I kicked the ball into the air and whooped with delight. On reflection, this must have looked pretty comical to anyone who spotted it and it's perhaps as well the game wasn't featured on Sky or Match of the Day. Vinny asked me what was up and I replied that I had won £400. After ensuring that I would buy him a drink after the game he advised me to make sure I didn't accept a cheque!

You always know when you are performing at the required level through the appointments which come your way. Such was the case when I was appointed to the Manchester United v Blackburn Rovers game at Old Trafford. I had refereed twice before at Old Trafford but never in the League, the previous fixtures being in the Coca-Cola and FA Cups. I have previously mentioned the intense rivalry between these two teams and of course I was aware that this might have been one of the factors contributing to the Cantona incident at Palace. The game was played on 30 November 1997 and, as usual, was an immense occasion. The entrance to a Premiership game these days is extremely well stage-managed and the atmosphere was built up to melting point. The game ended on this occasion in an easy 4-0 victory for Man United, Blackburn's cause not being helped by the sending off of Chris Sutton for a second yellow card. After watching the TV replay from a different angle, the second offence alone probably merited a red card as it appeared that it was an 'over the top' tackle which left Paul Scholes writhing on the ground. To this day Chris won't speak to me. Still, that's his problem, not mine.

ONE NIGHT AT THE PALACE

Christmas '97 would bring another televised game, with a little post-match surprise. I had just completed the Villa v Spurs game and was invited to the Directors' lounge, where I came across one of the most incongruous things you could wish to encounter in football. Live classical violin music, entertaining the post-match assembly in the Directors' lounge, is something you don't find everywhere. But at Villa, of course, they have Nigel Kennedy, the eccentric, often amusing (and sometimes less amusing) genius. As on this occasion, he is often to be found in the lounge after the game with his £2 million Stradivarius. Doug Ellis called for attention and introduced Nigel, who then launched into a solo performance. Although I am not ordinarily a fan of violin music, simply by being in the presence of greatness, I felt rewarded. When I got home and recounted the episode to my wife she asked whether Nigel had played the Four Seasons; 'How on earth would I know?' was all I could think given my total ignorance of such matters.

It is rumoured that Doug Ellis bought Nigel his first decent violin when Nigel was an impoverished young performer. Nigel takes great delight in repaying this debt of gratitude. 'Deadly' Doug Ellis, as his nickname goes, may well be a hard-nosed chairman when it comes to dealing with his managers, but I detected a great big soft spot for Nigel Kennedy and I believe their association is a source of great pride for Doug. Despite Doug's reputation for ruthless treatment of his managers, I also believed at the time that John Gregory wasn't far behind Nigel in the Ellis popularity stakes. How time has told!

As the season progressed various interesting matters arose, not the least being something that occurred in the Leeds v Bolton game at Elland Road. One of my all-time heroes is Peter Beardsley and Peter was on a loan spell with Bolton at the time of this game. I was horrified to find myself giving him a rare yellow card for a late tackle. Shortly afterwards I had to warn him that I might have to send him off for another careless tackle. I can only imagine how I would have felt if I had been the person to give him the only red card of such a distinguished career. Not to mention the fact that I wouldn't exactly have been the most popular person amongst my friends and relatives back home. Fortunately, Peter being the professional he is just curbed his boyish enthusiasm enough to get through the game without such a drastic event taking place.

BEARDSLEY IN THE BOOK

I had the great privilege at a later date to referee the Beardsley testimonial match at St James' Park. Peter had chosen for this occasion a game between Newcastle United and Glasgow Celtic, one of the teams he had supported as a boy. Usually testimonials represent a 'friendly' game but on this occasion Celtic had insisted on a Premier League referee, as they had dcelared their intention to take the game seriously for seventy minutes and to save the 'fun' for the last twenty.

As I approached the ground on the evening in question I found myself walking through a seething mass of Dennis the Menace lookalikes, who were spilling out of the local bars. Only the colour of the hoops was different. Even at this point, two-and-a-half hours before the game, some of them were being carried on the shoulders of their comrades! Although I was recognised by a number of the less inebriated, the comments were all friendly and good natured (much to my relief).

The Newcastle XI was to consist of mainly their first team of the time but was to be embellished by Kevin Keegan, Kenny Dalglish, Stuart Pearce, Chris Waddle and Paul Gascoigne, as well as Peter himself of course. Celtic soon eased into a three goal lead with Paul Gascoigne featuring as the main resistance. Paul was no doubt fired up by the hostile reception he received throughout from the Celtic supporters (a reminder of the infamous flute-playing gesture from his Glasgow Rangers days), as well as the rapturous response he was getting from the Newcastle fans. He was so wound up that I found it necessary to remind him of the nature of the occasion. True to their word, Celtic took their foot off the pedal with twenty minutes left and this led to the introduction of Kenny Dalglish and Kevin Keegan. Kevin proceeded to run around the pitch as if in his heyday. Before too long he whispered in my ear, 'How long have I been on Alan,' to which I responded, 'Two minutes Kevin.' He looked at me breathlessly and said, 'Never - I'm knackered!'

With four minutes left, I said to Tosh McKinlay, the Celtic defender, 'We haven't had a penalty yet, have we?' With a knowing look and a smile on his face he replied, 'No ref, but there's time yet!' Almost immediately, Alan Shearer went down under McKinlays 'challenge' and we had our penalty. To my dismay, Peter offered the kick to Kevin Keegan. Gladly, Keegan told Peter to take it himself. At this point I told Paul Lambert of Celtic to stand near me while the kick was taken. He couldn't understand why but I told him I had my reasons. Beardsley proceeded to lift the ball over the cross-bar and into the crowd. All was not lost, however, as I immediately blew my whistle and ordered a re-take as Lambert was standing inside the penalty area! Peter made no mistake from the second kick and everybody went home happy. A great night and a job well done.

There were some massive fixtures for me before the end of the season. In March, I was very flattered to be given the most important game possible in the Premiership with the allocation of the Manchester United v Arsenal game. This was top v second top. If United were to win they would have a virtually unassailable lead in the title race; if Arsenal were to win then they would be within striking distance. The prospect was mouth-watering. The kick off was 11.30 a.m. so that Sky could show the match around the world; an estimated audience of 80 million was expected to tune in.

The night before the game I stayed at the Copthorne Hotel just 600 yards from Old Trafford as I didn't want any anxiety about getting to the ground in good time the next day. After checking in at the hotel I went for my usual night-cap and suddenly discovered that Arsenal were staying at the same hotel. The place was also full of people going to the match. I found it quite nice to be recognised, with people asking for autographs, as this is not the sort of treatment you get from fans on match day. I spent some time chatting to Arsene Wenger and Pat Rice, their players being tucked up in bed of course.

The game was to be a spine-chiller. After a first half in which Vieira and Petit took a stranglehold on midfield, stifling United's progress and then prompting their own attacks, the second half became a much more open contest. With about twenty minutes left, Nicolas Anelka won an aerial challenge, dropping the ball invitingly into open space where the unmarked Overmars raced on to the ball and crashed it into the top right hand corner of the net. From this point, the famous Arsenal defensive mechanism kicked in. The tension mounted as United fought for the incredibly important equaliser. In the midst of all this Manu Petit turned to me and asked me how much time was left. When I told him 'Six minutes' he said, with a smile on his face, 'Make it one and I'll take you out on town tonight and we party.'

United, despite their efforts, could not break down the Arsenal defence; even when the determined and desperate Schmeichel decided to visit the

Arsenal penalty area for free kicks and corners, the impregnable Arsenal defence held firm. On his third excursion upfield, Schmeichel suddenly pulled up in some distress, having pulled a hamstring. This left the United goal wide open and Arsenal just failed to double their lead with a shot at an open goal from the half-way line. And then it was all over.

This result and the failure to score one goal cost United the title and no doubt many millions of pounds. This was the second time United had failed to lift the Premiership title since its inception and the second time I had been involved in key games affecting their downfall. So much for the allegations from Manchester City fans that I am a United supporter!

Every now and again in football something happens that seems totally out of context and this game provided one such moment. In the middle of this epic battle a figure appeared on the pitch carrying a plastic carrier bag. Lee Dixon and Nigel Winterburn used their man-marking skills to capture the individual. In the end he turned out to be a harmless little Irishman who didn't quite know what to do once he had got on to the pitch. It was a harmless incident but you can never tell when such events are going to turn out to be more sinister and you always have to take any incursion on to the field of play very seriously.

This game was soon followed by another Monday night Sky game between West Ham and Leeds, which Leeds lost 3-0. I issued six yellow cards to Leeds players, much to George Graham's usual dismay.

My own view is that a manager can't afford to have half his team booked in one match as the inevitable result of this sort of behaviour is that key players will be suspended at critical times of the season. Managers may blame the referee, or say their players let them down, but is there not also an argument which says that players' attitudes reflect the culture instilled by the manager and the coaching staff?

I returned to my hotel after the game and was enjoying a late drink when news came through that the Leeds team, who had set off for a flight back to Leeds immediately after the game, had been involved in a plane crash following take-off from Stansted Airport. News was slow in coming through and it was not until the next morning that I learned that there had been no casualties. I was so relieved that there had not been a tragedy and I was able to relax again. The passion of football is put into perspective when something like this happens.

ONE NIGHT AT THE PALACE

On the following Wednesday evening I was refereeing the FA Youth Cup semi-final between Leeds and Everton at Elland Road, and had the chance to meet some of the senior players involved in the plane incident. When I saw Gary Kelly and Ian Harte, we embraced, a spontaneous gesture of relief and joy that they had escaped unharmed. This brought home to me the mutual respect which can exist between people within the game. I spoke to Alan Sutton, whose definitive function at Leeds has always escaped me but who it seems has been there forever, and he told me of his experience. It sounded scary to say the least and makes you realise why some players refuse to fly.

I was soon involved in another big-match 4-0 scoreline, this time at Anfield when Liverpool beat Arsenal. The size of the scoreline was largely due to the fact that Arsenal had the title sewn up and had rested several key players. This cannot detract from a eight minute hat-trick scored by Robbie Fowler. This was a real hat-trick in that it involved goals with the right foot, the left foot and a header. People can say what they like about Robbie, and he unfortunately tends to provide them with plenty of ammunition, but what they can't do is deny his goal-scoring talents. Here is a player who, in my opinion, is far and away the most natural goal scorer I have been privileged to work with. The unfortunate series of ankle injuries he has suffered has, I believe, not only robbed him of many England caps, but also robbed the national side of a great predator. Robbie is still a young man and I sincerely hope he has better luck in the future.

I was yet again involved in a dramatic conclusion to the Premiership season with my appointment to a cliff-hanger between Chelsea and Bolton. This was one part of an equation which would decide who would go down into the relative obscurity of the First Division. The second part of the equation was the game between Everton and Wimbledon. To survive, Everton needed to win their game and required Bolton to lose at Chelsea.

Again, the games were synchronised so that neither team would gain an advantage by knowing the result of the other. This approach would remove the possibility of a repeat of the fiasco which condemned Sunderland to relegation a number of years earlier when, in a similar situation, Coventry City's kick-off was delayed by some twenty minutes due to 'crowd congestion'. This meant that Jimmy Hill's Coventry had an unfair advantage as they knew for the last twenty minutes that they only had to play out a 0-0 draw with Bristol City who also needed only one point to survive. The match reports talked of much passing the ball around in the centre circle and this arrangement sent Sunderland crashing into the old Second Division amidst much discontent in the football community generally.

Stamford Bridge was bathed in sunshine and this was Chelsea's last game of the season. This wasn't good news for Bolton as no team likes to lose at home on the last day as it leaves a bitter taste in their supporters' mouths during the summer. Chelsea were therefore not going to be coasting and in the end they won the game at a canter, 2-0. I had been expecting a stronger performance from Bolton and felt very sorry for their fans, who were now dependent on the result of the Everton game.

Meanwhile, there were dramatic goings-on at Goodison. If Everton failed to win against Wimbledon then Bolton would stay up and have a chance to consolidate their position in the top flight. In a see-saw game Everton clawed their way back from a two-goal deficit to level at 2-2 - a score-line which would have saved Bolton. However, as their Premiership status was slipping away, Everton were awarded a free kick which would result in a last-gasp winner, saving them and condemning sorry Bolton. An added touch of spice here is that the Everton winner was scored against Hans Segers, who many people thought might have saved it. The question of whether he had actually dived over the ball formed part of the soccer corruption allegations referred to earlier. Nothing was proven but the whole affair made everyone realise that possibilities exist for cheating and corruption in the game.

At Stamford Bridge the Bolton supporters were sitting with their radios glued to their ears waiting for the result from Goodison. When the news finally came through that Everton had won, the Bolton players and fans were devastated. With the combination of events Everton had escaped relegation and Bolton went down on goal difference, a desperate fate.

I was in the dressing room when I heard a knock on the door. It turned out to be Colin Todd, the Bolton manager. 'Can I come in?' he asked, 'my dressing room is not a very pleasant place to be at the moment.' He shook my hand and said, 'It's nice not to have to blame the ref, well done.' Taking the circumstances into consideration this was probably one of the best compliments I have ever been offered. Colin, as it happens is, like myself, from Chester-le-Street although we didn't know each other very well. I asked him if he would like a drink and we spent the next twenty minutes talking about home and anything else that crossed our minds. I don't suppose it was any consolation to him but at least it took his mind off things for a while.

I was sorry to see that Colin left Bolton later in acrimonious circumstances over the sale, against his wishes, of Per Frandsen to Blackburn. In one of those ironies of the footballing world Frandsen failed to make an impact at Blackburn and is now back at Bolton.

An interesting end to an eventful season.

12

BETRAYAL

THE SUMMER MONTHS WERE to see the beginnings of change. The Premier League had decided to appoint their own Referees' Officer and they had chosen Philip Don for the position. Philip was soon to introduce more stringent fitness tests and more intense medical checks. We were given targets to aim for in our fitness programme and the general approach was one of introducing a more professional regime.

It was ironic that at this time I was suffering from an occasional trapped sciatic nerve. This manifested itself as a pain in my hamstring muscles and led to considerable discomfort. Following manipulation of my hips, the problem would be contained for a while. Unfortunately the situation meant that I was beginning to miss the occasional training session so I became involved in a vicious circle of trying to maintain my fitness but risking possible problems with my back if I tried too hard.

It was during this summer of 1998 that I became president of the Association of Premier League and Football League Match Officials. This one-year appointment was to bring me into contact with many people, from all walks of life. I attended the PFA awards dinner and spent the evening in the company of Lord Taylor of Warwick, an avid Aston Villa fan and a very nice man. We found we had a number of things in common, with one of them unfortunately being death threats. He actually had a bodyguard with him at the event as he was being targeted for the 'crime' of being the first non-white peer in the House of Lords.

At the League Managers Association dinner I sat with a number of managers, including Joe Kinnear, Roy McFarland and Sam Allardyce, but it was Ray Graydon of Walsall who impressed me most. This was because of his politeness and a degree of refinement which somehow seemed misplaced in this environment. Another important appointment date was the Football Writers' Dinner. I am pleased to say that this was an occasion when friends and adversaries were all treated the same, so much so that even Neil Harman (now of The Times) bought me a drink. The previous legal dispute of a couple of years before was forgotten as Neil bought me a drink and suggested he would like to help me write my autobiography.

The appointment would also take me around the country on speaking engagements to various refereeing bodies. The worst of my representative duties however would be for tragic reasons, due to the premature passing-away of an up-and-coming referee called Carl Finch, who died of cancer at the age of forty. Before his illness Carl had been a paragon of fitness and health and it was desperately sad that he never reaped the benefit of his hard work over the years. Carl's death would affect me deeply and would remind me how lucky I was.

The pre-season meetings took place as usual at Keele University but this time with a difference. This was the first get-together with Philip Don in his capacity of Referees' Officer. This must have been difficult for Philip, as he had the responsibility of taking charge of twenty-two referees and trying to get his point across in a way that would be accepted by everyone. The one thing in his favour was that by and large we all wanted the same thing. On the other hand, referees by definition tend to be strong-minded people, otherwise they wouldn't be in such a job. Following a nervous start Philip recovered and came over quite well, in keeping with the respect we had for him as a referee.

The new season, 1998/99, started without too much controversy except for an outcry about the number of yellow and red cards. The attitude of the media at this point was one of confrontation. It seemed that almost all acts of discipline were being questioned by the press. This was not a particularly good time to be high profile but to be honest I revelled in the controversy and I really enjoyed trying to give explanations. To me all the debate and discussion is part of football and I wouldn't want it any other way.

After a few 'ordinary' games at the start of the season, I was excited to receive my first televised game of the new season, Leicester v Wimbledon. This was not a great game but was one which caused me a great deal of unexpected upset. In the first half Kenny Cunningham of Wimbledon kicked the ball upfield and the ball landed just outside the Leicester penalty area. Aided by the rain, the ball skidded on the surface and caught the

Leicester keeper Kasey Keller by surprise. Kasey, who was rushing out of his goal, caught the ball in his hands, around the midriff, slipping out of his penalty area in the process. The assistant, Nigel Green, raised the flag for a free kick and I was left in the position of deciding how to penalise Keller for what technically could be a sending-off offence.

Accepting that the keeper's actions were accidental I simply blew for a free kick. This to me seemed like a sensible course of action and seemed to be generally accepted. Little did I realise that in the Sky commentary box was a certain Philip Don and that he was in the process of castigating me for not sending Keller off. After the game my assistants, Nigel Green and Mike Cairns, fourth official Dermot Gallagher, match observer Keith Hackett and myself became embroiled in a debate as to the merits of my decision. The outcome was two people (including myself) in favour of my action, two in favour of a yellow card and one totally undecided. My view remained that if any card was to be shown then under the laws of the game it would have to be red. As there had been no clear goal-scoring opportunity I did not feel that a red card was warranted and I was therefore not uncomfortable with my decision.

At that moment into the dressing room walked Philip Don. He hadn't had the opportunity to say too much before the door opened again and in walked the Leicester press officer. Philip was hidden by the door and, unaware of his presence, the press officer proceeded to advise me that the press would like to see me to get my view on the Keller incident 'for which your boss Philip Don has slaughtered you unmercifully on the television.' I can only imagine the embarrassment that Philip felt as he lurked behind the door frame. I simply said that if my boss said I was wrong then there was no reason for me to comment. He then left the room followed quickly by Philip. I had been totally shocked by all of this and what I had heard had shaken me to the core. I felt isolated and betrayed. I found it disappointing in the extreme that here was I, a referee trying to do a difficult job in difficult circumstances, and I felt that I could at least have had the support of my own employer. When I got home, my wife was in tears as she had switched the television on at half-time and had witnessed the demolition of my professional reputation.

To give Philip his due he did ring me up the next week to apologise and said that, on reflection, a yellow card might have been in order. That is fine as far as it goes but of course by then the damage was done. Sky TV are hardly likely to be attracted to the possibility of getting Philip on the following week to admit his change of heart. I guess that's one of the things about refereeing, you just have to grin and bear the criticism whether you think it's justified or not. I have worked with Philip since this incident and find him hard-working and diligent. I hope for his continued success in the Premier League and like to think that he himself might have learned something from this incident.

Interestingly, I did get lots of support the following week, some from unexpected quarters including managers, fans, other referees and League officials. One Premier League manager said to me, 'If he had done that to me, I would have ripped his ******* head off and shoved it up his ****.' A sad state of affairs all round.

The next googly I received was from Philip's equivalent, Jim Ashworth, the Football League Referees' Officer. He asked me if I would referee Derby and Manchester City in the Coca-Cola Cup. Given the background with City, I wondered at first whether to accept this but very quickly decided I was not going to be frightened off. On the night, it turned out to be lively entertainment with the main chant of the evening being 'Who's the ******* red in the black.' In the event, the game produced six yellow cards and I ended up sending off Jamie Pollock of City for elbowing Baiano of Derby in an off-the-ball incident. From the resulting free kick Derby scored the equaliser and the game ended in a 1-1 draw. Another factor to endear me to City fans, I suppose.

After the game Joe Royle, now the City manager, had no complaints. When I told him why I had sent off Pollock he said, 'I knew it, I wanted to get him off before then but didn't get the chance.' An honest comment from honest Joe.

The following week it was back into the Premiership melting pot and my next big game which was Arsenal v Spurs - my third appointment to this acrimonious fixture. I had refereed on George Graham's return to Highbury, when he was with Leeds, but this time he was returning to Highbury as manager of the hated Tottenham. George decided again that rather than take a seat in the stand he would proceed directly to the dugout. As we lined up in the tunnel the fans were already having a go at each other and the atmosphere was electric.

BETRAYAL

George asked me if he could get to the dugout first and I ensured that he got pole position on the steep narrow stairs leading to the Highbury pitch. I recalled that when he returned as manager of Leeds he got a standing ovation. This certainly wasn't going to be the case here as he had committed the sin of all sins and defected to the despised opposition.

When we emerged from the tunnel all that could be seen was a mass of people in the West Stand waving brown paper bags. Football crowds have their own way of dishing out humiliation and on this occasion the paper bags were of course a reference to the 'bung' allegations of previous years. I had to laugh.

The game itself was notable for only one thing and that was George telling me that I had refereed well. Now that is something of a novelty but at least it shows he is capable of decent sportsmanship on the odd occasion. The result was a George Graham special, a wonderfully boring scoreless draw.

The FA Cup was now upon us and this brought me a first appointment at Griffin Park, home of Brentford, to take a replay against Oldham Athletic. This was to be televised by Sky and provided me with some anxiety as the field was a sea of water. Under commercial pressure, Sky were desperate for the game to go ahead. I wouldn't normally allow this to influence my decision but on this occasion both teams wanted it to go ahead too (because of the money). It's safe to say I was encouraged to allow the game to be played.

Once again, of course, the safety of the players was paramount in my mind. Having considered that, I did decide it was safe and the game did go ahead. It turned out to be a cracker with end-to-end play bringing the crowd to its feet. Brentford put up a good performance and the game ended all square at 2-2 after extra time, even though I had sent their captain off after sixty minutes for denying a goal-scoring opportunity. The game was decided on penalties with Oldham running out 4-2 winners. The reward for their success was a home tie against Chelsea, the consolation for Brentford fans being that they are the only club in the Football League to have a pub situated at each corner of the ground.

As the game had run over through extra time and penalties, it was quite late by the time the after-match briefing was completed. As I had not eaten I found myself wandering the streets of Ealing at 12.30 a.m. trying to find a half-decent restaurant. The only one I could find open was a Nepalese establishment and I sampled my first yak steak, or something. It turned out to be as hot as the match and I returned to my hotel with an inner glow in more ways than one. A splendid evening.

In October 1998 I was heading for a game at Chelsea against Aston Villa. I was travelling on the train with Stuart Loudon, who had taken the day off for the trip. We had just finished a nice, if over-priced, meal and were enjoying the remnants of a decent bottle of wine when the train lurched and then slowed to a halt. I remarked flippantly, 'Oh bugger, he's hit a cow.' I then compounded the situation by suggesting that the driver had gone to pick up the pieces.

Unknown to me, the train had actually hit a person who had decided to commit suicide by standing on the track, a tragic but apparently not uncommon occurrence on the East Coast main line. The train was not allowed to move for three hours while the brakes were inspected and specially freed and the coroner, doctor and clean-up unit had completed their very unpleasant work. I felt terrible having made a joke about the situation when someone had been driven to such desperate measures because of some problem in their personal life. After the three hours we joined another train while the staff of the original one were relieved from duty and offered counselling.

We arrived at the hotel at 1 a.m. in the pouring rain. It's important to mention the rain as this was going to become a problem for this game. I didn't sleep well, thinking about what must have been going through the mind of the unfortunate person as he waited for the train to come down the line. I also felt great sympathy for the train driver and his colleagues as something like that must stay forever in your mind and would no doubt have an effect on them and their family for years to come.

When I woke in the morning the rain was still pouring down. I was driven to Stamford Bridge and on arrival decided to inspect the pitch straight away rather than accept the customary hospitality. What I saw disturbed me and I realised there were going to be serious problems unless work was started immediately. I went straight to my dressing room, donned my kit and football boots and went in search of groundstaff and a football. Incredibly I couldn't find either. What an amazing situation, I thought, a major sporting event, with Sky about to beam the game worldwide, and the referee couldn't find a ball to test the pitch or any groundstaff to try and help.

BETRAYAL

After demanding some sort of action I got three or four groundsmen rounded up by 1.40 p.m., with four garden forks in various states of repair. When you consider the money poured into football and the high-tech aspects of beaming the match across the world, it's rather fascinating that clubs are still operating with clapped-out pitchforks. Despite all the implications of calling a game off I was determined to be objective and single-minded about this decision. Aston Villa were top of the league at the time and both teams, particularly Chelsea with their foreign stars, had players on display worth many millions of pounds.

There were mini-lakes in one of the goalmouths and the centre circle. Most worrying of all was a big pool of water down one wing where water was dripping off the stand roof. By now players were starting to mill around, some like Dennis Wise and Desailly saying there was no problem, some like Frank Leboeuf just wanting to know what was happening. Little Zola said to me, 'It's OK ref,' and I replied, 'I'm worried you might drown, Gianfranco,' to which he gave one of his toothy smiles.

At 2 p.m. I decided to put everyone out of their misery and called the game off. Of course, I hadn't reckoned on the reaction of Ken Bates, the Chelsea chairman. I like to think that the bombastic Ken is simply enthusiastic and that his bark is worse than his bite. Mind you, his bark can be pretty fearsome! At the time of the cancellation, Ken was lunching with Richard Attenborough in the Executive suite and only found out about the postponement through the public address system. By the time the Tannoy had finished the message, Ken had appeared at the pitchside frothing at the mouth. 'What a waste of a good lunch,' I thought to myself, whilst Ken proceeded to throw a tantrum. With his arms waving wildly around in the air, he was intent on reminding everyone who owned the '******* club!'

I decided it might be a good moment to go and speak to the press, and spent an hour in the press room giving the media something to write about. There were reporters from France, Italy and Spain as well as the English press. By the time I showered, changed and went upstairs it was 4.45 and the rain was still pouring down. I felt vindicated in the course of action I had taken but I guess there is always an element of luck in these decisions. It would no doubt have been a different story if the rain had stopped and the sun had come out, as sometimes happens after you call a game off.

ONE NIGHT AT THE PALACE

My lift took me back to King's Cross and, probably owing to the bad weather, the roads were quiet. As I had arrived early for my train, I decided to go into the Great Northern Hotel for a drink. Within five minutes someone noticed my Premiership blazer and started a conversation, saying the Brentford game he had gone to had been called off as well and wasn't the rain a bummer. When we parted, like long-lost friends, he said it had always been his ambition to meet me and how nice it was to have done so, and parted saying, 'See you again, Mr Elleray.'

During this season I did a presentation to the Referees' Association on the subject of foreign players in the English game. In 1992, at the start of the season, there were only seventeen foreign players in the English League; the current figure is in excess of 250. As I said earlier, this must have an adverse effect on the development of the game in this country. If you consider that most of the foreigners play in the Premiership and that on any one day there are only enough places in the starting line-up for 209 players that puts the problem into perspective!

There is an argument that the introduction of foreign skills will have a beneficial effect in terms of bringing out similar techniques in our developing players. This may be the case but at the same time you can train and be coached as much as you like but there is no substitute for first team action. The influx of foreign players has also had a dramatic effect on referees. This is in terms of language problems and also temperament issues. The foreign players have a different approach, different expectations, and most of the time they have superstar status - whether this is justified or not. This can often make the referee the bad guy when someone takes a dive or feigns exaggerated contact if the referee interprets it incorrectly.

On the other hand, the imported players invariably bring colour and flair to the game. One such player is David Ginola, whom I first came across at Paris St Germain and then of course at Newcastle and Spurs. The man is a footballing genius and a genuine nice guy. But why, oh why, does such a strong athletic player go to ground so easily and sometimes when nobody has touched him? Does he have a habit of tripping over a blade of grass, or does he not know how to fasten his laces properly? He was a hero at Newcastle but even their fans would shout at him when he fell over for no reason. I think it is simply a cultural thing, the players on the continent being encouraged to gain advantage at any cost whereas the average British fan likes to see fair play and not what they would regard as cheating.

Other contributions from foreigners include the mesmerising skills of Dennis Bergkamp. I consider it a privilege to have seen at such close quarters what this man can do. One day I was admiring his control and vision and it was only when I watched the game later on Match Of The Day that I realised just how quickly he had performed these pieces of skill. Then there is Zola, perhaps fading in recent years but whose accuracy and vision are a joy to behold.

One foreign player who has brought some humour to the game is Gus Poyet of Chelsea. Gus is Uruguayan but speaks several languages. He displayed his humorous side to me during a game against Aston Villa. There are always periods in a game when for whatever reason all the free kicks and throw-ins seem to go one way for a while. This was the case in this particular game when for about ten minutes everything seemed to go to Villa. Suddenly, after a challenge, Frank Leboeuf went to ground either in genuine or exaggerated agony (it wouldn't surprise me if it had been the latter). I stopped the game to allow the trainer to come on and I was standing around talking to Dennis Wise, Paul Merson, Didier Deschamps and Marcel Desailly about 'namby-pamby foreigners'. Fortunately Deschamps and Desailly have a limited command of English. Poyet suddenly burst into the company and shouted, 'You give us nothing ref, you give us a free kick, two free kicks or three free kicks or I kill you.' The look on everyone's face was a picture, with even Dennis Wise standing open-mouthed. Then suddenly there was a shrug of the shoulders and a smile and everyone burst out laughing. After that I couldn't help smiling every time I passed Poyet during the game. What they would have made of his comment in South America I'm not sure as I understand that it's now a criminal offence to shout 'Shoot the ref' after someone did just that.

This, my penultimate season, was progressing quietly, which I suppose was an indication that I was refereeing quite well and uncontroversially. The new fitness tests were in place and these added a new meaning to the term 'back on the treadmill'. I had to attend at Hillsborough on three occasions to carry out tests measuring fitness. The target was to arrive at a figure measured in VO2 max, whatever that might mean. The figure we were to aim for was ideally 50 or above. I was able to reach 47, which was considered more than acceptable. This measurement is arrived at by the experts attaching probes to the victim's chest and back and then placing a piece of breathing apparatus like that of an aqualung in your mouth and setting you off running on a treadmill. The speed increases to the point where you are unable to keep up with the pace and the reading taken at that point is the final measure. Other readings include haemoglobin and cholesterol and there is also an investigation into your diet over a three day period. The results are collated and you are given advice on how to reduce weight, etc. This helps to prove the point that referees don't just go out and run around on the day and that they have to take their fitness very seriously indeed.

A letter arrived from the FA at the end of March. Knowing it was semi-final time my heart was in my mouth as I picked up the letter. I was hoping against hope to get a semi. I tentatively opened the envelope and the blue booklet appeared together with the normal reply card. I could feel a little trickle of perspiration on my forehead and my heart was racing. As I read the text I could see 'semi- final, Manchester United versus Arsenal'. My heart leapt and then I noticed the small print 'reserve referee'. I went cold for a moment but then I thought how arrogant it was to expect a semi when there are many capable referees competing for the honour. I rapidly decided it was a privilege to be invited to participate at all.

It really did turn out to be a privilege as the first game was drawn and I was treated to two wonderfully exciting games. The replay turned out to be a piece of soccer memorabilia with that wonderful Ryan Giggs goal. He ran from his own half, beating at least four Arsenal players on the way, before despatching an unstoppable shot past the England keeper David Seaman. This was all the more dramatic as United were down to ten men at the time with Roy Keane having been sent off.

It was a wonderful experience to be present at such a memorable event and I am sure that the Giggs' goal will be shown on TV for many years to come. Like 50,000 others I will be able to say, ' I was there.' The only thing spoiling the occasion was the news that I had received on my mobile phone just before the game advising me that Carl Finch had died. I was devastated and again it put everything else into perspective. I decided not to tell the match officials before the game as I felt it would affect their concentration and they had a very important job to do. After the match, the referee and his team were euphoric at the way the game had gone and I let a period of time pass before I broke the grim news to them. They were as devastated as myself and agreed that I had done the right thing in keeping the news from them until the time was right.

Carl's funeral was attended by many people from all walks of the footballing community, so many, in fact, that the service had to be relayed outside the church. It was a highly emotional affair which left me very upset at the loss of a dear friend.

After this, I was badly in need of a pick-me-up and it duly arrived in the guise of a phone call from a chap called Joe Guest, the Referees' Officer of the FA. He started off by saying, 'I understand you like to keep mementoes from games you've done.' 'Yes,' I replied. 'Would you like a match ball from the F.A. Trophy Final?' he added. 'Of course,' I replied. 'Just one thing,' he said, 'you have to referee it first - you have been appointed to referee the Final at Wembley on 15 May, congratulations.'

Well, to the average Premiership and Football League fan, the Trophy may not seem like a big deal. However, to countless thousands of people all over the country who support their local non-league side this is a very big event indeed. When a local team makes it through to Wembley it brings a huge amount of civic pride and is wonderful for boosting morale, often in depressed areas. It is not unusual when driving around the country to see a town decked out with pennants and flags in their club's colours in the weeks before the final. Of course, any appointment at Wembley is a fantastic honour and I was on cloud nine for some time with this wonderful news. I couldn't help thinking of my Dad and how proud he would have been at the thought of 'his lad' refereeing at Wembley.

Before the final I had a date as fourth official at Middlesbrough who were playing Manchester United in the Premiership. My sister had just told me that my niece Gabrielle was a keen David Beckham fan and wondered whether I might be able to get his autograph for her. When I got home I switched on the computer and ran off a blank copy of a certificate with all sorts of stuff about Gabrielle, leaving space at the bottom for Beckham's signature.

On the day of the game I wondered how I would approach this as I had never before, as a referee, asked for an autograph. I was going out for a warm-up when I bumped into Beckham, who was doing the same. I mentioned the autograph to him and he replied that he would do it later. 'Fine chance,' I thought. After the game we were having a debrief in the referee's room when there was a knock on the door and Beckham walked in. He very politely interrupted and said, 'Excuse me, did you want me to sign something?' I got his signature, a young lady was made very happy and I registered a great deal of respect for Beckham in the way he had behaved with great humility and consideration. The young man takes a lot of stick and it is nice to know that he can be a polite and approachable individual.

The literature arrived for the Trophy Final: 'Travel down on the Friday night, stay at White's Hotel, Bayswater, do the match on Saturday and then you're free to go.' This surprised me as I thought it would be a two night stay, taking into account the travelling commitments. I decided to check with Joe Guest and was told that the details were correct and that, due to budget cuts, the FA Trophy officials would stay at Whites on the Friday and the FA Vase officials on the Saturday. A little ironic, I thought, when you see the escalating pay figures of players these days, but I wasn't going to dwell on it and let it spoil my big day. In fact, I had decided to have a blow-out on this one and had decided to take down the family, stay Saturday evening and book a meal for a party of sixteen family and friends at my favourite Italian restaurant in Lancaster Gate.

Having decided to be extravagant we travelled by train, first class, on the Friday. All the match officials met up together with their respective families and we decided we were going to have a fun weekend. The Friday evening was spent at a special dinner kindly organised by the Amateur Football Association for the match officials. This consisted of lots of speeches and photographs but was a very pleasant occasion.

On Saturday morning, we had breakfast and I exchanged autographs with Peter Andre, the Australian pop star, who was sitting at the next table and who was fascinated that I was going to be refereeing at Wembley in the afternoon. A black Daimler limousine then arrived to pick up the officials with another following for families. This indeed was a mighty day out.

I tried to be chatty as usual but this is difficult when you have butterflies in your stomach, your chest feels as if it's about to burst and your mouth is dry. The route is now etched in my mind. We drove through the streets with a little glimpse of the stadium here and there, then it was gone again. Pubs were busy with supporters, equally intending to enjoy a good day out. Around the roundabout at the side of the Wembley Hilton and then, as the car drew into the car park, it stopped directly underneath the twin towers, a football symbol all over the world.

This was a mind-blowing experience. Into the banqueting hall, and a break in tradition was allowed: the wives were permitted to wander around with us and we took them to the dressing rooms and onto the pitch. They got a good insight of behind the scenes and discovered the real size of the enormous Wembley pitch. Then it was time for the families to separate and the match officials to return to the dressing room for a massage from a local physio employed by the FA for the day. The business was about to start.

At 2.20 p.m. we took to the pitch for a warm-up. This was a referee's warm-up with a difference as we took a ball out with us. This turned out to be a source of amusement to the fans but I wasn't going to miss the opportunity of saying I had kicked a ball around on the famous Wembley turf. Back in the dressing rooms we were directed to be ready and at the tunnel by 2.52. At 2.50 I rang the bell: this is the moment of truth, I thought. 'No going back now,' as I had told myself on previous big occasions.

As I stood at the head of the tunnel I was worried in case I was grinning like a Cheshire cat; that's certainly the way I felt. The word was given and it was down to me to lead everyone out. Walking through the extendable Wembley tunnel is a strange experience: as you walk up the gentle slope, the inside of the stadium appears as a small orifice at the end of the tunnel. The light at the end of the tunnel, quite literally. All my effort over all those years and here I was leading two teams out onto the most famous pitch in world soccer. What a feeling!

On emerging from the tunnel you are immediately hit by the vast expanse of space and in fact it takes three minutes to get from the tunnel to the centre circle. This gives plenty of time for thought and all sorts of things ran through my mind: family, friends, doubts, more doubts and then the need to be extremely positive. On arrival at the centre circle we were introduced to the guest of honour, Jimmy Greaves. Hardly royalty, but some might think a more suitable choice! I have nothing against royalty adding to the atmosphere and occasion of a Cup Final but you do sometimes wonder whether they even know what sport they're watching.

Jimmy Greaves, in any event, is one of English soccer's great heroes. I can recollect some of the brilliant goals he scored back in the 1960s and

ONE NIGHT AT THE PALACE

70s. I remember vividly one goal in particular, unfortunately against Newcastle, when he ran half the length of the field, passing Bobby Moncur, the Scottish national team captain, as if he wasn't there and then leaving Willie McFaul, the United keeper, stranded as he rounded him at speed. He also scored an amazing 44 goals in just 57 appearances for England, including 13 in one season.

Jimmy's sense of humour also appeals to me. I found myself thinking back to the days when he used to co-host the TV programme 'Saint and Greavsie' on Saturday lunchtimes. Referring to when Brian Clough got into a fracas with a supporter Jim made reference to this being 'the first time the fan has hit the shit!' Another memorable snippet from those days was just after Saint had been banned from driving and was no doubt hoping to keep the news low-profile. As the show opened, the first thing Jimmy said to a very sheepish St John was, 'Did you have long to wait for a bus, Saint?' What a character, and what a privilege to meet him under such circumstances.

It was now time for the National Anthem, which was sung with enthusiasm by the 27,000 fans - out of time, but with enthusiasm. The teams were introduced, Kingstonian from London and Forest Green from Gloucestershire. Both are giants in the amateur world, with Kingstonian in particular having a very famous background. Just as I was about to start the game a Kingstonian player asked, 'Was that you who sent off Cantona at Palace, ref? What a night that must have been!' Like it or not, that incident was to remain infamous and a talking point whenever I met people, even in the centre circle at Wembley.

The game was played with lots of skill and endeavour but it remained goal-less at half time. Then, after 70 minutes the deadlock was broken with a cracking drive from the edge of the area by Tarkan Mustafa, the Kingstonian full-back. I would imagine that would be a moment that sticks in his memory for the rest of his life. No more goals were scored and Kingstonian were the victors. Now it was time for collecting the medals.

Climbing the thirty-nine steps to do this is a wonderful feeling, the pinnacle of anyone's career. You see faces you know in the crowd, people from clubs and Football Associations, as well as family and friends. For a moment I felt as if I had arrived in heaven. When I reached the platform there was Greavsie handing out the medals and, as he gave me mine, he said

166

in his well known Cockney accent, 'I'd like to say well done ref.' There was a pause as I waited for the punchline, but when I eventually thanked him he said, 'No, I mean it, bloody well done, you had a great game.' He then turned to the chap next to him and said, 'I don't believe I've just said that to a bloody referee.'

It was only when I got back to the dressing room and opened a bottle of champagne that I realised how tired I was. In walked Joe Guest with the match ball to add to my medal and my day was complete.

After picking up the family it was off to book in at a different hotel and get ready for our night out. When we were sat down at our table for sixteen at the Concordia Restaurant I was amused to see Joe and the FA Vase officials at a nearby table. While our table made merry, Joe and company were having a very sober time on soft drinks and quiet discussion. I guess we tormented them quite a bit seeing as we were in very high spirits. A good end to a good day.

We returned to our hotel where we managed to consume another couple of bottles of champagne before retiring. We got up the next morning bright and early - well, perhaps early - and headed off to Kings Cross to get the 9 a.m. train so that I could be fourth official at the Newcastle v Blackburn game. There was no way I wanted to be anything more than fourth official on this day in view of the way I was feeling. I had a nasty moment or two just before the game when Jeff Winter approached me, following his warm up, to say that he felt a twinge in his suspect calf muscle. I was mortified and replied, 'You must be ******* joking.' He was quite serious, however, and told me to be on standby to take over. This was quite literally a sobering experience and I was hugely relieved that he managed to last the match.

The close season had arrived and with it a new set of instructions from the Premiership hierarchy in terms of fitness tests. It was now decreed that we would have to be capable of sprinting 50 metres in under 7.5 seconds, twice, followed by 200 metres in under 32 seconds, twice, and finally covering at least 2700 metres in 12 minutes. This came as a bombshell to me as I was approaching my forty-eighth birthday and my last season. I didn't see any problem with the 50 metre dash or the 12-minute run but I was a bit concerned about the 200 metres. Still, I thought, I'm going to have to go for it.

ONE NIGHT AT THE PALACE

The Riverside at Chester-le-Street, now home to the Durham County Cricket Club and one of the most scenic grounds in county cricket, was to be my training ground. As this was also where Newcastle United trained I would be doubly inspired. My first attempt at the 50 metres amounted to seven seconds so I reasoned that with a little bit of work there should be no problem with doing this twice. The first attempt at 200 metres was 35 seconds with the second being 34 seconds. I think panic set in at this stage and thereafter this distance caused me to hit something of a brick wall.

I decided to have no break from training and indeed to step it up to work on the 200 metre sprint. Everything was going quite well and I had it down to 32/33 seconds when disaster struck. As I raced around a bend I felt a pain like being shot in my left leg. It was my hamstring, my worst fears coming true. Fortunately I took the right action and stopped immediately, getting ice on the leg at the earliest opportunity. I would have to rely on the physio to do the rest.

This was in May and I had my fitness test proper scheduled for June. I panicked again when I reminded myself that this was my last season. If the injury was to persist, everything could be fouled up and I might never get the chance to referee in the top flight again. This appalling thought made me all the more determined to achieve the targets set. The treatment was laborious and painful and although I managed to resume light training after two weeks it was restricted to the 12-minute run.

After four weeks I was able to start sprinting again but I was nowhere near my best. The fitness test had to be postponed twice and was eventually rescheduled for 3 August. Talk about cutting it fine - my first game was due to be Arsenal v Leicester on 7 August. If I failed the test it would be at least another month before I would be allowed to take it again. This would mean missing six games, games which I would never be able to catch up on in view of my impending forced retirement.

When the time for the test came I decided to go down to Loughborough the night before and stay in at a hotel near the University to ensure that I arrived as fresh as possible rather than drive down on the day. Of course luck would have it that the next room in the hotel seemed to be occupied by a couple who were doing their own fitness tests all night.

On the 3rd, I was hoping for rain as this would help to cool me down. Instead I got blazing sunshine and temperatures in the 80s. The track at

Loughborough is bowl-shaped and there is no respite from the heat of the sun, particularly when there is no breeze to speak of. The start and the finish of the runs were being timed by laser technology so it was all very exact with no room for 'Well you nearly made it, Al, let's say you squeezed in.' I was determined to show, in any case, that I could do the necessary and that no new regulations were going to stop me.

One advantage I had on this occasion was that I was in competition and I had someone running alongside me. I achieved the 50 metres requirement with no problems. My first attempt at the 200 ended in 30 seconds - two seconds within the time-frame allowed. Now I had to do it again after a short rest. This was my last chance, I just had to do it. Although 200 metres doesn't normally seem like a long way it seemed like a marathon and I was gasping for air and feeling dizzy. I could hear everyone shouting, 'Come on, come on, you can do it.' With one last push I crossed the finish line in 31 seconds - 1 second within the required time.

A huge sense of relief, not to mention euphoria, spread throughout my entire body and now I knew I only had the 12-minute run to do. This distance was more my forte and I actually offered to pace the others so that they could get through in time. At the finish I had covered a more than adequate 2850 metres and passed the test.

Off we went to the Students' Union bar for a well earned reward of bacon, eggs, chips and beans. On the way, I wondered if subconsciously, during training, I had been saying to myself that the minute I passed the fitness test then my last season would be under way and that my mind had been rebelling against this reality. Perhaps there was the more accurate realisation that I was getting too old for it all.

13

THE JOY AND THE PAIN

HAVING SPENT THE SUMMER getting through the fitness test, I was now able to concentrate on preparing for what would be my last season as a referee. My enjoyment in this season would be enhanced by another change in the rules, this time to the benefit of officials.

It had been decided that referees appointed to a game more than 120 miles from their home would be required to stay overnight in a hotel provided and paid for by the Premier League. This was another sensible measure to achieve increased professionalism and try to take some of the strain off the officials. It would enable all the match officials to meet four hours before the kick off and be transported by people-carrier to the ground. The new system was, for me, tremendous. I usually stayed overnight beforehand in any event but now it was officially organised and the accommodation would be in better hotels than I was used to.

It was down to London for the Arsenal v Leicester game, my first of the season, and I stayed at the splendid Hendon Hall Hotel with the rest of the officials. I was able to utilise the meeting on the Saturday morning to go through my match briefing and explain what I required of my colleagues and how we would work together as a team. We then got on the 'team bus' and enjoyed a comfortable journey to Highbury. All the pressure and stress of driving through the centre of London was removed and we arrived at the ground feeling comfortable and relaxed.

The game turned out to be somewhat dour and the most difficult aspect of the day turned out to be in having to differentiate between had Heskey 'fallen' or 'was he pushed?' The problem confronting referees with players going to ground easily is that sometimes we get the legitimate ones wrong, as was the case in this game. Heskey had been on the floor about six times already when he competed with Grimandi of Arsenal in an aerial challenge, resulting yet again with him falling to the ground. I determined there had been no offence and allowed play to continue. Seconds later the ball was kicked out of play by Arsenal and I asked Heskey whether he required treatment. He said he did as he had hurt his neck. Although somewhat sceptical I allowed the physio to come on and to my surprise and consternation Heskey was removed on a stretcher wearing a neck brace.

I had been really cheesed off with Heskey and had thought he was trying to con me yet again and I therefore felt somewhat guilty when he was taken off to hospital. It was a classic case, though, of someone crying wolf once too often.

Although Leicester deserved a draw they were beaten by an own goal in injury time. After the game I wondered whether I would ever be back to Highbury and, in the uncertainty, decided to say my farewells to everyone associated with the club. This was to be a long season of farewells and these first ones made me feel quite emotional.

I was in reasonable shape considering I had spent half the summer trying to recover from injury and I had not had any pre-season matches at all. I was now working hard on trying to regain my form and fitness and I am pleased to say that my efforts would prove successful.

On the horizon loomed Liverpool v Watford and another encounter with Graham Taylor. Fortunately this time I would not need to speak to him as the excellent Kenny Jacket had taken over the role of communicating with the officials. I can't say I was disappointed at not having to deal with the smirksome Taylor.

The game itself would go down as one of the greatest smash and grabs I have seen. After an early goal on the break from Watford, Liverpool used all their might to try and steamroller the opposition, only for them to be thwarted time and again by the resistance forces operating under Watford's colours, marshalled by central defenders Robert Page and Mark Williams. Watford survived heroically and walked away with the three points, much to the dismay of the Kop.

One of the interesting aspects of this season was the introduction of radio headsets. The experiment was brought in at the start of the season in August, but by November it was in total disarray. Some referees were allowed to stop using them but I agreed to persevere until the end of the season to ensure the system was given every chance. To the average fan, it probably appeared simply a case of the referee putting on a headset a few minutes before he took to the pitch. The reality was that the equipment arrived in a bright yellow metal case and consisted of three radios, a headset, microphone and charger. The assistants would each have a headset and waist belt. Initially the sets wouldn't work and they all had to be reprogrammed. They also had to be encrypted to avoid external sources picking up what was being said. Not a big concern really as they wouldn't transmit in the first place!

Eventually the technical problems were overcome and, with a thorough reception check pre-match, they did work. The big problem, from the referee's point of view, was not only that these things were bulky and heavy but also that there was a set procedure to follow. It was necessary to press the 'speak' button, speak, say 'over' when finished, then let go of the button (one button depressed stopped all the others transmitting). Anyone who has ever refereed a game at any level will appreciate that in the middle of a game you need to concentrate tightly on the game and not on things such as radio procedures. The experiment was therefore doomed to failure and was abandoned at the end of the season, much to everyone's relief.

Another significant change to the laws of the game empowered the fourth official to bring to the attention of the referee anything which occurs on the field of play which has gone unnoticed by the three officials relating to serious foul play or violent conduct. At this time he would use a new hand-held device to 'buzz' the referee. This was something I welcomed and came about as one of the positive impacts television coverage has had on the game.

Back home in the North East the local television company, Tyne-Tees, had expressed a wish to accompany me to a Premiership match, filming from home to ground, and then back home again. I sought permission for this from the Premier League and this was granted, except for any filming in the ground as the Premiership contract with Sky precluded this. A bit petty, I thought, but never mind, who am I to comment on big business deals? The game they chose was Coventry City, a team I had not refereed at all in the previous season, versus Manchester United.

The television crew arrived at 9 a.m. on the day of the match and asked for a shot of me in the house sitting on the three-piece suite. I was a bit embarrassed to have to tell them that I didn't have a suite as I had just moved house and we were actually living on sun-loungers at the time! As that was out, they therefore decided on some tacky shot with red and yellow cards and then a shot of me getting the car out of the garage. A cameraman accompanied me for twenty miles as a passenger in my car, filming as I drove. I dropped him off at a rendezvous point and sped on to the hotel, followed by the rest of the crew. They filmed the pre-match meeting scenario, carried out an interview with me, did a short piece at the ground and then, after the game, concluded with a short piece back at the hotel.

The film was due to be shown the following Sunday and I looked forward to seeing it. It was, in fact, put back three times for some reason. They did eventually run it three weeks later and to my amazement it contained interviews with Alex Ferguson and Gordon Strachan. Although I was unaware they were going to do this it worked out all right as I must have had a half-decent game in view of the comments they made. Neither of these two fiery characters is renowned for their generosity of praise for referees. Strachan said, 'It was a good performance from the referee; it was nice to see a referee not wanting to be the centre of attention.' Ferguson said, 'Yes, he had a good game, he's getting better with experience.' Coming from Alex it's difficult to know how to take that but I'm happy to accept it as a compliment.

The season was flying by and so much was happening on and off the field, new house and all that goes with it, last season of refereeing, thoughts about the future etc. My mind was in a whirl. Soon it was October and I was handed two very contrasting fixtures within four days. The first game was Halifax v York City. This was a Yorkshire derby and I thought there would be a bit of tension. I wasn't wrong.

When I arrived at the ground I was talking to a local chap who was telling me about the bad blood between the teams. Apparently three Halifax players had fallen out with the player/coach Peter Butler and had transferred to York. This indicated the possibility of an evening of retribution and revenge. At the pre-match briefing I was instructing everyone to be vigilant and to be aware of the situation. At this point the door opened and in walked three scruffy-looking individuals. I was about to give them a piece of my mind when one of them said, 'Don't throw us out, we're police officers' and with this he produced a warrant card. 'We're here to make sure nothing happens in the tunnel area' and he went on to elaborate on what I had already heard. It's nice to know that the police were so on top of the situation but it reinforced the sort of tensions that must be existing. I mentally thanked the Football League for giving me this plum game! Seriously, I suppose I was flattered that they felt fit to appoint me to handle such a potentially fiery encounter.

The atmosphere in the tunnel was tense but I was watching everything like a hawk as I led the teams out onto the pitch. I didn't say anything out of the ordinary to the captains at the toss-up and the game got under way with York kicking off. The ball was immediately booted upfield and I observed the three York players in question homing in on the Halifax player/coach. To their amazement they found me right on the spot ready to observe any misdemeanours. I think they got the message and they backed off. It was a tension-filled night with lots of errors but with a lot of endeavour and a fair share of physical encounters. Although nothing serious took place it was no surprise that the four yellow cards I had to produce that night went to the three York players and Peter Butler.

For the end of the game I had arranged for one of my colleagues to be in the tunnel and the other at the entrance to the tunnel. However, when I got there they were not in sight. The next thing I knew I was in the changing room myself, having been whisked away by the police in the same way that my colleagues had apparently been despatched a few minutes earlier. Although we were unable to witness any of the events in the tunnel, the noise of raised voices and people being 'moved' around could clearly be heard. The police were obviously anxious to deal with any trouble in their own way without the match officials having to be involved. Soon afterwards the police returned and said, 'Job done, nothing to report, we're off now.'

The second part of the double bill of fixtures was altogether different. From a grim Yorkshire dog-fight I was moving on to a high profile London derby in the form of Chelsea v Arsenal. I travelled by rail to Richmond in Surrey and booked in at the very nice Richmond Hill Hotel. I was thoroughly enjoying the luxurious benefits of the new travelling arrangements. In the evening I went down into Richmond for an Italian meal, taking advantage of everything the good food guides say about pasta being what you need to store up energy. I made sure I had my share and also felt obliged to indulge in a little red wine as I understand this too is good for the constitution.

THE JOY AND THE PAIN

The meeting the following morning was great fun as this season we were working in pre-selected groups. This meant that we got to know each other very well and consequently there was much more leg-pulling and humorous intervention. This, I am sure, creates a healthy atmosphere and good teamwork amongst the referee and his colleagues. Into the bus and off we went towards Stamford Bridge. The traffic was horrendous and it took an hour and a quarter to travel seven miles. Eventually we arrived and to my dismay it was raining heavily. I had recollections of my last visit here when Bill and Ben and their little forks couldn't stem the floods gathered on the pitch. I got a distinct feeling of déjà vu and prayed that I wouldn't be faced with a similar dilemma today. Like that last game this was to be televised live on Sky internationally, but not in England.

I went for a cup of tea and the security man, Paul Hater, who I know well, said, 'I think you should go and have a look at the pitch.' 'Bugger off!' I replied. Paul responded to this with a genuine impassioned plea to go and have a look. To be honest I think there was part of me which just didn't want to go out there, something subconscious wanted to stop me from seeing what I didn't want to see. I summoned up the courage to go down the tunnel and, on reaching the pitch, discovered to my dismay that the heavens had opened and the rain was coming down in sheets. This time, however, the ground staff were much better prepared and they were coping very well with a sodden pitch which featured occasional puddles.

The game went ahead and full credit was due to everyone involved for getting the match under way. And boy, was it worth it, what a game. For long periods Arsenal were completely missing from the game and this allowed Chelsea to coast into a two goal lead. With about fifteen minutes to go I penalised an Arsenal player and Davor Suker said to me, 'But ref, relax, the game's over.' Moments later Kanu managed to pull one back for Arsenal and Suker ran past me on his way back to the centre spot saying, 'Maybe, just maybe.' A few minutes later Kanu grabbed the equaliser and Suker ran past me shaking his fist and shouting, 'Game on ref, game on.'

The best was yet to come. From a hopeful crossfield pass, Kanu chased Albert Ferrer towards the corner flag. Under pressure Ferrer kicked the ball against Kanu and it rebounded into the corner flag area. Ferrer was grounded and Kanu gave chase, collecting the ball beside the goal-line and the corner flag. Ed De Goey, the Chelsea keeper, had come out of his area to close the distance between him and Kanu. He suddenly thought better of this and started back-pedalling towards his own area so that he would be able to use his hands. Kanu, closing in, and now being confronted by De Goey, sold him a wonderful dummy and moved through the small gap vacated by him. There was a seemingly impossible angle between Kanu and the goal which was guarded by two defenders standing on the goal line. The next event is best encapsulated in the words of the Sky commentator, Martin Tyler: 'What's he going to do now? Score, that's what!'

Kanu had somehow contrived to wrap his size 14 boots around the ball and curl his shot over the heads of two defenders to score what can only be described as the best goal I have ever seen. It was a phenomenal piece of skill and was made all the more dramatic in that it sealed an Arsenal victory, coming from two goals down with only fifteen minutes left. It was also Kanu's hat-trick. Amazing.

The Kanu goal reminded me once again that foreign players do bring wonderful skills to our game, and my next match of consequence was also to feature imported talents very considerably. The game was West Ham v Sheffield Wednesday at Upton Park. A piece of added spice here was that Paolo Di Canio had left Wednesday in acrimonious circumstances and was now about to face them for the first time as a West Ham player. In a wonderful piece of diplomacy Harry Redknapp had decided to make Paolo the West Ham captain for the day.

I was looking forward to the game because I felt that Wednesday's lowly League position belied the way they were playing and I knew that West Ham always try to play football. I was pleased this was another televised game because the viewers, as well as myself, were to be treated to a seven goal spectacular. There was also plenty of incident, some of it involving me. I had to send off Danny Sonner of Wednesday for a foul on Di Canio, the yellow card being Sonner's second of the game. Wednesday insisted Di Canio had dived but my belief was that Sonner had caught him so I had no choice and off he went. It was 2-1 to Wednesday when Trevor Sinclair raced into the box and Wim Jonk stuck out a foot. Down went Sinclair, he had been tripped, I awarded a penalty and no-one complained. Di Canio scored to make it 2-2. Andy Booth then powered in a superb third for Wednesday. What entertainment! When would it all stop? The game eventually ended with West Ham the winners by four goals to three.

THE JOY AND THE PAIN

I was making my way back to the dressing room when a Sky employee shouted, 'Sinclair dived for the penalty, Alan.' 'No way,' I responded. 'Come and have a look,' he said. Intrigued, I went to the interview area where the monitors were located and was shown a view of the incident from the rear view camera. Sure enough it was clear that as soon as Jonk made a move to tackle, Sinclair dived. In effect he had conned me. As this had decided the result of the game, it was particularly disastrous for Wednesday, who were eventually relegated. I was upset at having been deceived and felt really bad about it.

Back at the hotel I was having a drink when who should walk in but Trevor Sinclair. Now, I've known Trevor since his days at Blackpool so I shouted over to him, 'Hey, what's this diving in the box, Trevor?' I found his response interesting. 'I was just trying to get out of the way,' he said, 'I hope I haven't caused you any embarrassment.' 'Not me,' I said, 'I'm used to being called a prat, it's yourself you've embarrassed.' With that thought we parted company.

I would like to think that the incident might influence Trevor in the future. It would be interesting to know, however, whether such gamesmanship is instigated by a player's own personality and values or whether they are pressurised by managers, coaches or team-mates in seeking to deceive the referee.

The season was now half-way through and it was time for my second health check. So another day off work, thank you British Telecom for your understanding, and off to the Holme Pierrepoint National Centre for Watersports near Nottingham. The results turn out to be slightly down on the previous check, quite normal at this stage of the season, I was informed. I asked for a training schedule as I wanted to show an improvement when it came to the time for the third and final check. The old man wanted to go out on a high note rather than being perceived as unfit and over the hill.

On a freezing cold Tuesday night in December I found myself in Lancashire, heading for the Reebok Stadium in Bolton for a Worthington Cup 5th Round tie. The prizes were getting bigger at this stage of the season and the reward for the evening's victors would be a place in the semi-final. Having never been to the Reebok before I got a real thrill as a view of the stadium opened up in front of me from the motorway. The design is fantastic and the structure looks like a spaceship from a distance, I found myself humming the theme music from 'Close Encounters' as I approached. On arrival I found that the stadium is every bit as impressive as it looks. A splendid effort by Bolton and their architects, the only thing letting the side down being the pitch. The surface was threadbare in places and appeared to have transplants from Blackpool beach in many parts. As Bolton were playing Wimbledon I joked to my colleagues that the state of the pitch would be irrelevant to the Londoners as the ball would be in the air all the time. This was probably an unfair comment but it's hard to shake off old reputations.

It was a snowy, freezing evening but the pitch was made playable due to the undersoil heating. Here was an interesting situation, normally the referee leads both teams out but at the Reebok there are two tunnels, one for the home team and one for the visitors. I decided to resolve this by getting the fourth official and the senior assistant to lead out Bolton, while the other assistant and I would lead out the visitors. The game started, as might have been expected, with Wimbledon, as the Premiership side, imposing their authority as they took the lead through Carl Cort in the first ten minutes. Although I thought Bolton were about to be overrun, I reckoned without Eidur Gudjohnsen, a player I had not really seen before. He was beginning to become a one-man threat to Wimbledon and he exploded into devastating action mid-way through the first half, carrying the ball past four defenders in a mazy run into the penalty area, leaving himself with just Neil Sullivan to beat. He did this with ease to score a goal which was a genuine contender for goal of the season.

This gave Bolton a boost of confidence and in the 38th minute Bob Taylor was moving to head the ball in the penalty area when I detected a shirt-pull which prevented him getting his feet off the ground. I awarded a penalty, which was duly despatched, putting Bolton 2-1 in front. As we trooped off for half-time the Wimbledon lads were saying, 'That was a tough call Al, watch the video later and you'll be embarrassed.' This was amongst other unmentionable pleasantries, of course.

I didn't have time to worry about this as my mind was taken off it by a comment from one of my assistants saying he had pulled a calf muscle. We spent the half-time break getting treatment for him at the same time as I was making arrangements for him to be replaced by the fourth official. The trickiest part however was to be replacing the fourth official.

THE JOY AND THE PAIN

The call went out over the Tannoy asking if there was any qualified referee in the ground, and if so, could he or she please report to reception. Eventually, one of the Bolton stewards, complete with luminous jacket, came to the dressing room and volunteered his services. I then spent the next ten minutes of the now extended half-time interval explaining how to operate the electronic substitute board and outlining the other duties he would have to perform. This completed, we took the field and started the second half.

As we were taking the field I passed Sam Hamman, the Wimbledon owner, who delighted me by saying, 'Don't worry Alan, it was a definite penalty, no problem.' This was much appreciated and demonstrated Sam's genuine qualities, particularly when it was the incident which ended up costing Wimbledon the match and a place in the semi-final at Wembley.

On the way home I was doing the usual, analysing in my mind every decision, every tackle, and every comment. It suddenly dawned on me that there weren't going to be many more nights like this. This feeling of sadness was to become a recurring theme throughout the rest of the season. Although it was a desperate feeling I undertook to remain positive and decided to enjoy every minute of every game I had left.

Christmas came around once again and I decided to continue my sequence of Boxing Day appointments, making it eleven out of sixteen. Most of these had necessitated me leaving home on Christmas Day and this would be no exception. I was off to Derby for a Midlands clash with Aston Villa. I think the players must have eaten too much turkey, they certainly played like turkeys, and I wondered whether I should just have stayed at home and played with my Christmas presents. I was pleased that the crowd had a good time. They were in festive spirit with their seasonal songs and colourful outfits which made it seem almost worthwhile.

I woke up on 1 January thinking, 'My God, it's 2000.' We had survived Armageddon but for me I was fearing much worse than that. I was now really on countdown to retirement and the thought scared me.

My first appointment of the new millennium was a trip to London for the Spurs v Liverpool fixture on 3 January. This was to be a difficult game as George Graham had his players really wound up for this one and Liverpool were on a run of fine form. On the pitch the movement was fast and furious and the skill levels, as you would expect, were very high.

However, the gamesmanship was at an even higher level than the skill factor and it became very difficult to determine what were genuine fouls and what was play-acting. On one side we had Smicer, Berger and Camara all falling over as if shot by a high velocity rifle and on the other we had Iversen, Tarrico and Freund all blowing around like paper bags in the wind. They all made Ginola look big and strong, which he was on this occasion, as it happened. He was at times unstoppable. When people like David play to the best of their ability like this it is a privilege to be on the same pitch and to be in a position to view the speed of movement and thought.

Spurs ran out 1-0 winners but the game could have gone either way. Despite the fact that Spurs won the game I had still apparently upset George Graham with four yellow cards for his team. George had long since ceased complaining personally to me about such things as he could obviously see I wasn't going to bow to his whims and that I would continue to apply the laws of the game in an impartial manner. Instead he adopted a different approach in saving his comments for the official report which all managers make out after the game. He decided to mark me 1 out of 10, the bottom mark possible. Interestingly, the Liverpool camp, the team who had actually lost the game and to whom I had issued three yellow cards, gave me 9 out of 10 and made comments like 'totally impartial' and 'did not allow himself to be fooled by gamesmanship.'

The most disappointing thing I find about the sort of behaviour displayed by George is that managers who behave childishly like this when completing the match report miss the opportunity to be constructive. They reject the chance to help create a climate of communication and understanding. Most referees welcome a situation where they can accept feedback and then sit back and look at ways of improving their performance.

Interestingly, in the lounge after the game, I was talking to Martin Boddenham, the match observer, when David Pleat, Graham's Tottenham colleague, came over and interjected. Looking at Martin he said, 'What gives someone like you the right to assess a man of his quality, a man at the top of his profession and performing well?' With this he turned and walked away, leaving both Martin and myself bemused. I'm not sure what brought on the outburst but it seemed rather strange in view of the report Graham had given me.

THE JOY AND THE PAIN

Following the Spurs game I went down with flu, probably as a result of George Graham putting a curse on me. I missed the Arsenal v Leicester FA Cup game but bounced back the following week. I had decided to intensify my training as I had two games of great significance coming up and I was conscious that I would have been slightly weakened by the flu.

The first game was Aston Villa v Chelsea and if I say that the score was 0-0, then I have given the game more coverage than it deserves. There was one aspect of note, however, and that was the emergence of a young player called John Harley. John showed great maturity for his age and is someone I expect to see a lot of in the future. I remember hoping he was a good linguist otherwise he wouldn't have much company in that Chelsea team, apart from Dennis Wise, of course, who does try to speak a kind of English.

I was now looking forward to my next game, which would be Manchester United against Coventry City. The ground capacity at Old Trafford had just been expanded to 62,000 and this would create a new record for the Premiership. The game was scheduled for 5 February and I was gearing myself up mentally for the occasion at home on the Friday evening, when the phone rang. It was Jim Ashworth, the Football League Referees Officer.

After the usual preamble, and some waffle involving abbreviations like APL and FLMO, I was just about to tell him to cut the bullshit and get to the point. He pre-empted this, however, and continued 'You know you wanted to referee in London on the weekend of the 26/27 February. (I had requested this in the hope that I would then be able to stay over and watch the Worthington Cup Final) I think I can get you released from your fourth official appointment at Sunderland if you want me to,' he went on. I began to wonder what he might have in mind and started to think about who was playing at home that weekend. He then stunned me by adding, 'How do you fancy reffing the Worthington Cup Final?'

I was speechless. Yes, some people had tipped me for the game but there again I had become used to disappointments in this business. Nine years previously I had been tipped for the FIFA panel and six years previously I had actually been nominated, only to be rejected as too old at forty-two!

I took nothing for granted these days. After considering the situation for perhaps a tenth of a nanosecond I found my voice again and squeaked, 'Thanks Jim, I think I can fit that in.' I went on to tell him, in a more serious vein, that I would be greatly honoured and that I was very flattered by the invitation.

I went on to ask who would be my assistants. Jim said, 'Don't worry about that for the moment, just bask in the glory of the appointment. We'll be doing a press release about your appointment for tomorrow's papers and the rest of the team will be announced on Monday.' I think that is probably when it dawned on me that I was to be the first referee to take a match at Wembley with a female assistant, an historic event. It had to mean that Wendy Toms was deservedly going to be appointed to run the line for me.

What was clearly going through Jim's mind was that if the news of Wendy's appointment was released at this time it would overshadow my moment of glory. This was a considerate approach which I appreciated. It was also a judgment which was very sound, as would be proven by the reaction of the media to Wendy's appointment over the coming week.

Delighted as I was, I realised that I needed to focus on the immediate big game and I drove to Manchester with a big grin on my face. The phone rang almost continually that evening with well-wishers wanting to congratulate me. I was most grateful for people taking the time to do this and I was particularly touched when one of my assistants for the Manchester game, Alan Sheffield, appeared the next day with a card from himself and his wife Carol, accompanied by a bottle of Moët champagne. I was beginning to feel pretty emotional at this time; it was really great to have all these good wishes for the final but I began to realise that the burden of expectancy on me was going to be quite high. I started to wonder whether I was worthy of such an appointment when you consider the good referees around and the fact that many of them had never been to Wembley. Here was I being invited back for the fourth time.

I was aware of the support I would have from my family, friends and old colleagues such as the Gateshead Referees' Society, an organisation of which I had been the Chairman for seventeen years. I also felt emotional knowing how proud my father would have been. I put all of this to the back of my mind and concentrated on the job in hand the next day. And what a cracker it turned out to be.

THE JOY AND THE PAIN

Manchester United started slowly, as they often do, and Coventry looked quite good. Then United stepped it up a gear and smoothly moved into a two goal lead. Coventry pulled one back through Cedric Roussell and an exciting edge came into the game. United increased their lead to 3-1 and I expected that to be the end of the competition. However, Coventry kept at it and Roussell reduced the arrears once again to give United a nervous time in the last ten minutes. An uncomfortable victory for United but a cracking game.

The training schedule given to me by the experts was beginning to pay dividends and I was determined to be in the best possible shape for the Wembley appointment. I was training for at least an hour, four days a week, on top of one, or sometimes two, matches each week. What I didn't realise was that I was not letting my body get enough rest and that I was asking it to do too much.

My next game was the match between Middlesbrough and Aston Villa. This game was particularly important for Boro as they were in a lowly position in the league and the fans were becoming disenchanted with the management. I was looking forward to the game, not least because there were to be great individual talents on display in the guise of Benito Carbone and Paul Gascoigne. The latter would be particularly interesting as he possesses fantastic skills but because of his over-enthusiasm can be hard to handle.

The team-sheets confirmed both maestros were playing and I was extremely pleased. As the teams were lining up for kick-off I felt a nip on my backside. Without turning round I said, 'Whoever it is, you've got a week to get off.' Then, twisting my neck to see who it was behind me, I was not in the least surprised to see the beaming smile of Gazza. 'He's on form tonight,' I thought. 'He's on my side, this will be OK.' I'm afraid that conclusion turned out to be wildly incorrect.

After two minutes Paul tackled an opponent, hurting his own shin in the process. I offered some sympathy and the chance of some treatment but he indicated he just wanted to get on with things. He is a fighter, there's no doubt about that. The game was going really well for me but not for Boro, who were struggling at 2-0 down. Being at home, the tension was rising dramatically with the crowd getting restless. In the 39th minute the inevitable happened and the Gazza self-destruct button was pressed again.

ONE NIGHT AT THE PALACE

A clearance landed at the feet of George Boateng of Villa, who raced forward to mount an attack. He was being closed down by two Boro players, Gazza and Summerbell, and the next thing I knew there was a collision caused by a push from Summerbell. I awarded a free kick and went to take up a suitable position. Suddenly Boateng was clutching his face and it was clear he required immediate attention. At the same time Gazza appeared to be collapsing in stages, firstly grabbing his left arm in obvious pain. He was trembling and moaning, 'Aave broke me arm, aave broke me arm.' He was in some distress and only calmed down when the paramedics administered oxygen.

My immediate reaction at the scene, with Boateng holding his head and Gazza holding his arm, suggested to me that Gazza had been guilty of violent conduct and had I seen it I would have had to send him off. Fortunately George was alright and on reflection I am pleased that I didn't have to dismiss Gazza. Although he has been accurately described as 'daft as a brush' (by Bobby Robson, I believe) you can't help liking him and, as a person, he is the most genuine and generous individual you could wish to meet. Even while in tremendous pain and before the oxygen was administered he had gone across to Boateng and apologised and tried to see that he was OK.

What a pity that he has a wild, destructive streak. I am sure this is caused not through malevolence but by rushes of adrenalin due to his over-excitement. Unfortunately, this can have dire consequences for fellow professionals. The onus is on referees to ensure the protection of players from lunging tackles and flying elbows and in this respect I'm afraid Gazza is one player certain to keep the referee on his toes.

At the end of the day Villa ran out easy winners by four goals to nil. It had not been a good day for Boro in any sense, with a humiliating home defeat being exacerbated by Gazza's injury, which would keep him out for months.

Wembley was getting ever closer and the excitement reached new heights when the travelling details were received. I had lots to think about: I needed to make arrangements for tickets for the family and I had decided that as my mother had never seen me referee 'in the flesh' before, it would be fitting to get her to Wembley for my finest moment. However, in the end we agreed that as she was eighty years old it would not be reasonable to expect her to be able to manage the stairs at Wembley and we had to abandon the idea. Arrangements were made to ensure she would be in front of a TV showing the game; at least she would be there in spirit, as would my late father.

I increased my training yet again. As a result I was feeling tired a lot of the time and I was eating food like it was going out of fashion. I decided it was hard work, this getting old.

In the run-up to the final I had to visit what, for me, was new territory with a game at Northampton. Without disrespect to either team, I have to say that it was difficult to regard Northampton v Brighton as a major event when my mind was on Wembley. However, I was professional enough to realise that this game meant a lot to the followers and players of both teams and once I got my head around it I gave the game the same degree of importance as any other.

The season was not going to end at Wembley but it would be the pinnacle of my career. I had thought the FA Trophy final was a great honour but this appointment was second only to the FA Cup and would be accompanied by lots of hype and a capacity Wembley crowd. The TV and radio interest in the final was now building up and a lot of attention focused on Wendy and, to a degree, on my perception of women in football.

I happen to believe that if you're good enough it doesn't matter what gender, race or religion you are and I don't mind saying so. Unfortunately some of the avaricious media people, desperate for a controversial story, are prompting all the time for a slip of the tongue. They were pursuing not just Wendy and I on this subject, but also Paul Armstrong, the other assistant, and Phil Richards the fourth official. Fortunately we all managed to avoid embarrassment and, as the day approached, the situation became a non-issue.

By the Tuesday before the game I had given my last interview and was looking forward to relaxing and concentrating on my preparation. One or two people were questioning the validity of the Dave Challinor long throw. There was nothing to report on this, however, as the man quite simply has a prodigious throw and it is a perfectly legal weapon in Tranmere's armoury.

The training was a relief from the media attention and the mental pressures and I was feeling tired but physically strong. The build up to the event was exciting for my two boys, Ben and Carl, who were now twenty-one and eighteen respectively; they were both feeling very proud and looking forward to the day.

On Saturday 26 February, instead of going to my original appointment as fourth official at Sunderland, I packed my bags for London. Margaret and I were travelling down on the Saturday with the boys following on the Sunday. We drove to the railway station childishly singing, 'We're all going to Wembley' as excited as any fans going down to cheer their team.

On arrival at the Copthorne Tara Hotel in Kensington we were greeted by Jim Ashworth, who would be our host for the weekend. Margaret and I took a stroll along to Kensington Palace; walking along Kensington High Street I noticed what a fresh crispy afternoon it was and I hoped that the conditions would be like that on match day.

At about 5 p.m. the League officials called us to a meeting at the hotel. We all had our partners with us, with the exception of Paul Armstrong whose wife was expecting their first child. I would have to be gentle with Paul this weekend as he would obviously be on tenterhooks. The League people went through the procedures and paperwork surrounding the logistics of the final and I was amazed to find myself being asked what my fee was for the match. Perhaps I should have tried it on!

A meal was arranged for the evening and we were to be joined by Jack Taylor, who was now working for the Football League commercial department. The evening was almost surreal and I felt as if people were watching all the time. I suppose I got a feel for what it must be like to be famous. I'm not sure that I would like that sort of attention all the time and I began to understand why people in the public eye sometimes lose their cool when they are being stared at or pestered for photographs. I also felt that people in the immediate company were looking at me, wanting to follow my lead on whether to be serious or humorous. Anyone who knows me will know that I much prefer the latter approach. I was very careful about what I had to eat and drink and ended up going to bed at 10.30.

I was delighted to wake to a rather grey day and I was equally pleased when I reminded myself that the kick-off time had remained at 3 p.m. despite the fact that the match was being televised by Sky. This meant my preparation and routine was consistent with most match days.

An 11 a.m. meeting was held with League officials. This time they outlined their hopes and aspirations for the game and I was pleased to say they basically only wanted us to do our jobs correctly with minimum fuss. The cars arrived at 11.30 and I discovered I was to travel to the ground in a stretch Mercedes limousine with darkened windows. It brought back memories of my Marseilles adventure.

As we left the cars on arrival at the ground I could hear shouts of 'Good luck, ref', there were requests for autographs, but most of all there were hundreds of shouts of 'Good luck Wendy'. This was to be her day as much as mine and I appreciated the amount of pressure she must be under. One mistake and it would be all over the newspapers the following day. I would like to think I did everything I could to put her at ease.

Up the stairs we went to the Banqueting Hall, which was all decked out in green and gold, the corporate colours of the sponsor, Worthington. Our guests were already there, properly seated at pre-arranged tables in the main hall. I ensured my three colleagues soaked up the atmosphere. Yes, I was excited but I was also getting a buzz from the obvious excitement of the three newcomers to Wembley who were agog at everything they were experiencing.

We said our temporary farewells to our wives and partners and I steered my team down to the dressing rooms. The first job was to find the room allocated to Wendy. I had to remember this was a first for Wembley. Her room turned out to be downstairs whilst ours was upstairs. There were many reasons to be pleased about Wendy's appointment but one spin-off was that it gave myself and the others more room in the broom cupboard which was the Wembley ref's room.

Timing and precision are paramount before any match but in a cup final it is even more important. I took the responsibility for keeping my team relaxed and distracted and decided to take them out for a walk on the Wembley 'turf'. Whilst the pitch was in acceptable condition it was nowhere near the standard of the season before. The groundsman explained to me that this was due to the fact that the match was so early in the year and the grass hadn't started growing. In places it was like walking on mud with no cushioning at all. At this point we were able to soak up the atmosphere which was building up in the ground.

I sent Wendy to her dressing room and told her to get changed and then to meet us in the main changing room. There was a lull between getting changed and the appointed time for a massage. I therefore produced from my holdall a TV quiz book with which we proceeded to have some fun for the next twenty minutes. It might seem a strange thing for people in the crowd to imagine but as they were all getting worked up about the approaching kick-off the officials were sitting arguing the toss about which of the Teletubbies likes to wear a hat!

At 2.25 we donned our warm-up tops and we went out on to the pitch, using the next ten minutes to soak up the atmosphere of the now almost full Wembley. As I was about to return to the dressing room I heard a voice I recognised from the crowd. It was Peter Jones, the Premier League referee from Quorn, a life-long Leicester fan and a great friend of mine. He wished me well and he gave me a good luck hug, and then it was back to the dressing room.

With eight minutes left to kick-off we headed for the tunnel. I could hear and sense the hustle and bustle which always surrounds a big match like this. The managers appeared with their respective players, I found myself analysing the handshakes and the glances into my eyes, imagining things that weren't there. I felt I was ready for this and didn't have any concerns at all.

Jim Ashworth appeared and reminded me that he would lead us to the edge of the grass and then it would be up to me to take over. He also warned me that the pyrotechnics surrounding the teams taking the pitch would be a bit on the loud side. My heart missed a beat as I thought of all the attention surrounding the game; I felt a little twinge of apprehension but this was soon put in place by thoughts of the job I needed to do before we even get to kick-off. I was more worried by the preliminaries than the game itself.

Emerging from the tunnel the first thing that hit me was the noise. Unlike the Trophy final this was a full house of 75,000 people, all shouting for their own team. In a way this is more of a fans' final than the FA Cup as there is a greater allocation of tickets to the true supporters. The next sensation was the fireworks. The noise and the smell of gunpowder was overwhelming and I thought for a second I was in a battle zone. Probably an inappropriate reference but all I could think of at the time to describe the noise.

My mind did start to wander at this stage as various flashbacks cropped up. I recalled earlier parts of my career, particularly visiting my father in hospital to tell him of my elevation to the Premier League, to Cantona jumping into the crowd and to the Manchester City supporters who had sent death threats to my home.

By the time I had thought about the 120 or so cards I had received from well-wishers, the march to the centre circle was complete. John Aldridge, the Tranmere manager, was next to me and said, 'I don't know what to do, I've never done this as a manager.' 'Don't worry,' I said, 'the good thing about being a manager today is that you're last in line and the captain gets to do all the work.' We were introduced to Iain Napier, Chief Executive of Bass, who fortunately did not ask my opinions on his beer; Peter Middleton, Chairman of the Football League; and John McKeown, the Football League's Chief Executive. For the second time in nine months I heard the National Anthem sung with gusto and out of tune.

We posed for photographs, I received the signal from Sky and we were off. In the sixth minute Tranmere's Clint Hill, the footballer with a name like something out of 'Rawhide', scythed down Stefan Oakes of Leicester. I remembered the words of the League officials: 'Just do your job as normal.' I was thinking 'red card' but in those few seconds which a referee has to make such important decisions I thought of the fans who had travelled all this way and paid so much money to see a Wembley final. I wondered if I could perhaps justify keeping it to a yellow card instead. I decided, perhaps generously, that I could and Clint survived, but only with the biggest bollocking a player has ever received from a ref at Wembley. I am pleased to say I had no more problems from Clint.

I was all over the pitch, in advance of play, on the touchline, in the goalmouth, wherever I felt that I could make the maximum contribution. I was delighted that all the hard training had paid off. I was reaping the reward and really enjoying myself.

In an even and open contest, the first goal came Leicester's way, the ball was played into the Tranmere area and, with the dexterity of a forward, Leicester skipper and central defender Matt Elliott swept the ball home. Later in the first half, Leicester's Robbie Savage was hacked down unceremoniously by Tranmere's Nicky Henry close to the touchline beside the technical area. I was in the process of issuing a yellow card and I became aware of someone shouting in my ear. It was John Aldridge 'politely' suggesting it was a good tackle. I told him his presence was not required so he should sit down, and I continued to carry out the caution. On completing the formalities I glanced over to the touchline and saw that Aldridge was still around, at which point I said in an exasperated tone, 'Are you still here?' The message was received and away he went - for the moment.

Half-time arrived with the score 1-0 to Leicester. My colleagues and I went back to our dressing room where we discussed events of the first half. I first enquired of Paul how he felt things were going. I deliberately asked him first as I didn't want to over-emphasise Wendy's position. I knew that Paul hadn't had any problems in the first half and I would then have more time to speak to Wendy if she wanted to talk in more depth. As it turned out, both my colleagues were feeling very comfortable with things and from my point of view I was very pleased with their performance.

The majority of the time was spent talking with Phil Richards, the fourth official, who wanted to tell me about the antics of John Aldridge on the Tranmere bench. Apparently, Aldridge had been up and down like a jack-in-the-box. This, for no reason other than his team were losing and two of his players had been booked. I told Phil that if Aldridge persisted to let me know and we would 'get rid of him'.

The second half got under way and Tranmere, as expected, lifted their performance in an attempt to get back into the game. In the 57th minute, as they pressed for the equaliser, the ball was played forward into the corner of the Leicester penalty area. I followed the play only to find the ball promptly returned, with interest, into the Tranmere half. I turned and gave chase, anxious to keep up with play.

As I ran at full stretch I felt a sensation in my right leg, in the lower calf region. At first it simply went tight, but this was rapidly followed by a sensation of warm fluid running down the back of my leg. Suddenly I could move no more and the tightness exploded into searing pain, the worst pain I have ever experienced. I could feel the agony right through to my fingertips. I tried to walk and simply fell to the ground, much to everyone's amusement in the crowd and commentary boxes. Except that is for my friends and family, who understood what I must have been going through.

I managed to avoid stopping the game till the ball went out of play at which point I blew the whistle and found myself immediately being attended to by Neil Mason, who was doing the massages for the day and who had been waiting to get on to treat me as soon as he could. He straightaway diagnosed the severity of the problem and informed me that I had suffered a tear in the Gastrucnemius muscle (large Calf structure) and that I would have to go to the small hospital in Wembley Stadium. I was about to become the first referee to be carried off on a stretcher at Wembley, a distinction I would rather have avoided. The fourth official, Phil Richards, approached me with the immortal words, 'Are you alright?' If I hadn't been so incapacitated I would have throttled him. As it was, a sense of duty kicked in and I said, 'Re-start the game with a throw-in to Leicester. Do you have a note of the cautions?' 'Yes,' he replied. I then added, 'There are 32 minutes left to play, get your concentration going and start in your own time.'

As I was being carried to the hospital there were many emotions running through my mind and body. I had been injured before but I had never required a stretcher. Had I let people down? Would this be the last game of my career? Then I felt embarrassed, for no other reason than a referee's misfortune is everyone else's delight. Then I felt sorry for myself. All of this subsided, though, as the searing pain in my leg got worse and worse.

The gloom lifted ever so slightly when Martin O'Neill, the Leicester manager, motioned to his section of the crowd to give me a round of applause, a nice gesture. I should add that no such generous gestures came from the opposing manager John Aldridge, whose behaviour that day would lead to a disciplinary hearing.

The stretcher took me to the tunnel where I was put into a wheelchair and carried up the stairs by the paramedics to the hospital. I could feel every single vibration from every one of their footsteps. The duty doctor, a young lady who was clearly not a football fan, carried out an examination in a most painful manner and then proclaimed, 'Tubigrip to the leg and then to the changing room to get dressed and rest.'

My face must have been a picture because she then said, 'What's wrong?' 'I am going for my medal,' I said firmly. 'You're not climbing those steps,' she said equally forcefully, 'You'll make the injury worse.' 'If you want to stop me you'll have to break my legs,' I responded. As she stood there shaking her head, Jack Taylor, who had escorted me to the hospital, said, 'Look love, patch him up and let him get his medal, it's the least he deserves.'

The leg was bandaged in such a way that I could walk but only with a severe limp. I was therefore transported back to the dugout in a wheelchair where I watched the rest of the game through glazed eyes. I hadn't shed a tear yet, that would come later.

On taking my seat in the dugout, I was amazed when I was informed of what had been going on in my absence. The first matter which had to be sorted out was to find a replacement for the fourth official. The ground was apparently half-full of Premier League and Football League referees and assistants and there was, in fact, something of a queue. Steve Brand from the Wirral, a Premier League assistant referee who had been sitting close to the dugouts, got there first.

Shortly after my departure Phil made his first decision of consequence as referee. Heskey was running through towards the Tranmere penalty area when he was apparently tripped by Clint Hill. Phil decided that, as Hill was the last defender, a red card had to be shown for denying a goal-scoring opportunity. In any event, if it was deliberate trip it would have been a second yellow card. The dismissal of Hill was, however, hotly disputed with the Tranmere players suggesting that Heskey had dived.

At the time of the dismissal, the Leicester substitute, Theo Zagorakis, had started clapping when Hill was walking from the pitch. He apparently later said that it was genuine applause for a fellow professional. Unfortunately, Aldridge had decided otherwise and confronted Zagorakis, having to be pulled away by the new fourth official.

David Kelly, the Tranmere skipper, had then fired in an equaliser that Tranmere deserved, at which point Aldridge leapt to his feet in celebration. He then ran across to Zagorakis and apparently slapped him across the face causing an almighty ruck, which again the fourth official had to sort out. I think Steve must, by this time, have been beginning to regret getting to the head of the queue.

I was also informed later that Mr Aldridge had been witnessed ridiculing me as I was carried off, apparently inciting the Tranmere crowd to do the same. This from a man whom I had helped at the beginning of the game when he had been unsure of what to do. I can understand managers getting excited and losing their temper but I can't accept behaviour such as described to me in this incident. Aldridge was formally charged with a number of offences and was subsequently 'punished' with a fine. Some would say he got off very lightly.

THE JOY AND THE PAIN

The game concluded, almost incidentally as far as I was concerned, with Leicester winning 2-1 after Matt Elliott scored his second goal and secured the Man of the Match award to boot. When the final whistle went I joined my colleagues in the middle of the pitch. Congratulations were interspersed with commiserations before a few Leicester players, including Flowers, Lennon, Savage and Sinclair, came over to wish me well, which was good of them. The Leicester manager, too, added his good wishes.

It was Tranmere who were first up to receive the medals, then Leicester to receive the cup and their medals. We were guided up behind them in an effort to keep things running smoothly and, as my hobbling got worse, I began to wonder if I had made the right decision trying to get up those thirty-nine steps. I didn't want to get in the way of others or compound my embarrassment by collapsing on the staircase or in front of the royal box. I eventually made it and I knew immediately it was worth all the pain as I looked out at a capacity crowd in a state of uproar, representing a riot of colour and commotion. It was a fantastic sight, made even more special by the knowledge that I had taken part, even if I hadn't been able to perform for the full ninety minutes.

After receiving my medal, I descended the steps and on the way down I spotted my wife Margaret. I simply touched her on the shoulder as I went past, knowing that if I stopped I would probably break down, which would not have been the thing to do in front of a 75,000 crowd. I managed to retain my composure until I met Margaret again in the Banqueting Hall. We hugged each other and shared each other's disappointment.

My sons were emotional too and when I found out later that certain TV commentators had made light of my misfortune I couldn't help thinking what a pack of toads certain sections of the media can be. Are officials not human like other individuals participating on the day? This lack of respect and consideration seems to be something peculiar to the British media and doesn't appear to happen abroad. The whole episode was admirably summed up by Judith Don, wife of Philip, who simply said, 'Bugger'. I couldn't have put it better myself.

The evening celebrations would be muted unless I did something about it so I put on an act to ensure that things were not spoilt for my colleagues who, after all, had carried out their duties admirably, including Wendy who had performed with distinction in difficult circumstances.

ONE NIGHT AT THE PALACE

I prompted Paul Armstrong to keep ringing about the baby, of which there was still no news. Phil Richards, who had taken over in the middle and had done so well, was in a difficult situation, being ecstatic but also uncertain as to how to treat me. He had received the unexpected honour and experience of refereeing at Wembley and must have been on a high but he was also very aware of how I must have felt. To break the ice I decided to get him to talk us through his experience on the field. He did this in a very entertaining manner and this set the scene for the rest of the evening and everyone had a good time. It was still, though, one of the most difficult days of my life.

The next day we were heading home. Our car arrived to pick us up and we needed to collect the boys from the Kensington Palace Hotel. I asked the concierge to get me the number of the hotel so that I could ring the boys to tell them we were on our way. I rang the number and then took part in a strange conversation which went something like, 'Could you put me through to Mr Wilkie's room, please?' To which the response went something like, 'I'm sorry sir, I don't think Her Majesty has any guests of that name.' It's amazing what a difference a wrong number can make! An amusing end to a very mixed-up experience.

Travelling back home the disappointment kicked in. Sky TV rang as I was being driven to King's Cross and asked for an interview. I thought it might help lift the gloom and agreed to meet a crew at my home at 4.30 that afternoon. While I was on the train going home Tony Toward of Newcastle United rang to commiserate and offered the services of the club's physiotherapy facilities; a brilliant gesture I thought. I agreed to call in on the following Thursday.

At home, I was sitting in my study waiting for the Sky TV crew to arrive when a transit van drew up and parked outside my front door. As I watched with astonishment, the roof of the van appeared to move and a large satellite dish suddenly appeared and started tracking the appropriate satellite. I felt as if I was back on the set of 'Close Encounters'. Having just moved into the house recently, I was trying to keep a low profile so as not to cause any disturbance or annoyance to the neighbours. Never mind, at least I meant well.

Two interviews followed, one going out on Sky News, the other for Sky.com TV. It is the electronic age after all. The latter was to be a remote interview which entailed the crew setting up a static camera on a tripod, then fitting me with a microphone and a receiver ear-piece. This would enable me to both speak to and listen to Dave Clarke and Kirsty Gallagher in the studio. What was unnerving was the fact that I could hear them but could not see them, whereas they could both hear and see me. The disadvantage of this was demonstrated when I was wired-up waiting for the broadcast to start, sitting there wondering what was going to happen, when all of a sudden Kirsty's voice sounded in my head - 'Don't look so sad Alan, we'll try and cheer you up.' I thought, how nice, only for Dave to issue those fateful words, 'Are you alright?' bringing back to me the moment when I wanted to strangle Phil as I was lifted on to the stretcher.

The interview over, the crew cleared up all the cabling and lighting, but remained outside my house for about an hour and a half. They were apparently sending various pieces of footage they had taken from their interviews earlier in the day at the Riverside training complex where Alan Shearer had announced that he would retire from international football following Euro 2000. It would seem I was destined never to get the headline on my own.

14

THE END OF THE ROAD

ON THE FOLLOWING THURSDAY I called in to see the Newcastle physio as arranged and he told me the leg was so inflamed that he couldn't even examine it properly. I was advised to come back the following week. In the meantime I was invited to the Newcastle v Chelsea game on the forthcoming Saturday. At St James' Park all the usual comments and leg-pulls came flying my way. I took these in good humour, having become accustomed to anything anybody could throw at me. By the end of the game my leg had swollen so much that I could not straighten it properly. On arriving home the pain was so severe and the swelling so large that I became very concerned.

On Sunday I went to hospital where a thrombosis was diagnosed. At this point, thoughts of refereeing again seemed insignificant, I simply wanted to get out of this in one piece and be able to walk again. After the diagnosis and urgent treatment, rapid improvement was made and, after ten days, I was able to walk again. I decided to attend the Lilleshall Sports Injury Centre in Shropshire for a week to ensure I got the most appropriate treatment to get me back on the road to refereeing again. Having overcome the scare of a serious medical problem I was now very conscious that time was ticking away on my last season and I was determined to make the most of what time was available. The Premier League, when I advised them of my visit to Lilleshall, offered to pay the bill which was very much appreciated.

On Monday morning I checked in and underwent a thorough medical examination. To my delight I found out that I was in a reasonable state of fitness, which was encouraging after a three-week lay off. At first, the injury was something of a mystery and I was advised I shouldn't have been as active as I had been in recent weeks. However, I was hungry for more matches and I wasn't to be put off. I worked hard all week, did everything asked of me, sometimes twice, and I felt everything was going well. For company I had Ramon Vega of Spurs, Dave Brammer and Mick Walsh of Port Vale and Costass, a Cypriot recently released by Bolton.

My inspiration at Lilleshall, however, was to be in the form of a much younger player, a lad called Simon who was twenty years of age and who had for the last two years been battling to regain fitness following a cruciate ligament injury. His career was virtually over before it had started. So sad, but Simon's cheery demeanour and determination made me put everything into perspective and I resolved to battle on and not allow myself to feel depressed about my own situation.

That week I rowed, cycled, hopped, trampolined, swam, ran in the water and did just about everything else you could think of apart from abseiling naked down the north face of the Eiger. Thursday came round and I was let loose on a football pitch for some running at three-quarter pace. All of a sudden at the end of my eighth run the calf went very tight and I got a dreaded feeling of relapse. I set off back to the gym dejected. To my relief I was reliably informed that this might only have been due to fatigue and that I had been working very hard, for a chap my age, that is. I'm not sure why they always find it necessary to add that last bit.

Following another thorough examination, the injury was confirmed as a substantial calf tear, probably caused by over-training in the weeks leading up to the final. Ironic really, when I had been making such an effort to be in tip-top shape for my big day. I suppose it could have been worse and the muscle could have torn before the event and I would have missed the final altogether. I decided to be grateful for small mercies.

The week at Lilleshall did wonders for my confidence in the injured leg and its recovery. I would be very anxious for a while, however, whilst out on training runs. Due to the injury I was cancelling appointments left, right and centre. The one that I regretted missing most was the Leeds v Chelsea match which would have been a repeat of my first Premiership game. However, I was now back at a good level of training with the leg feeling fine except for a sensation of numbness surrounding the calf muscle.

My target for making a comeback was a game at Preston against Cardiff. If I could make it, it would apparently be a record recovery from such an injury. Not bad for an old man. The week of the game arrived and I declared myself ready. I turned up at Deepdale and everyone reminded me, in the nicest way, about my injury saying how painful and disappointing it must have been. I tried to act calm and collected but inside I was feeling sick with anxiety and concern. I needed a mental diversion so I decided to concoct a prank on one of my assistants. He needed to use the loo just before the bell was due to go to indicate the teams must leave the dressing room to take the pitch. While he was doing the necessary, I and the others sneaked out of the room and hid outside. On returning from the loo he was panic-stricken, thinking we had taken the field without him. Flush-faced he ran down the tunnel but suddenly realised there was no activity pitch-side. When it dawned on him what was going on, the tunnel reverberated to the shout of 'Bastards, Bastards'. Childish, I know, but good fun nevertheless.

The game was of poor quality, but that was secondary to me. I managed to see the game out and completed a total of 97 minutes. I felt confident now about making Southampton the following week. The rest of the season was mapped out for me. If I could keep going I would go to Southampton, followed by a crunch relegation battle between Bradford and Derby, and then I would be fourth official at first Sunderland and then Newcastle. My career would then conclude in grand style with my last match as referee being Manchester United against Spurs at Old Trafford, where it was expected that United would be presented with the League championship trophy. And finally, I would end my active days as fourth official at Sheffield Wednesday, against my old friends Leicester City.

The Southampton game was against Watford and was noticeable for two events. Firstly, at the end of the game every player shook my hand and thanked me, and secondly, Matt Le Tissier handed me his shirt, 'For old times sake.' The fact that the players were so generous delighted me but my performance can't have been so wonderful as the assessor gave me my lowest mark of the season. It was nice of the players not to mention that I'd apparently been rubbish on the day!

I was now getting back to full fitness and soon it was Good Friday and time for the crunch game between Bradford and Derby. Everyone was aware that this was the game which could decide the relegation battle and you could feel the atmosphere building. A tight little ground, supporters packed in, a soft boggy pitch and the nerves of the players noticeably jangling.

THE END OF THE ROAD

At Bradford, the tunnel is very narrow and you can't avoid close proximity with the other people involved in the game. No-one looked at their opponents, they either looked at me or at the ceiling and everyone was shouting, getting psyched-up for the game. The reality of such games is that the result can make or break people's careers whether they are a player or manager. The air was somewhat blue, as it tends to be at moments of high tension, and I found myself shouting, 'Come on lads, a bit of decorum, we have two young mascots at the front here.' This fortunately restored a bit of sanity to the proceedings.

Although I was aware that there was likely to be many incidents in this game, I couldn't have anticipated quite what was to come. This turned out to be one of the most amazing games of my career with eight goals, four penalties, eight yellow cards and one sending off. Apart from that, nothing much happened!

The first half got off to an incredible start with Derby taking the lead after twenty-four seconds. They went two up after nine minutes. Bradford pulled the deficit back to one goal with a penalty which saw Rory Delap of Derby sent off. I had awarded a free kick to Bradford which was flighted in to the far post where Robbie Blake ran to meet the ball, only to be pulled back by Delap at which point Blake made contact with the ball as well. As I blew the whistle, the ball flew into the net. The Bradford players were pleading with me to let the goal stand but unfortunately I had made a decision and it was irreversible. I sent Delap on his way and prayed that the penalty would be converted. Dean Windass stepped up and powered the ball into the back of the net, much to my relief.

Surely with Derby down to ten men after 15 minutes, Bradford would take advantage. However, Derby went 3-1 up shortly afterwards when I awarded a penalty for a trip on Malcolm Christie. This was converted by Craig Burley. Bradford hit back with a super strike from Windass from 30 yards and then made it 3-3 when Peter Beagrie cut in from the left and struck a powerful shot with his right foot. This wasn't to be the last action of the first half though, as Bradford dramatically took the lead to go in 4-3 up at half-time, with Windass completing his hat-trick. The Bradford goal was scored right in front of the Derby fans and of course it was all my fault. As I left the field with my assistants we were pelted with nuts, sweets or whatever else they could get their hands on, which fortunately included nothing too hurtful.

The second half, amazingly, was just as frantic but without the goals. That is until I awarded Derby their second penalty, this time for a hand-ball. No complaints from the Derby fans now, I noticed. Burley stepped up and scored his second from the spot and the score was level at 4-4. Four minutes from the end Daryl Powell, the Derby captain, went down in the Bradford box and I awarded yet another penalty. By now the Derby fans must have thought I was a hero. Craig Burley stepped forward to take the shot that would surely ensure Derby's survival in the Premiership. Stuart McCall of Bradford in the meantime came forth with the utterance, 'You have just relegated us.' As at the Leeds-Middlesbrough relegation game I felt like saying, 'What have you and your team mates been doing about it all season? Don't blame me for your rubbish performances.' This would probably not have been a good way to finish off my career and I fortunately decided that silence was the best course of action. After the second Derby penalty Craig Burley had said to me, 'For Christs' sake, don't give us another penalty, I'll probably miss.' As he placed the ball I wondered whether this might just be the case. Up he stepped, and with Derby's survival at stake, he hit the shot hard and low but it hit the keeper's legs and rebounded to safety. The anguish in Craig's face was clear and he was distraught. He wasn't to know that, in the event, both of these teams were to survive, with the disaster of relegation falling to the crazy gang of Wimbledon.

Rare as 4-4 draws are, it wasn't the first time this had happened to me at this ground as nine years earlier Bradford and Bolton had reached the same conclusion. On that day, however, I only awarded three penalties, although I managed to send three players off. It must be something in the Bradford air.

One of the pleasures of visiting Bradford is that Geoffrey Richmond is one of the most charming chairmen you could wish to meet. He is a self-made businessman, who apparently sold his Ronson lighters empire to Dunhill for an extremely large amount of money. There is nothing Geoffrey likes better than to regale his guests with entertaining conversation in the lounge. He is very affable and will always ask you if you have any guests you want to bring into the executive lounge. The nice thing is that his demeanour doesn't change if his team has lost, he is still the perfect host. My recollections of Geoffrey go back a long way, of course, as it was the same man who was horrified at the prospect of 200 pies going to waste when he was chairman of Scarborough back in 1984/85!

My next two appointments would see me visit my two local clubs, Newcastle and Sunderland, as fourth official. Sentimental journeys both. When I went to Newcastle, I recall Alan Shearer asking me what had gone on at Bradford and was I on speed or something? Then he added in his Geordie accent, 'On the other hand I suppose it was you, like.'

With these appointments out of the way it left me to conclude my active career at the top level at a fitting place and an even more fitting occasion - Old Trafford 4 May 2000 at 1130 a.m., live on Sky. The presentation of the League trophy would be made at the end of the match to the all-conquering United team, who by now had already sewn up the title. As I entered the ground via the South Stand tunnel, there were hundreds of security people. On enquiring how many people are employed on match day I was informed that it is in excess of 4,000, taking into account the food stands, parking attendants etc. A phenomenal business.

The dressing room, as usual, was too hot so we wedged the door open to get some cool air. We went out to inspect the pitch which was in lush condition, this being the third pitch to be laid this season owing to poor drainage. Everyone seemed to know it was my last game and some of the stewards wished me good luck. I pride myself on the fact that throughout my refereeing days I tried never to get big-headed and always treated everyone with respect regardless of their position. I think this was reflected in the genuine comments made on this occasion. I went out for a longer than usual warm-up, giving one fan the chance to shout, 'You should give up refereeing Wilkie, you're too fat,' as he sat there eating his meat pie at 11 o' clock in the morning.

As players from both sides smiled, nodded or gave me some other acknowledgement, I thought to myself, 'I will miss this.' As the Sky staff checked the time with me, I told them not to worry, 'Just tell me when you want me.' I was returning to the dressing rooms when I spotted David Ginola standing isolated in the tunnel. I shook his hand and asked how he was. 'I have been better,' he replied, 'How are you, your leg healed now?' 'I think so,' I said, 'I'm sorry you're not playing, this is my last game.' 'I cannot play,' he said and added plaintively, 'I wish you a good game and a good life.' I realised something was wrong between David and his manager and with subsequent revelations into his last days at Tottenham I can understand why he was so desolate. It was a very sad end to his Tottenham days.

In the dressing room I took a moment to compose myself and then it was all systems go. The knock on the door came and it was John Smart, the Sky floor manager, and we moved out into the tunnel to line up. Next the jewellery check, and then the bit I thought would never come, the end of my refereeing career. But what a place to finish, 62,500, a new record crowd, and a worldwide audience of 100 million people. It's mind-boggling to think that people in countries like Zaire, South Africa and the Falkland Islands crowd round television sets to watch these matches and here I am, in the thick of it all, playing a major part. Whoever would have imagined this as I started my first game as referee on a sunny Sunday morning in Chester-le-Street when the Old England pub took on the Relton Working Men's Club?

Old Trafford was basking in sunshine and the indications were that it was going to get hotter, so water and fluid were made available. The game started and it was fairly even for a while, until Teddy Sheringham scored the first goal against his old side. This is it, I thought, the Spurs resistance will crumble and United will put on an exhibition. Not a bit of it. Spurs stepped up a gear and Chris Armstrong scored a spectactular headed goal. 'We're in for a close thing,' I thought to myself. And so it was until David Beckham scored a sensational goal from 25 yards leaving Ian Walker flat-footed. United made it 3-1 in the second half with a Solksjaer goal and it was all over. United were celebrating in style.

The introduction of six substitutes changed the face of the game but it did give us the chance to view some up-and-coming talent. For United there was Ronnie Wallwork (infamous already for 'attacking' a referee in Belgium), Greening and Wilson, who will do well in the future, I am sure. For Spurs there was Ledley King and Luke Young, both of whom I mentioned earlier, and I am certain they will go far. They also had Matthew Etherington and Simon Davies, bought recently from Peterborough, and I am sure we will hear a lot more about these two youngsters.

We were now into the last five minutes, and I needed to indicate to my fourth official how much time was to be added. As the ball went out for a throw-in on the half-way line I ran across and told him, 'Three'. To ensure no misunderstanding he repeated, 'Three minutes'. 'No, three years,' I said dreamily, wishing this really was the case. The three minutes passed and suddenly it was time to blow the whistle. My eyes filled and my throat dried up. Yes, I had one more game left but not as referee and I would never return to Old Trafford. Not to take part anyway, and the feeling of sadness, as well as pride, was overwhelming.

I regained my composure, shook hands with the players and it was off to the dressing room, but not before David Beckham came over to wish me well and we walked to the tunnel together. He would return to this pitch many more times. For me it was the end of an era.

As I always did, I shook the hands of my colleagues, thanking them for their efforts. Well, I managed the handshake but when I tried to say thank you I found I couldn't speak. A moment or two with my head under a towel was required before I was back to normal. There was a knock at the door and a signed Spurs shirt appeared, 'With grateful thanks from Tottenham Hotspur.' A cursory search failed to find George Graham's signature. Another knock and this time it was Arthur, the Man United kit manager. I was presented with Ryan Giggs' European Champions League shirt auto-graphed by the team, together with a bottle of Man United champagne. I was overwhelmed by the thoughtfulness of both clubs. The champagne found a good home when I presented it to Tyneside Juniors, a club of which I am President, to be used as star prize in a fund-raising raffle.

We decided that as it was trophy presentation day, we would get changed and rejoin the party. By the time we emerged, the Carling platform had been erected on the pitch and the dignitaries were in place. So as not to cause an obstruction I sat on the side of the pitch, which sloped down to the track. My colleague Andy Garratt wanted to take some photos as he had never been to Old Trafford before, let alone this close to a major celebra-tion on the pitch. As he was clicking away I asked him if he had noticed who was sitting almost next to me. He hadn't realised that I was just feet away from Victoria Beckham and young Brooklyn. With some embarrass-ment he forced himself to take a photo, he would not have been forgiven by his family if he hadn't done the necessary.

The celebrations over, we made our way back to the hotel where I was presented with another surprise. My colleagues had laid on a party for me - quiet, but in its own way, a very special occasion.

ONE NIGHT AT THE PALACE

That only left Sheffield Wednesday v Leicester City. This was a strange occasion as my heart told me that my career had finished the previous week. Wednesday won in some style, 4-0, but it was to no avail as they were already relegated.

Wednesday were very generous and they presented me with an autographed shirt and ball. The thing that will live with me longest though is the memory provided by the losing manager, Martin O'Neill. He was annoyed and frustrated with his team ending the season on such a poor note but that did not stop him coming to see me, shaking my hand and saying, 'Congratulations on your retirement, we always believed you were one of the best referees around, could we offer you a players shirt as a souvenir?' I was very flattered by this and asked for Neil Lennon's shirt, Neil being a player I admire a great deal. This was duly delivered to the dressing room, still dripping, and would be autographed later. So ended my active career after sixteen years as a servant of the Football League and Premier League.

On returning home I was delighted to receive through the post a Patrick Vieira shirt, fully autographed by the Arsenal squad, with a note saying, 'With best wishes from all at Arsenal.' A nice gesture from a classy club.

I may have had some disappointments over the years but I have also seen tremendous generosity and warmth from people within the game. This applies to the fans too, whose humour probably just about overshadowed their abuse! I will miss it; thanks for the memories everyone.

EPILOGUE

Life After Ref

EVERYONE HAS A DREAM. I lived mine - not many people are that fortunate. What would happen now, I wondered? Would everything be an anti-climax? How would it affect my life? I would soon find out.

During the close-season I spent time dwelling on what might lie ahead. Just at the thought of it I was feeling a great emptiness and it was with dread that I read newspaper reports about the approaching season. I tried to relax at home, I made a nuisance of myself and I imagine I really got on Margaret's nerves. I was really twitchy and couldn't settle at all.

During the summer months, when I would normally be waiting for my letter of retention to the Premier League, I received an invitation to become an assessor on the Football League. Only by accepting this position would it be possible, if selected, to become a Premier League Match Observer. The criteria for both positions is similar, you must have been either a referee or an assistant on the respective Leagues, and have come to the end of your career by virtue of reaching normal retirement age.

The Premier League invitation, in turn, arrived and I was then delighted to be able to accept the positions for both organisations. The duties involved in the respective roles are different, with the Premiership Match Observer being more wide-ranging and having greater responsibility on match day.

The Football League duties are restricted to reporting on the performance of the referee and his assistants and also on any breaches of regulation observed. The Premiership responsibilities extend to commenting on any discipline carried out by the referee, condition of the pitch, observations on TV coverage, organisation of stretchers around the ground, medical teams, behaviour of the crowd, conduct of the teams and a report on the post-match press conference. In case this is not enough, there is also a section called 'other observations'!

The section covering crowd behaviour is interesting as, through the UEFA Fair Play scheme, a place can be gained in one of the European competitions by virtue of sportsmanship. There is a form to complete covering a club's approach to the game and general behaviour. This details any cautions and dismissals, attitude to attacking football, respect to both opponents and referee, and finally a mark is awarded for the behaviour of the personnel on the bench. All of these determine a final fair play mark.

Most importantly, though, a report on the performance of the referee and his assistants is prepared, encapsulating all that was good about their performance, then offering any advice of shortcomings. In an effort to develop consistency in writing style and the matching of marks to reports, I was paired with two senior experienced observers, Peter Willis and Roger Dilkes, for my first two fixtures.

The Football League and the Premier League agreed to jointly prepare a weekend training session in which all the new recruits would be tested for the accuracy of their reports. This entailed ten assessors/observers attending a match and producing independent reports for discussion the next day, when the poor referee would also be present. After that, it would be out into the big wide world alone. In the event, everything went without mishap and a sigh of relief was expressed by all concerned.

It was in late July when the fixtures arrived and I saw that my first game was to be Leeds v Everton at Elland Road. Dermot Gallagher would be the subject of my first assessment. 'Might as well start at the top,' I thought. Dermot fortunately made my first job very easy as he had a splendid game. One of the difficulties of this role, however, is that the people I am reporting on are my friends and I have shared with them over the years the bond of a very difficult job. Mutual support has been one of the things that have helped us all get by when the bullets are flying. Having said that, there is no room for sycophancy and I will do whatever is necessary to maintain the standards of English refereeing, which I passionately believe is still the best in the world.

I recently spent seven hours over one report involving someone whom I class as a good friend. There were things that needed to be said and I didn't want to shirk the responsibility. At the same time I did not want to demoralise or alienate the person involved. As I said much earlier, as referees, it is important that we can be open and honest and, when it is necessary, look upon our mistakes as learning points for the future. I look back to when I had the feedback on my own performance from

EPILOGUE

Gerry Jones for that game at Barrow and how I decided to take the criticism constructively and get back on the right track. I now like to think I will be able to help the development of up-and-coming referees. It is not my job to catch out referees but to give them constructive advice and, I believe, coaching.

I think I am making the mental transition to observer reasonably well, considering there are always going to be pangs of regret every time I watch a kick-off and feel the pain of not being out there controlling things. I believe the fact that I was able to battle back after the Wembley injury to take another four top class matches helped considerably. This enabled me to finish my refereeing days with a feeling of achievement rather than a feeling of disappointment.

It would have been nice, of course, to have finished on a high note by seeing the Cup Final through to completion but, as they say, 'Life is never perfect.' I'm certainly not going to complain.

There is a saying in football: 'All the best referees have retired'. I suppose I should be flattered now that I am among that fraternity! I don't believe it is true, however, despite the comments I have been getting like 'This guy's not as good as you' and 'They don't make them like you any more'. Whilst this is very nice I believe there are some good young referees around and if I can help to make them better than I was then I'll be a very happy man.

I am looking forward to putting something back into refereeing and, as my playing injury led me into something I loved, perhaps my retirement from refereeing will turn out to be the catalyst for something just as rewarding. I certainly hope so.

One final thought: I am now becoming somewhat worried that I seem to be getting as enthusiastic for my new role as I was for refereeing. I had better not mention this to my wife!

FOOTNOTE

Alan Wilkie has since been appointed as a full-time official of the Football Association in the capacity of Regional Manager - Referees, North. He retains his observer/assessor role, now known as Match Delegate, for the Premier League and Football League.